QUALIFIED

QUALIFIED

How Competency Checking and Race Collide at Work

SHARI DUNN

HARPER
BUSINESS

An Imprint of HarperCollins*Publishers*

HarperCollins books may be purchased for educational, business, or sales promotional use. For information, please email the Special Markets Department at SPsales@harpercollins.com.

FIRST EDITION

Designed by Emily Snyder

Library of Congress Cataloging-in-Publication Data has been applied for.

ISBN 978-0-06-335406-7

24 25 26 27 28 LBC 5 4 3 2 1

This book is dedicated to the past,
the present, and the future.

Not everything that is faced can be changed, but nothing can be changed until it is faced.

—James Baldwin

CONTENTS

INTRODUCTION

If I didn't define myself for myself, I would be crunched
into other people's fantasies for me and eaten alive.

—Audre Lorde

BLACK WOMEN ARE the canaries in the workplace coal mine,
and they have been signaling for years that something is
devastatingly wrong. Not just for them and other people of color
but for all of us, and our success as a country depends on us
fixing it.

The workplace can be and often is complicated and hard for
anyone to navigate. American office politics are the stuff of dra-
mas and sitcoms alike. But Black women are not only dealing
with the same burdens as everyone else; they are also facing
uniquely specific ones. Over the course of my consulting career
and in my work life, I've heard from Black women across industries who all report eerily similar "experiential arcs," which see
them either blocked from advancement or being turned against
by colleagues once they are in senior roles. From nonprofits to
government agencies to corporate spaces, Black women are reporting, almost verbatim, the words and phrases being used
about and against them in conversations, assessments, and offi-
cial reviews: "too ambitious," "too intimidating," "too angry," "too
confident." And this isn't just what a few Black women think or
feel. Surveys, research, and unemployment data seem to confirm

that something is amiss. Lean In's research on Women in the Workplace is the largest of its kind, with over 40,000 women surveyed across 333 businesses. In 2020, their research confirmed a troubling but evident truth: "In all of Lean In's research . . . we see the same general pattern: Women are having a worse experience than men. Women of color are having a worse experience than white women, and Black women, in particular, are having the worst experience of all."[1]

We've been seeing the impact of those experiences on Black women and other women of color showing up in the data over the last few years. In 2020, a survey by Working Mother Media found that 50 percent of the women of color surveyed planned to leave their jobs due to bias and lack of support.[2] Four years later, March 2024 data from the US Department of Labor seemed to confirm that Black women were indeed having "the worst experience of all." That data revealed a "significant" rise in unemployment for Black women over the age of 20, from 4.4 percent to 5.6 percent, which drove the overall Black unemployment rate up to 6.4 percent, almost double the unemployment rate for white Americans.[3]

As you read through this book, I encourage you to remember what renowned Nigerian novelist Chimamanda Ngozi Adichie calls "the danger of a single story."[4] "Well, *I* don't discriminate." "*I* am a good person." "*I* know plenty of Black women and other people of color who are succeeding." I don't dispute that a number of people have found a way to navigate the average American workplace and not just survive but thrive in their roles and climb the corporate ladder. But we don't know the physical or emotional price they may have paid to reach that level of success.[5] So, as you read this book, it will be important for you to balance the success not only of people you know or know about but also your own success against what the research, resulting data, and experiences of millions of Black and other people of color reveal. And what all of that information reveals is stunning. It will take the vast *majority* of Black Americans between one and three *centuries* to reach economic and employment parity with white Americans.[6] Contrary to what may be popular belief, this shocking fact is not because Black Americans are lazy, or don't care about education, or because they are unqualified. We didn't get here by accident; it took intentional, systemic effort to hold back the progress of Black Americans specifically and other people of color generally, and it will take intentional, systemic effort to change it.

The canaries sent me on this journey to unearth the roots of what these women are seeing, hearing, and experiencing in the workplace. But over the course of writing this book, I began to see that what is plaguing Black women at work is impacting not only them but also Black men and other people of color. It is also negatively impacting white people because what is plaguing Black women is effectively undermining our collective efforts to build a dynamic, innovative, and inclusive workplace and society.

But to answer the question—What *exactly* is happening to Black people and people of color in today's modern workplace?—I needed to identify the specific mechanisms at play. This was so I could identify the problems *and* know how to fix them. For example, bias and racism are behind housing discrimination, but there are specific mechanisms at play, such as redlining, mortgage loan discrimination, and recently uncovered appraisal discrimination. And we need that specific information to provide specific remedies. It's the same within the workplace; we can say unconscious bias or racism or discrimination, but how exactly is it happening, and what form is it taking in today's modern workforce? In the American workplace, like the housing industry, I found there is an extra, invisible weight being shouldered by Black and other people of color and a series of blockages that are actively holding them back. It's systemic, and it impacts all of us. I call it competency checking.

"Do you know the fireman's carry?" Nakeia Daniels, PhD, asks me.[7] In early 2024, Daniels was appointed the new director of the Oregon Department of Veterans Affairs, the first Black woman to occupy the position. It's an incredible opportunity but a loaded one. "They teach it to you in the military so you can carry a whole person on your back while you're running for safety. That is how I describe the weight of things like competency checking." Competency checking is an expression and tool of systemic racism used in the workplace to "confirm" or discount the capabilities and qualifications of Black people in particular and people of color in general. It acts as a means of setting and maintaining a higher bar for hiring, retention, and advancement, or, in worst-case scenarios, a means of blocking certain people from being hired at all.

There are three primary ways competency checking is deployed in the modern workplace. The first is the **assumption** of Black intellectual inferiority and/or a lack of qualifications. This can manifest in low expectations, marginalization, and extreme micromanagement. (More simply: If someone assumes, consciously or unconsciously, that all Black people are intellectually inferior, they may question the person and their qualifications more closely during an interview and once hired pay much more attention to their work while looking for any mistakes.) The second method of competency checking is the **expression**, particularly of surprise or unease, with open displays of Black intelligence, which can trigger requests or demands to confirm how it was acquired and whether it's the result of rote memorization or actual, integrated knowledge. This can manifest as dismissal, quizzing, argument, and tokenization. (If a Black person knows something that their white coworker doesn't already know, the coworker's reaction isn't "I didn't know that!" but more often "How do *you* know that?")

The third method of competency checking is **activation**, specifically the feeling of fear when confronted with a Black person who holds any authority, especially someone in a leadership position. This can manifest as requests for identification, undefined feelings of unfairness, anger, unease, and what I would describe as an "autoimmune level" rejection of Black leadership. While competency checking can happen to other people of color and, to some extent, white women, there are specific historical and cultural reasons why Black people seem to bear the brunt of it. This book is an exploration of these methods, when, how, and why they were created and implemented, and how they continue to have an outsize impact on Black people and other people of color at work.

The idea that it is not incompetence that is holding back Black professionals is for many a foreign concept. That's understandable, given that the narrative surrounding Black people—and the reason the workplace looks the way it does today—is that they don't value education or that there's no one in the hiring pipeline because there are so few qualified Black people, or that Black people want special treatment. What's interesting is that both anecdotal and empirical evidence suggests that Black workers *are* getting a type of "special" treatment, just not the type that many people think.

In 2019, the Economic Policy Institute (EPI) released research that revealed the impact of race and racism in the workplace. That year was a hot labor market, and the US saw the longest economic expansion in its history, with over 100 consecutive months of job growth and more than 21 million jobs added. But the EPI's analysis of Bureau of Labor Statistics and Local Area Unemployment Statistics (LAUS) and US Census Bureau data uncovered some surprising things: Per their report, "Black workers are twice as likely to be unemployed as white workers overall, even Black workers with a college degree are more likely to be unemployed than similarly educated white workers." That unemployment "gap," apparently, is "a pattern that has persisted for more than 40 years. In fact, this 2-to-1 ratio holds in practically every state in the nation where Black workers make up a significant share of the workforce."[8]

I believe that gap is linked, especially when it comes to new hires and leadership, to competency checking. And it starts with a name. In 2024, the *New York Times* reported on research from the National Bureau of Economic Research about the impact of a "Black" or "white" sounding name on job applications. In a 2019 study, researchers sent 80,000 fake resumes for 10,000 job openings at 100 companies. The resumes were modified to imply different racial and gender identities, using names like "Latisha" or "Amy" to indicate a Black or white woman, respectively, and "Lamar" or "Adam" for a Black or white man.[9] According to the resulting data, "on average, candidates believed to be white received contact from employers about 9.5 percent more frequently compared to those thought to be Black."[10]

This type of research is known as an audit study, and it was the largest of its kind in the United States. Ultimately, it found that "the results demonstrate how entrenched employment discrimination is in parts of the U.S. labor market—and the extent to which Black workers start behind in certain industries."[11] It's not all doom and gloom: some companies showed little to no bias when it came to screening applicants for entry-level positions. And while there is much to learn from the companies that "got it right"—and we will look at what they did right in this book—we must remember that this study pertains solely to entry-level positions that do not require a college degree or extensive work experience. So it does not cover aspects of career progression or advancement opportunities within these companies, which are equally critical to understanding the full scope of how competency checking shows up in the workplace. FedEx, for example, was identified as a company that showed little to no bias in entry-level hiring and yet has both settled a class-action lawsuit and been sued for race-based discrimination related to "promotions, discipline, and pay practices."[12] Reinforcing the fact that just because a company has been able to identify and account for one of the trees that makes up competency checking (race-based name bias) doesn't mean they are seeing the forest.

That competency checking of Black Americans, particularly against those looking for advancement, is still woven into the fabric of the modern workforce is borne out by additional data coming from the EPI. "Even when they are employed, Black workers with a college or advanced degree are more likely than their white counterparts to be underemployed when it comes to their skill level—almost 40% are in a job that typically does not require a college degree, compared with 31% of white college grads."[13] These workers have the education, experience, and skill to excel, as well as qualifications that are often equal to or exceeding their white counterparts, but time and again, competency checking blocks their path. I spoke to Adam Levitt, cofounder of the law firm DiCello Levitt, about what his firm is seeing when it comes to the legal consequences of racism and discrimination at work. Adam shared that "the types of discrimination we're seeing are not just about being denied opportunities but about being subjected to a different standard once in those roles." Absent specifics for the sake of client confidentiality, Adam gave me an example of a case he worked on, which proved "Black employees were systemically under-evaluated despite outperforming peers, illustrating a broader pattern of racial bias in performance reviews."[14] Constantly being held to a higher standard because of arbitrary goalposts and false assumptions about Black inferiority leads to the denial of competency, qualification, and ultimately of humanity.

I have noticed a clear difference in the reactions and responses from Black and other people of color versus some white people when I describe the concept of competency checking. When presented to Black and other people of color, there is often a sense of relief, validation, and, in one memorable instance, spontaneous applause. When people and their experiences are recognized, what tends to be felt is an overwhelming sense of relief. However, when discussing the same issues with some white people, there is confusion, pushback, and a tendency to play devil's advocate to refute the truth of the data and people's lived experiences. I think this is because, for so long, when it came to the lack of diversity in the workplace, Black people and other people of color were blamed for their own exclusion. They were told to get in the "pipeline," lean in, get a mentor (or better yet, a sponsor), wait their turn, get an education (but not too much), and stop feeling like an imposter. Even if they do all that, they can still find themselves and their achievements erased with as little as a choice comment in a meeting or a backdoor complaint to HR.

Such was the situation every Black person in the United States working in finance found themselves in, in 2020, when Wells Fargo CEO Charles Scharf was quoted saying, "While it might sound like an excuse, the unfortunate reality is that there is a very limited pool of Black talent to recruit from."[15] Scharf made this statement during the summer of unrest following the murder of George Floyd, in response to questions about why Wells Fargo had so few Black people in high-level executive positions. His assessment came as a surprise to (and angered many of) the over 700,000 Black people working in finance and insurance nationwide and specifically the 6 percent of Black Americans who were working exclusively in finance.[16]

Two things can be true: First, Black people make up 13 percent of the US population and should be more robustly represented in finance. Second, there *is* an existing pipeline of Black professionals if you are actually looking for them.

What Scharf either ignored or missed is that it is the blockages in the pipeline, not the number of people, that are preventing what should be, based on today's numbers, a natural and robust flow of diversity in the workplace. One of the blockages we'll look into later in the book is referral-based hiring, which usually ends up acting as a "shadow" talent pipeline that almost exclusively favors white people.[17] Ironically, in an interview for the *Financial Brand*, Scharf himself revealed the power of that system: "[His] father, a broker at Loeb Rhoades . . . had been lobbying his son [Scharf], who was a senior at Johns Hopkins, to send his resume to Commercial Credit. He had read that (Sandy) Weill, (Jamie) Dimon, and Bob Lipp, former President of Chemical Bank, were in the early stages of building Commercial Credit into something big. A family connection helped get the resume in front of Dimon, who offered Scharf a job the same day he interviewed him."[18]

We have been trying to treat workplace racial bias—as expressed through competency checking—with the wrong medicine at the wrong time for years. Think of it this way: An infected, gaping wound can't be treated with just a Band-Aid. A bandage is a tool for a cut or a scratch, applied after the wound has been cleaned out and disinfected, but not before. My intention with this book is to get us to see past ill-timed Band-Aid actions—ineffective corporate DEI initiatives, "color-blind" solutions, individual mentorship, among others—and provide the hardworking antibiotic that will clean the wound that is racism in the workplace in the United States once and for all.

I do this because diversity is, quite literally, natural. There's diversity in nature, plants, and animals, all necessary and interconnected. There's diversity inside us, from the microbiomes in our guts to our unique gene configurations.[19] All that diversity keeps the ecosystem—the planet's and ours—running smoothly.[20] The absence of diversity in any system means we have an illness, an imbalance.[21] And our workplaces reflect that. More to the point, our country reflects that. The year 2020 made some confront America's dark and not-so-distant past, with results that continue to run the gamut between revolutionarily positive to violently angry backlash. But the fact remains, the only way we embody America's belief in "E pluribus unum" and become one country made up of many is by removing the Band-Aid and applying the medicine to the wound. We do this by choice: Choosing inclusion. Choosing equity, which is supposed to be a cornerstone of our society, especially our legal system. The reason we have a criminal justice system that guarantees the accused the right to an attorney is to ensure that the law is being applied *equitably*.

The fact that so many Americans say they are against these things is, to me, a sign that this long-standing infection is getting worse, not better. Unfortunately, there is no quick fix or a single treatment option that can answer hundreds of years of systemic oppression, and it is ludicrous to expect one to exist. We have placed unrealistic expectations on current modalities such as DEI and have demanded a type of competency checking–based perfection on the execution of this work. Are there people practicing DEI who are not good at their jobs or who have done "harmful" work? Sure. But are there also business, strategic planning, and hiring consultants who aren't good at their jobs and whose work is harmful because they choose not to confront systemic racism within their processes and educational tools? Yes. But we don't outlaw business, strategic planning, and hiring consultants, so why are we trying to outlaw DEI? Simple: because admitting there's a problem requires us to confront our shared past, and for some, that comes with an unbearable amount of shame, and for others, it comes with barely contained hatred, both of which come disguised as "anti-woke" rage. These are people who have used rhetoric and obfuscation on personal and national platforms to hijack the terms, malign the methodology, and confuse the debate so that people believe diversity is the illness, inclusion is exclusion, equity is biased, and up is down.

At the end of the day, it doesn't matter what we call the pursuit of racial equity in the United States—those who oppose a diverse, inclusive, and equitable society will fight against it. This sophisticated rhetoric machine has, in only a few years, managed to convince millions of people, who ardently believed in it, that "the American Dream" has become a nightmare because *they* now feel like the ones on the outside, pushed out by a supposed "takeover" of people looking for handouts and special treatment. But there is no attempted "takeover"; rather, it's simply the people who have always been here asking, in no uncertain terms, for their fair share of a dream that has never truly included them before now. And when it comes to workplace discrimination as expressed through competency checking, we have repeatedly been applying bandages and then, when the infection returns worse than before, declaring the wound untreatable and the treatment ineffective. This is not a slam on DEI initiatives. It is simply an acknowledgment that, on its own, it can't cure what's wrong.

That is precisely the purpose of this book. *Qualified* is not about how to get a mentor or how to create a "DEI lense" or a series of generic platitudes about how to deal with constantly being called "surprisingly articulate" in the workplace. This is a book about how to achieve a diverse workplace and how that can only be accomplished by confronting the infection that is anti-Black bias in America. This book is your guide to dismantling the insidious assumptions that have come to define who is "qualified" and to help you identify, cleanse, and heal the race-based assumptions that are holding Black people and other people of color back in the workplace today.

While this book primarily addresses the impact of competency checking on Black people and other people of color, it's crucial to understand the broader implications of tackling such issues. Combating race-based bias necessitates a slower, more deliberate approach—encouraging us to focus, pay attention, and engage in critical thinking. This process not only helps dismantle systemic injustices but also cultivates a society that values thoughtful deliberation and thorough analysis in addressing complex problems. By applying these rigorous methods of scrutiny and reflection, we stand to gain a society that is not only fairer but also more adept at solving a wide array of challenges, thereby benefiting everyone.

QUALIFIED

CHAPTER 1

Competency Checking Defined

You always told me it takes time. It has taken my father's time, my mother's time, my uncle's time, my brothers' and my sisters' time, and my nieces' and nephews' time. How much time do you want for your "progress"?

—James Baldwin

THE COMPETENCY CHECKING of Black people doesn't begin in the workplace. It starts early, and in my case, it started the moment I was born.

My paternal grandmother wanted to name me Harriet. My mother—no offense to Harriets out there—did not. But because my grandmother was on her way to the hospital, my mother was under the gun to come up with a name. This was the late 1960s, and she quickly thought of Shari Lewis, a famous ventriloquist with a puppet named Lamb Chop, and how much she liked the name and that exact spelling—with an *a*. The white nurse taking the birth certificate information, however, wasn't familiar with this spelling and told my mother that it was incorrect; she said it was spelled *Sheri* with an *e*. My mother insisted that she wanted it spelled with an *a*. Years later, I found out that the name on my birth certificate was, in fact, *Sheri*, as the nurse had said was correct. So, while I wasn't directly competency-checked, I nonetheless had to deal with the consequences of it happening to my mother by going to court to change my name to what it should have been all along.

It seems easy to write off my mother being competency-checked on the spelling of her own child's name as an unfortunate run-in with a busybody nurse fifty-plus years ago. But in doing so, you would miss one of the trees that make up the vast forest that is competency checking: the way white supremacy feels empowered to question, supersede, and challenge Black agency, authority, and intelligence.

In the same way it can happen to a new mom trying to name her child, it can happen to a credentialed educator who is charged with training other teachers. John Daves, PhD, shared with me the complexities and challenges he faced while leading training initiatives as a Black professional in predominately white educational institutions. "When we had faculty meetings," said Daves, "sometimes teachers would directly ask me about texts, and a white woman in the group would answer as if I wasn't there. I'm in a vulnerable position. I haven't gotten tenure yet, and I'm the only Black person here."[1] In this instance, the resistance toward Black knowledge and intelligence was not necessarily overt but manifested in ways that undermined his authority and questioned his competency. In another instance, the resistance was overt. This manifested in faculty members who were uncomfortable with Daves's proposed innovative teaching methods, going directly to the head of the school with their concerns instead of coming to Daves. That circumvention of Black authority—by going to a VP, a CEO, or a board of directors—is a reoccurring theme among the Black leaders I've met in the course of my consulting work. To move past the resistance, Daves had a white teacher present his training. "Having a Black person who is in charge of them made them feel intimidated, so I put a white teacher in front of all-white teachers. . . . I had to show [my competency] through other people."[2]

Even world-famous singer and rapper T-Pain (real name Faheem Rashad Najm) found that celebrity isn't enough to eliminate competency checking. While speaking about his love for country music on TikTok in 2024, T-Pain revealed that while he has collaborated on and written a number of country songs, he had to, much like Daves, hide or obscure his leadership and presence in the process. "I done wrote a lot of country songs, [but I] stopped taking credit for it because, as cool as it is to see your name in those credits . . . the racism that comes after it is just like, 'I'll just take the check.'"[3]

Daves, T-Pain, and my mom all understood broadly that racism was at the core of what was happening to them. They understood this because they had already experienced a lifetime of racism, as expressed through competency checking. For Black children, it starts early. Society teaches Black children that no matter how exceptional, intelligent, or high-achieving they are, white supremacy can and will question their knowledge and accomplishments and instead put far more effort into spotlighting their flaws and limitations—real, perceived, or otherwise. In an ideal world, we should all understand that intelligence manifests itself in many ways. Some people are great spellers but have a hard time with public speaking; some people are excellent with their hands, like the uncle who can measure by sight and paint like a pro but finds it hard to convey their process. These are normal variances in human ability, but for Black children, a normal difference can become all-encompassing and be seen as proof of the fallacy of Black intellectual inferiority.

Dr. LaShorage Shaffer, associate professor at the University of Michigan–Dearborn, has studied at length a type of misidentification that happens with Black children. In an article on "Confronting Special Education's Race Problem," Dr. Shaffer gives an example based on what she has witnessed of how Black children's inquisitiveness can be misidentified as challenging and disrespectful while white students' inquisitiveness is not. "The Black student may even notice the white student getting positive feedback from the teacher. And even though he's receiving a different response, he's going to keep trying. . . ."[4] Dr. Schaffer says the Black child sees the difference but cannot fully grasp what is happening, so they keep doing what they see the white child doing, asking questions to try to get the same positive feedback, but they don't get it. They *can't*. At that point, Shaffer says, the Black child is in danger of being misidentified as difficult or challenging or as needing special education testing.[5]

These unfair interactions can, in some cases, trigger a phenomenon known as the **stereotype threat**. In a published study from 1995, psychologists Claude M. Steele and Joshua Aronson define the term as "being at risk of confirming, as a self-characteristic, a negative stereotype about one's group."[6] Put another way, people who are aware they are being stereotyped can sometimes, due to overwhelming psychological pressure, live up to that negative stereotype. A young Black child is told that Black people don't read very well; the child is given a reading test, and they don't do well. A Black adult gets a new job and is told they got it because of **affirmative action**—their fear of living up to the stereotype of only getting a job because they are Black may cause them to perform poorly on a project. Aronson and Steele explain that the risk of confirming negative stereotypes about an individual's racial, ethnic, gender, or cultural group creates this high cognitive load and reduced ability to perform academically or in the workplace.[7]

For me, the issue is more about the actual environment in which Black adults and children function or struggle to do so. According to Shaffer, the idea that Black people are "cognitively substandard" (what I call a **foundational fallacy**) is really the issue, and that it persists, resulting in everything from teach-ers having lower expectations for Black students to more fre-quent and severe discipline for behaviors incorrectly perceived as challenging.

Black kids in this situation are, in fact, responding logi-cally to a constant barrage of competency checking. Even when they are performing equal to or above their white peers, Black children can see that they are not getting the same response or treatment. While I understand the logic behind the stereotype threat, it runs the risk of the same misidentification that Shaffer noted happening to Black children: people end up punished—or punishing themselves—because they believe they have (based on external stimuli) failed by getting "psyched" out by the threat of being stereotyped. However, the reality is they are, in fact, being blocked by the destabilizing presence that is competency checking and race-based blockages.

The only way to change this is to train ourselves to be able to spot, name, and disrupt what is happening when someone is competency-checked. We must dig into why it is happening, how it's happening, and what we can do to change things for the better. But we must be open to that change. Too often, we see these conversations as an either/or: If one group gets the opportunity to participate, my group will lose something. But what if we reframe our understanding of what is possible? I often wonder how many good jobs don't exist because Black entrepreneurs have been sidelined, dismissed, or ignored. How many opportunities for growth could American companies be missing out on because they refuse to consider other—namely, nonwhite—points of view? How many dead or dying industries could have been saved if Black people weren't systematically prevented from acquiring wealth, especially generational? One way to break through the what-ifs that plague us as a society is to face them head-on.

The Fiction

I remember being in a training session with a group of people, and two people in the group, a white person and a person of color who was not Black, pointedly said to me that they thought we should only consider merit and not special treatment when addressing the issues we were discussing, related to race. The person of color rather pointedly said, "I've worked hard for what I have and didn't get any handouts." Implicit in those exchanges was the assumption that by acknowledging the impact of race-based blockages on Black people specifically, we were lowering standards and providing handouts to unqualified people.

If we are to address what holds Black people and people of color back in the workplace, let alone rectify the issue, we must first understand that the issue has never been about actual incompetence but a deep fear and suspicion of Black competence and success. Specifically, a fear and suspicion that is deeply rooted in the notion that if given the same opportunities as white people, Black people might use their intelligence and success to do to others what has been done to them: violence, disenfranchisement, and discrimination.[8] This suspicion is what is at the core of competency checking as it is expressed through discomfort and mistrust of Black intellectual ability, authority, and overall competence. However, many people who do not believe that competency checking exists (or who want to deny that race matters) blame programs like affirmative action for the assumption of Black intellectual inferiority. One of the staunchest proponents of this false narrative has been Supreme Court justice Clarence Thomas. Justice Thomas, who ironically has admitted to walking through the doors that had to be forced open for him by affirmative action, seems to ignore that the assumption of Black intellectual inferiority is a pernicious, long-standing fiction that predates affirmative action by hundreds of years.

So, what is the root of the "fear" of Black competence and success I mentioned above? Any time one group seeks to oppress another, they create a series of fictions to justify their actions, gross generalizations that make them seem noble and help to keep up the appearance of their humanity while undermining the humanity of the "other." *This group is sneaky,* so they are the reason for our problems. *This group is violent,* so we must use extreme force against them. *This group is not like us; they don't share our emotions, our intelligence, or our color. Therefore, they are not human,* and we may treat them inhumanely. After enough time has passed, these fictions become assumed facts, part of our culture, policies, practices, and beliefs, so deeply entwined with our ideas of who other people are that they become "just the way it is."

Those fictions have created a scenario where it can be so strange and disconcerting to see Black people in or in charge of traditionally white workplaces that those places can end up treating Black and other people of color the way a body treats a transplanted organ—by attacking what appears to be a foreign presence. The "antibody" deployed to oversee and sometimes reject Black people is competency checking.

When we think of segregation in the South, we tend to think of overt discrimination laws to do with buses and, most famously, water fountains. What we don't consider is that until fifty-six years ago, a byzantine set of laws and accompanying etiquette called Jim Crow dictated all elements of Black life. This was the law of the land in the South and in most northern states, where Jim Crow was both actual law and de facto, enforcing the same basic social hierarchy across the country.[9] These were laws and customs designed to maintain the fiction of white supremacy, a key element of which was the assumption of white intellectual superiority. In his book *Jim Crow Guide to the U.S.A.*, Stetson Kennedy highlighted the elements of Jim Crow etiquette that related to the ways Black people were forbidden from expressing or showcasing their intelligence, knowledge, or competency in day-to-day interactions:

1. Never assert or even intimate that a White person is lying.
2. Never impute dishonorable intentions to a White person.
3. Never suggest that a White person is from an inferior class.
4. ***Never lay claim to or overly demonstrate superior knowledge or intelligence.*** (emphasis added)[10]

As ludicrous as these laws and etiquette practices seem, a violation could have deadly consequences. "The intent of Jim Crow etiquette boiled down to one simple rule: Blacks must demonstrate their inferiority to whites by actions, words, and manners."[11] These rules helped set up and reinforce a foundational fallacy in American thinking: that Black people lacked critical intelligence and reasoning skills. These people were so ignorant that they failed to see the irony inherent in the fact that Black people could not openly display these skills without punishment. It reminds me of the cruel game older siblings sometimes play—taking the younger sibling's hand, slapping them with it, then telling them "stop slapping yourself." For Black people during Jim Crow, it meant being forced into a game where your life could depend on you pretending to lose.

Jim Crow as a construct was designed to uphold the larger lie of white supremacy. Neither emancipation, civil rights legislation, nor affirmative action laws have fully eradicated it. Rather, it has undergone a metamorphosis and become the aforementioned forest that is covert racism.

When we consider the workplace, are we to imagine employers twirling their mustaches and refusing to hire Black people for jobs commensurate with their experience because of conscious bias? In some cases, yes, and we can't run from that. We must use all legal, moral, and economic tools to force aside those people blocking the door to employment and advancement, as we did those blocking the schoolhouse entrance to the "Little Rock Nine" in 1957. But whether consciously or unconsciously, those holding Black applicants, employees, and managers to a higher standard are doing so through a series of competency checks that has led us to a situation where everyone—individuals, companies, and society—loses out. That the country's most highly educated Black workers are still less likely to be employed in a job that is consistent with their level of education and expertise dispels the notion that they don't meet the qualifications or want special treatment. That the trades remain a largely closed and hostile club for Black people shows it is not a lack of motivation but an active blocking of entry that is behind the so-called talent-pipeline problem.

Take the confirmation hearings for Supreme Court justice Ketanji Brown Jackson. On paper, Justice Jackson is one of the most accomplished people appointed to the bench. She is an Ivy League graduate with extensive clerking and judicial experience and two prior successful Senate confirmations. While other Supreme Court nominations have been contentious, Justice Jackson faced questions that other nominees have not. Her treatment was so out of bounds that the *New Jersey Law Journal* (*NJLJ*) editorial board felt compelled to write about it: "[Former Fox News host] Tucker Carlson had never asked for the LSAT scores of any prior candidate, including Amy Coney Barrett, Brett M. Kavanaugh, and Neil M. Gorsuch."[12] From my vantage point, Carlson demanding Justice Jackson's LSAT scores is a textbook example of the second foundational form of competency checking: surprise and/or unease at displays of Black intelligence paired with demands for confirmation as to how that knowledge was cultivated and how deep it goes, otherwise known as **extreme vetting**.

The *NJLJ* went on to say, "Judge Jackson graduated magna cum laude from Harvard University and cum laude from Harvard Law School, where she served as a supervising editor for the *Harvard Law Review*. She clerked for three judges, including Justice Stephen G. Breyer. She served 15 years as a public defender and eight years as a trial court judge in the U.S. District Court for the District of Columbia. . . . To connect the candidate's LSAT scores and her qualifications to serve on the United States Supreme Court is nothing more than a racist slur."[13] Pay attention to this paragraph and note, as I did, that the editorial board not only felt the need to prove Justice Jackson's competency; they had to list it all.

What Justice Jackson endured is something Black folks experience daily, in the workplace and in life, albeit outside the media glare and often, though not always, on a smaller scale. This day-to-day competency checking can show up at any time, though it is frequently more insidious and harder to spot. It can take the form of asking a Black colleague to prove what they say is true or requiring them to show how they came to a conclusion while not asking the same of others. Or the pushback against Black authority, as was the case with a Black manager at an Equinox gym in Manhattan who won an $11 million racial discrimination suit because, among other things, "one of her supervisees, a white man, refused to accept her as his supervisor."[14]

White employees feeling empowered to competency-check their Black managers and business leaders is not uncommon, as Daves's example showed. Many corporate, nonprofit, and governmental leaders who might express shock and disgust at the examples above are practicing competency checking in their recruitment, hiring, and retention efforts, hindering the earning potential of Black Americans.[15] Take, for example, the story of Alicia Moore, a professional with an MBA and, at the time, eight years of experience working in nonprofits, community engagement, and philanthropy. While looking for a new job several years ago, she met with one recruiter whom several companies she was interested in utilized in their hiring. "Every time I would ask about a job," she told me, "she [the recruiter] would come back to me needing 'more,' but she could never really define for me what that 'more' was."[16] Even though Ms. Moore had experience in the field, she had hoped to get into grant-making; the recruiter, Moore felt, functioned as an impediment between her and potential employers. According to Kimberly B. Cummings, founder of a career and leadership development company for women and people of color, "While ultimately the final hiring decision is up to the hiring manager, recruiters have the first line of sight to all candidates in many organizations. . . . If biases exist within a recruiter, the slate delivered to the hiring leader won't have a chance of being diverse."[17]

Alicia Moore's experience was not an isolated incident. I had a similar experience with the same recruiter. In 2011, I sought to transition from television news, my career of almost a decade. Journalism had been my fifth successful career pivot. Before that, I had been a practicing attorney and worked in Washington, DC, as a director for a national nonprofit, and eventually ran a national philanthropic foundation in New York City. After transitioning careers, I worked as a development director for a television production company before becoming a news anchor. I brought this breadth of experience to the recruiter, who was seeking to fill a community relations/ PR manager position at the local branch of a national banking institution. However, instead of highlighting my combination of skills and abilities, she focused on what she felt I lacked to qualify for this position. It didn't matter that I had years of media experience and had run a division of a national membership organization that involved outreach, training, and designing and implementing a communications plan (which is still in use almost two decades later). She still seemed uncomfortable with me and refused to present me as an applicant to the client because I didn't have the exact direct experience, never mind the fact that former journalists are often hired for PR, community relations, and nonprofit work.[18] Many journalists I worked with went directly into those careers upon leaving the newsroom. While not one of them had my combination of education and experience, they overwhelmingly shared a characteristic that I did not: they were white.

The story of the recruiter is not just about a "bad actor," or maybe subjective feelings Moore and I had. Research shows this phenomenon is very real. A key element of competency checking is holding Black people to higher standards for employment. According to the *Journal of Applied Social Psychology*, "The Shifting Standards Model (SSM) can help explain this. Simply put, you shift the requirements or 'standards' based on who it is."[19] SSM is one part of explaining race-based differences in subjective evaluations and compensation and is an expression of competency checking. If you fundamentally don't believe that Black people have the ability or competency to do a certain type of work, you might unconsciously or consciously deploy SSM even when faced with information that proves otherwise.

Dr. Trevor Bates, the former president of a small college in Ohio, experienced this in real time. Despite his significant achievements, including spearheading a comprehensive and ultimately successful campaign that raised $15 million in eighteen months and implementing strategies that dramatically increased staff compensation, Bates consistently encountered skepticism and resistance. In our conversation, Bates noted the moving goalposts and the ongoing questioning of his capabilities: "I think the bar always moved. And it was interesting because, when I was there, we launched the college's first-ever comprehensive campaign. People said, how is that possible? We've never raised that much money. How does he know how to do that? How did that happen?"[20] Instead of support and praise, he found surprise and shock when he managed to address financial issues that had long plagued the institution.

That shifting sand Dr. Bates and Alicia Moore and many other Black folks find themselves standing on in the workplace isn't just in their imaginations. The "legal memo experiment" is another example of this in action. The consulting firm Nextion wanted to determine if legal partners were more inclined to notice and comment on errors made by Black employees. To accomplish this, 60 partners across 22 law firms agreed to participate in a writing analysis study. They were given copies of a memo peppered with intentional errors and asked to analyze it. Half of the reviewers were told the memo was written by an African American man named Thomas Meyer, and half were told the writer was a white man named Thomas Meyer (this was done to account for race-identifying name bias).[21] Even though the memos were identical, the reviewers found more errors (including things that were not errors) in the memo they thought was written by a Black man and found fewer errors in the memo they thought was written by a white man (overlooking actual errors). The reviewers paid more attention to and raised their standards for the author they thought was Black and paid less attention to and shifted their standards to a presumption of qualification for the author they thought was white. As a result, they said the white candidate had "good potential" and "good analytical skills," while the Black candidate was criticized as "average at best and needing a lot of work."[22] As a result of this type of competency checking, Black employees like Bates and Moore frequently find themselves being asked to provide an impossible "more," in this case, to be "more" white in order to be judged fairly.

The SSM could also help explain why people may seem to praise certain groups for doing the same thing expected of other groups. Because it is assumed Black people are inarticulate, one expression of competency checking is the continuous shock and surprise at a Black person who is "well-spoken." Or why, in the case of the legal memo experiment, a Black employee might get more criticism for doing something seen as normal for other groups, such as misspelling a word. Spelling errors lowered the evaluation of the "Black" legal memo writer, whereas spelling mistakes by the "white" writer seemed to have no real impact. The Nextion study was small, and some have criticized the results based on that fact. But when we combine that study with what we know about implicit bias and the SSM, the trees that make up the forest that is competency checking begin to come into view.

Twice as Hard

Ideas about Black intellectual inferiority and supposed laziness have yet to be excised from our collective mind. In my consulting work, I have had white people and sometimes people of color, when talking about diversity in the workplace, say that they "don't think it's fair for unqualified people to get jobs." These statements are rooted in the idea that Black people are inherently, even scientifically unqualified, seeking "special advantage," and, of course, are rooted in the idea that whiteness by its very nature is a sign of qualification.

Is it any wonder, then, that some white people and even

other people of color might look around their professional spaces and see few to no Black people and assume that some of the fiction around Black intelligence must be true? And when they encounter a Black person in spaces they previously haven't been in—or have only recently entered—they might be suspicious of that person's intelligence and ability. Paradoxically, is it any wonder that some Black people who have, to a degree, succeeded in this current system want to distance themselves from those fictions? And in doing so, those Black people might place the blame not on those who created and benefit most from the system but on those who, like them, are most severely impacted by it.

Again, the most prominent example of someone who seems to embody this thinking is Supreme Court justice Clarence Thomas and, more recently, South Carolina senator Tim Scott. Both Black men emphasize their personal stories as reasons for their success—they "overcame," so why can't everyone else? They downplay their lucky breaks and the role the fight against anti-Blackness has played in their lives. They seem to see themselves as standing outside of history.

In the case of Tim Scott, does he think the sixty-three Black state representatives that made up most of the South Carolina legislature during Reconstruction simply didn't try hard enough in the face of Jim Crow, a system of racial terrorism that would be the law of the land when Scott himself was born in South Carolina in 1965? Based on his theory of overcoming, it seems others should have tried harder, and they, too, would have had the same results as he did.

Does Justice Thomas not see the impact of the systematic racism faced by his grandfather on *his* limited financial fortunes today? The disruption of generational wealth can be seen in the racial wealth gap, which Calvin Schermerhorn, a professor of history at Arizona State University, writing in the *Washington Post*, says has remained functionally stagnant since emancipation. According to Schermerhorn, "The typical Black family today has just 1/10th the wealth of the typical white one. In 1863, Black Americans owned one-half of 1 percent of the national wealth."[23] Schermerhorn goes on to say, "The cause of that stagnation has largely been invisible, hidden by the assumption of progress after the end of slavery and the achievements of civil rights. But for every gain Black Americans made, people in power created new bundles of discrimination, largely hidden from sight, that thwarted, again and again, the economic promise of emancipation."[24] Is Justice Thomas unwilling or too embarrassed to admit that it is this fact, not some failing of his admittedly hard work, that places him at the mercy of handouts and duplicitous support from wealthy friends like billionaire Harlan Crow, people whose families were not smarter or more hardworking than his grandfather but who were whiter?[25]

Both Thomas and Scott engage in the politics of respectability, which requires Black people to align as closely as possible with the dominant culture and distance themselves from the "negative" aspects of their own culture to prove their worth. Both Black excellence and respectability were meant to help Black people advance against an onslaught of hate, terrorism, and psychological torture. Both concepts posit that if we behave flawlessly, keep our composure no matter the insult, persist in proving "them" wrong, and pass every competency check, we will be seen as equals or, at the very least, garner unassailable if begrudging respect. Those who can achieve these ideals are considered deserving; they are the "talented tenth," a concept created by the white founder of Morehouse College— historically a school exclusively for Black men—and championed by W. E. B. Du Bois. It states that one in ten Black men who possess "superior natural endowments, symmetrically trained and highly developed, may become a mightier influ-ence, a greater inspiration to others than all the other nine."[26] The concept of the talented tenth is not only sexist but, at its core, classist and racist. It assumes those who cannot reach these lofty goals haven't tried hard enough. For many white Americans, this idea continues to find resonance because it aligns with the old adage, "pulling yourself up by the boot-straps," a persistent notion that overlooks the fact that many people don't even have boots, never mind that it is literally, physically impossible to pull yourself up off the ground by your shoes. It also serves to hide unearned advantages by pillorying the poor and working class as solely responsible for their own suffering while ignoring the fact that many wealthy people are only so by accident, either of birth or inheritance. Most people are not going to win the life lottery and vault to success from zero, but we hold to this notion to obscure the truth: no one "makes it" without help.[27]

The burden of carrying all this weight and disproving the negative manifests in a saying that most Black Americans are familiar with: "You must work twice as hard to get half as far/ much" as white people.[28] Because of competency checking, that saying is technically true, but that does not make it right or fair; even our highly treasured Black excellence, meant to challenge stereotypes and the resulting competency checking head-on, withers under examination as just another iteration of respectability. The ability of Black people to endure, to suc-ceed against odds that would crush others—from slavery to the terrorism of Jim Crow to the persistent discrimination and mi-croaggressions we face daily—is to be valued, understood, and praised. But it comes at a cost because meeting these unreal-istic standards doesn't leave much room for Black *humanity*, which encompasses excellence, normalcy, *and* mediocrity.

When thinking about this particular aspect of competency

checking, I always come back to the episode of the former ABC hit show *Black-ish* in which Dr. Rainbow Johnson mentors her son's girlfriend, who is applying to medical schools. To encourage her Gen Z mentee, Rainbow, a Gen X Black woman, uses a quote often misattributed to Harriet Tubman: "'If you hear the dogs, keep going. If you see the torches in the woods, keep going.' Isn't that lovely?" To which her Gen Z mentee replies, "Um, whew, it's something."[29] While Rainbow sees that quote as inspirational, her Gen Z mentee is horrified at the idea that achieving her dreams will require the same stamina and skill as it did to escape from enslavers hundreds of years ago.

Follow the Leader?

That "something" that the Gen Z mentee in *Black-ish* is referencing is, on some level, the type of stamina, skill, and preparation that Black people must actually bring to the workplace and public spaces daily. When Dr. Fatima Cody Stanford, a seasoned medical professional, boarded her Delta Air Lines flight from Indianapolis to Boston in November 2018, she was fully prepared for, but not expecting, the competency check that was inbound. When a fellow passenger began to experience a medical emergency, Stanford sprang into action. She had barely begun to help when a flight attendant approached to check her credentials. "Are you a doctor?" Stanford had her medical license stored next to her driver's license, ready in case anyone asked to see it. The flight attendant took her medical license for further inspection and returned shortly after, as Stanford was stabilizing the patient, with a barrage of questions. "Are you a head doctor?" "Are you actually an MD?" "Is this your license?"[30]

What was so telling about what happened to Dr. Stanford is

that two years earlier, in 2016, another Black doctor was similarly checked on a Delta flight. Dr. Tamika Cross was a resident ob-gyn when a medical emergency took place in the air. According to Cross, the flight crew told her, "Oh no, sweetie, put [your] hand down. We are looking for actual physicians, nurses, or medical personnel. We don't have time to talk to you."[31] In the wake of the incident, Delta executives met with Cross, apologized, and repealed the policy requiring flight attendants to verify medical credentials. To date, there is no report of a white passenger experiencing this kind of pushback during a crisis.

Surely the flight attendants on Dr. Stanford's 2018 flight were aware of the policy change. But they still felt compelled to interrogate a Black person during a precarious moment. Who deemed them qualified to examine a doctor's medical license? How are nonmedical professionals even equipped to spot a fake? It's completely nonsensical but reinforced by the fiction that Black people are inherently inferior—less intelligent, capable, and not deserving of high titles, such as Doctor. Dr. Stanford has multiple degrees and hundreds of accolades and was, at the time, employed by Harvard Medical School. Yet the fact that she was a Black woman "colored" these flight attendants' perception of her and her capabilities. Why? Because we are all actors playing out a script written long ago. Actor A is performing on behalf of society, a self-elected authority who imposes biased and unrealistic standards and forces Actor B, in the role of Black people, to constantly produce and prove their competency. In the eyes of a society dominated by whiteness, it's not enough for Black people to be accomplished; we must be extraordinary to deserve our place in a society that still privileges whiteness above all else. If Black people are getting any "special treatment," it is by being held to higher and often impossible and unrealistic standards in the workplace and everyday life.

The Path

It is crucial, then, as we close this chapter, to understand that the path to dismantling competency checking is not through the examples of an exceptional few but through the recognition of the rights and humanity of all. It is not enough for any of us to say we reject the narrative of Black inferiority. We must also confront and dismantle the ways in which this fiction continues to impact Black people and other people of color in this country, specifically in the workplace. It is not enough for some to succeed; the goal must be for everyone to have the opportunity to succeed *and fail* without the threat of being labeled a stereotype, individually or collectively.

One of the ways to bring about that particular change is to look more closely at our shared history.

CHAPTER 2

The Roots of Competency Checking

They would show their free papers, but nobody paid any attention to them.

—Sarah Hopkins Bradford, *Scenes in the Life of Harriet Tubman,* 1869

AMERICA IS A very young country. Because of this, and for many other reasons, we fail to appreciate or fully comprehend just how close the past is to our present or how much of an impact it has on us. Some refuse to see it; others— sometimes aggressively—seek to downplay it. Slavery as a legal, capitalist institution was abolished 159 years ago, but it existed on this continent for 246 years before that. During that time, assumptions about enslaved people grew like deep-rooted, creeping vines, winding through and intertwining with every element of America's laws, practices, policies, mores, and beliefs. As a systemic equity consultant, it's my job to find ways to make these connections clear, so I frequently turn to analogies and sometimes I mix metaphors to get my point across. So, here's another way to think of this: We can all conceptually understand that a house built on a poor foundation (cracked, lopsided, shoddy, etc.) is inevitably going to experience structural problems (sagging roofs, warped floors, and more). So it is within our systems, whether governmental, educational, business, or personal. Much like a house, human systems originally built on poor foundations of faulty thinking, erroneous assumptions, and lopsided benefits will cause problems in the present *and* the future if left unaddressed.

Of course, at this point, when I am working with clients, a devil's advocate usually shows up with a few questions. "It was common or accepted practice for builders to use straw for foundations back then, so how can we judge them by today's standards?" Or "That was a long time ago, and we've changed how we build houses, so why continue to talk about it?" My answer to both of those questions is that we have to talk about it *because* many of those "new" houses are built on those same old faulty foundations, bringing the past undeniably into the present.

Consider Samuel Cartwright, a physician in the antebellum South whose ideas—codified by his status, background, race, and wealth—had a devastating impact on the lives of enslaved people and generations of their descendants. "The Negro is not deficient in memory but in reason and imagination," he claimed. "In their moral and intellectual character, as seen in Africa, the Negroes are on a level with children. . . . Children have been well called 'little savages,' growing, like the Negroes, in the ratio of their instincts, and not by instruction."[1]

Cartwright also created fictional diseases like "drapetomania" and "dysaesthesia aethiopica" to answer the question of why enslaved Africans wanted to be free and to justify the use of physical torture against them because of their "inherent and pathological laziness." Cartwright never questioned these fictions. Instead he used them to confirm the story that enslaved people were "not human like us" and thus could be treated however the white ruling class liked. The use of physical torture to force the enslaved to work past the breaking point was based on the idea that Black people did not feel pain in the same manner as white people. According to this fiction, the skin of Black people was thicker, their nerve endings less sensitive, and therefore they could endure more pain, so more pain would be inflicted on them.[2]

Cartwright wrote these things in 1851, but we didn't just stop believing them when President Abraham Lincoln issued the Emancipation Proclamation in 1863. In a 2015 study on pain management, half of a sample of white medical students and residents proved to be operating under the exact same assumptions as their predecessor. "[A] substantial number of white laypeople and medical students and residents hold false beliefs about biological differences between blacks and whites and demonstrates that these beliefs predict racial bias in pain perception and treatment recommendation accuracy."[3] This is a clear and heartbreaking example of the devastating and lopsided result of not working to fix this faulty foundation that we continue to build upon.

If the beliefs about the Black body are still a part of our cracked, faulty foundation as a country, so too are the beliefs about the Black *mind*. And all these fictions upon which we have built our society, and that will eventually give birth to competency checking, are rooted in the most pernicious fiction of all.

Race

If you've been paying attention to the ongoing conversation about racism in America, you may have heard the phrase "race is a social construct." And it's true. There is only one race: humans. The rest of it is fictitious, made up out of whole cloth. There are no significant biological differences between humans that would justify separating them into racial categories. But the *fiction* of race is real, born from the inextricable collision of law, economics, policy, and practice. In the words of Ta-Nehisi Coates, "Race is the child of racism, not the father."[4] White Americans looking to justify what would otherwise be considered crimes against humanity created a story to prove that what they were doing—enslaving and subjugating other people—was, in fact, good and proper. A significant part of that was the creation of the first political identity group—whiteness—as a racial identifier. Like early American colonists, Europeans thought of themselves by their titles, religion, ethnicity/country, and even their occupation (like "smith" or "baker"), but not by the idea of race.[5] Black or Negro, a term derived from the Latin word *niger*, meaning black, was used by the early Portuguese slave traders to describe their human cargo, but even this wasn't about their race so much as it was a visual descriptor.

Bacon's Rebellion is one of the clearest examples of the collision between law, circumstance, economics, policy, and practice that arguably helped establish race as we think of it today. In 1676, Nathaniel Bacon, a wealthy planter in Virginia, wanted to execute a raid on Native lands; the governor, William Berkeley, said no. Enraged, Bacon assembled a group of indentured servants, enslaved people, and landless folks to carry out the raids. He promised them freedom and land if they would join him in rebellion. This ragtag group ultimately managed to burn Jamestown, Virginia, to the ground.[6] Obviously, Bacon's Rebellion was not a rebellion against slavery or the disenfranchisement of indentured servants. It was, however, the reason why certain laws were enacted. Virginian leaders, through legislation, began to draw stark distinctions between its newly identified white and Black inhabitants.[7] Many historians believe this was the ruling class taking measures to divide the laboring class along racial lines to prevent such united rebellions in the future.[8]

One of the more significant laws was designed so that children born of enslaved women would inherit their legal status. This devastating change meant that descendants of enslaved people would forever and always be slaves; there would be no path to freedom, or the freedom whiteness allows. The repercussions of this would reverberate through society for generations and continues to affect how we think about race to this day.

This doctrine of *partus secuitur ventrem* ("that which is born follows the womb") soon spread from Virginia to all twelve other colonies. The law exempted white biological fathers from relationships or obligations with or to children who came about because of the rape of enslaved women; it was this denial of paternity to enslaved children that secured the enslavers' right to profit from their labor.[9] In theory, this would then mean that children born of white women with Black fathers would be considered white. However, antimiscegenation laws that targeted Black men's relationships with white women while ignoring the ongoing rape of enslaved Black women were written to prevent *that* type of "race mixing."[10] Now we have a legal basis for what will become the "one-drop rule," meaning one drop of "Black blood" makes you Black, a construct that in reality continues to this day.[11] All of this was designed to make sure that those now identified as Black would never have access to the privileges, benefits, and opportunities that come with whiteness.

Historian Ira Berlin notes that at the same time we codified slavery, we codified freedom. "[W]e normally say that slavery and freedom are opposite things—that they are diametrically opposed. But what we see here in Virginia in the late 17th century, around Bacon's Rebellion, is that freedom and slavery are created at the same moment."[12] We can go further and say that in codifying the fiction of race, we were also creating what would become the American Dream—a dream that, in reality, is an illusion for most; as the comedian George Carlin once said, "It's called the American Dream because you have to be asleep to believe it."[13] Whether real or imagined, that "dream" was to be reserved only for those who were recognized and identified as white.

While most working-class white people then and now aren't landowners, the dream was that one day they too could be and become a part of a class from which they had previously been excluded. As Robin D. G. Kelley, Distinguished Professor and Gary B. Nash Endowed Chair in US History at UCLA, said: "Many European-descended poor whites began to identify themselves, if not directly with the rich whites, certainly with the idea of being white. And here, you get the emergence of this idea of a white race to distinguish themselves from those dark-skinned people whom they associate with perpetual slavery."[14] A key part of that American Dream became the maintenance of superiority and dominance, through legal, cultural, and practical means, over those now identified as Black.

As Howard Zinn explains in *A People's History of the United States*, "after Bacon's Rebellion [the Virginia Assembly] gave amnesty to white servants who had rebelled. . . . At the same time slave patrols were established in Virginia. . . . Poor white men would make up the rank and file of these patrols."[15] That previously poor whites had naturally seen no difference between themselves and enslaved Black people would become lost to history and be replaced by the unnatural filter of race that historian Edmund Morgan calls "a screen of racial contempt."[16] This "screen" would warp everything that came after it and make the unnatural seem natural. If this new concept called the white race was to be the sky, limitless and filled with potential and possibilities, then Blackness would be degraded as the necessary ground upon which all those who entered whiteness could stand to build and achieve their dreams.

The fiction of whiteness was accepted quickly, widely, and deeply. In fact, some of those who later would reject and fight against physical enslavement still accepted race-based discrimination.[17] Even after the abolition of chattel slavery, custom and intervention by the Supreme Court extended a cultural and legal version of slavery. This came about in the form of the Thirteenth Amendment, which allows for involuntary servitude as part of criminal punishment. And except for a brief period during Reconstruction, Jim Crow would enforce racial superiority and segregation, helped by everyday terrorism, including lynchings, and come to dominate life in the South, creating what historian Douglas A. Blackmon has called "slavery by another name."[18]

Reconstruction, the decade following emancipation when the federal government tried (and failed) to account for the harms of slavery, opened a small crack where it seemed possible for Black people to rise beyond the racist stories that had been told about them. During that time, a persistent group of newly freed Black Americans in the South and newly empowered Black Americans in the North, working with white allies, pushed and propelled themselves into business, education, politics, and integrated communities.[19] Those efforts were met with language that is directly connected to what we hear today amid the pushback against diversity, equity, and inclusion (DEI) and so-called "woke" policies.

If any of us ever think of the terms *carpetbagger* and *scalawag*, we might think of the movie *Gone with the Wind* or remember seeing the terms in our high school history books. What we don't know, because we aren't taught it, is that these terms were originally deployed by southern Democrats who opposed Reconstruction efforts. They were rhetorical flourishes used to delegitimize these efforts and maintain their prewar social order.[20] Most of us believe that carpetbaggers, named for how certain people carried their belongings in large bags made of carpeting materials, were opportunists looking to exploit the region's postwar turmoil for personal gain. But the true story shows the power of rhetoric to change perception. Many carpetbaggers were former Union soldiers, teachers, missionaries, and businessmen who moved to the South to assist in rebuilding efforts, start businesses, or take part in politics.[21] Of course, there were people among them hoping to make money, but many were there because they were committed to Reconstruction and the establishment of civil rights for freed slaves. It's the same story with scalawags: white southerners who cooperated with the federal Reconstruction efforts and the Republican Party who were accused of solely collaborating with the northern Republicans for personal or political gain. In reality, some were former Unionists and Whigs who opposed secession, while others were Confederate veterans who recognized the Confederacy's defeat and sought to rebuild their region.[22]

During Reconstruction, both carpetbaggers and scalawags played significant roles in the newly established, Republican-led governments, which were promoting rights and opportunities for newly freed Black people in the South. They often supported progressive measures such as public education, civil rights, and infrastructure development.[23] However, through rhetorical sleights of hand, they became the villains of a story told by those who sought to restore the antebellum social and legal order. Many modern historians have challenged the negative portrayal of carpetbaggers and scalawags because, despite their varied motivations, they contributed to significant, albeit short-lived, progress in civil rights during the era of Reconstruction.[24]

But that is not a story most of us have ever heard. "Falsehood flies, and the truth comes limping after it so that when men come to be undeceived, it is too late; the jest is over, and the tale hath had its effect: . . . like a physician, who hath found out an infallible medicine after the patient is dead."[25] Those words by the political satirist and writer Jonathan Swift ring as true today as they did over three hundred years ago when they were written. The rhetorical pushback against the advancement of Black people specifically has taken many forms and used many a Trojan horse to cover what's inside: anti-Blackness.

While Reconstruction-era terms like *carpetbagger* and *scalawag* carry specific historical meanings, parallels can be drawn with contemporary resistance to DEI initiatives. Much like Reconstruction, DEI has not been and cannot be a cure for hundreds of years of systemic racial discrimination. Again, that is too much for any single methodology to achieve. However, understanding the roots of resistance through recognizing the historical patterns of oppression and opposition to social change can help form tactics that better address this contemporary pushback. This is imperative because the pejorative use of *carpetbagger* and *scalawag* during the Reconstruction era and the current backlash against "woke" DEI initiatives show how rhetoric is used to delegitimize efforts toward societal progress and maintain existing power structures. The vilification of carpetbaggers and scalawags partly contributed to the eventual downfall of Reconstruction efforts, leading directly to the rise of Jim Crow laws, which had devastating economic and emotional consequences for Black Americans. Similarly, the current backlash against DEI could hinder progress toward a more inclusive and equitable workplace and society, which on some level appears to be the goal of those leading the charge to reframe these initiatives as "divisive."

The backlash to the success of the formerly enslaved during Reconstruction was swift and brutal. Reconstruction opponents also mischaracterized those efforts as forcing equality through external imposition, which is a historic through line. Without the legal intervention that was to become Jim Crow, it's possible that these past 157 years could have seen the unraveling of the fictions about Black intelligence and status in American society and their disentanglement from our collective national narrative, but it was not to be.

The Compromise of 1877 marked the end of Reconstruction as federal troops were withdrawn from the South and southern Democrats regained political control.[26] This would result in the rollback of civil rights gains made during Reconstruction, expansion of the "Black Codes," and the ushering in of Jim Crow. It's important to note that Jim Crow and its customs and laws were a regime of such extreme domestic terrorism that the Nazis—who had borrowed from the US genocide of Native Americans in their own Holocaust—came to study it. The writer James Q. Whitman connects the citizenship and anti-miscegenation laws of Jim Crow as directly relevant to the two principal Nuremberg Laws—the Citizenship Law and the Blood Law. However, there were elements of Jim Crow, including the "one-drop rule," that even the Nazis felt were too extreme.[27]

Lost on the Timeline

Named for Columbia professor William Archibald Dunning and his students, the Dunning School's theory sought to recast the advances of Reconstruction as failures.[28] As they saw it, the issue with Reconstruction was that it allowed these seemingly unqualified and incompetent Black Americans to participate in the civic and political life of the United States, again echoing almost verbatim critiques made about DEI allowing "unqualified" Black people into higher education, aviation, and sometimes, it feels, even existence. The Dunning School blamed Black people rather than white terrorism for the end of Reconstruction.[29] This narrative ignored the widespread resistance faced by Black and white Americans during and after Reconstruction as they tried valiantly to bring about a more equitable society. The Dunning School's influence on the views many held about Reconstruction was prominent for much of the early to midtwentieth century, and it appears, given our national tendency toward willful ignorance, that its theses are still a major influence for many.

The Supreme Court ruling in *Brown v. Board of Education* on May 17, 1954, legally ended a key element of Jim Crow— "separate but equal." But the ruling could not erase the "screen of racial contempt" erected after Bacon's Rebellion or unwind hundreds of years' worth of the policies, practices, and beliefs that, as of 1954, had been weaving their way into the fabric of America for 334 years. Even in the face of that reality, many Black Americans were finding ways to succeed against these odds. I call these descendants the vanguard, the generations before mine who insisted upon equal citizenship and pulled off feats of social and economic justice—acts of extreme bravery, valor, and accomplishment. However, they were still operating within a system that was explicitly designed to prevent them from sustaining, let alone passing down, any of the fruits of their achievements. That some in the vanguard were able to do so is a testament to their spirit, intellect, and skill as organizers and community members.

But it would be another decade after the passing of *Brown* when civil rights legislation would even begin to lay out the instruments designed to prune back those deeply rooted vines of thought and practice that make up who we are when it comes to race. When I bring this up to some white people, the common refrain is, "Well, that was a long time ago." But was it? Or are we lost on the timeline? The last two major pieces of race-based civil rights legislation—the Fair Housing Act of 1968, prohibiting discrimination in the sale, rental, and financing of housing based on race, color, religion, sex, national origin, or familial status, and the Civil Rights Act of 1968 (also known as the Indian Civil Rights Act), which finally extended civil rights protections to Native Americans, guaranteeing them the same constitutional rights as other US citizens—passed in April 1968, just three months after I was born.

This means those born in 1968 were the first truly "free" generation of Black Americans, and even then, more like first-generation immigrants than people whose families have toiled, feared, loved, and died in this country for over four hundred years. By this, I mean legally free from the customary and legal-based discrimination that regulated such areas as housing, the workplace, and even matters of the heart (*Loving v. Virginia*[30]). Of course, we knew then, as we know now, that those legal changes did not magically erase hundreds of years of violence, terror, lies, and beliefs about the descendants of the formerly enslaved. That environment of oppression and its requisite laws, policies, practices, and beliefs would persist, adapting with the times to maintain the status quo.

The Promise

"If you can convince the lowest white man he's better than the best colored man, he won't notice you're picking his pocket. Give him somebody to look down on, and he'll empty his pockets for you." So said President Lyndon B. Johnson, who was born and raised during the American apartheid that was Jim Crow. And while he did advance some of the greatest governmental strides in civil rights legislation during his time as president, he was still as culpable as any other white person raised under that fiction. In that quote, he is articulating a key promise of whiteness, of the American Dream: that Blackness should never be above you, more successful than you, smarter than you, or better than you in any way.

That agreement—that whiteness is superior and that anyone who does not have the privilege of living within it is inherently inferior—is at the root of many of the issues Black people and other people of color face in the workplace today. This agreement was built on a set of fictions, the most pernicious of which has to do with Black intelligence.

Historically, to maintain this fiction, slaveholding states forbade enslaved people from learning to read. "In other words," writes Scott L. Miller, "they passed compulsory ignorance laws."[31] By doing so, they installed a systemic process of deprivation that would be used to justify the fiction of Black intellectual inferiority for generations. Many enslaved people learned to read anyway, but as became a pattern in American life, to debunk racist fiction they had to take serious risks: severe corporal punishment, being sold away from family, reenslavement of free Black people, and even death to do so.

The question, then, is, if Black people were biologically and inherently intellectually unequal to white people, why was the ruling class so afraid of Black literacy? Because reading could lead to expressions of intellect, which would undermine a key racist assumption—intellectual inferiority—that was used to justify slavery. If an enslaved person could learn to read and write, it would contradict the fiction of them being innately less intelligent or capable or, more simply put, less human. Once slavery ended, one might say the worst fears of those who benefited most from white supremacy were realized.

Not enough people know that prior to *Brown v. Board of Education* and the civil rights legislation of the 1960s, there were other attempts to lay out the tools to prune the vines of racism from society. During Reconstruction, two amendments to the Constitution and the first-ever piece of civil rights legislation were passed: the Fourteenth and Fifteenth Amendments to the Constitution, and the Civil Rights Act of 1866. The Fourteenth Amendment is the reason all Americans alive today are citizens because it granted citizenship to all those "born or naturalized in the United States," including formerly enslaved people, and provided all citizens with "equal protection under the laws," while the Fifteenth Amendment legally secured the right to vote for Black men.[32] A note here: Native Americans were not included in the Fourteenth or Fifteenth Amendments or the Civil Rights Act of 1866 as they were considered a separate nation with their own government. In a perverse irony, 158 years later, those seeking a "new Jim Crow" are using the Civil Rights Act of 1866 to accomplish "[the] dismantling of race-specific programs that promote 'diversity, equity and inclusion,' or DEI."[33] Those seeking to abolish the tools that have *barely* begun to provide redress for the three-hundred-plus years of legal exclusion from economic and political life claim they are seeking a "color-blind" society. However, I believe their true goal is a society that *ignores* the impact of color and race on Black and other people of color to the advantage of white people. That more than a dozen lawsuits are currently using this framing to go after Black advancement in education, the workplace, and the entrepreneurial space, where Black people are barely represented, reveals the true aims of these groups, a restoration of white supremacy, and the establishment of a new Jim Crow.[34]

The current misuse of the Civil Rights Act of 1866 is a stark reminder that it takes *more* than legal tools to change things. It took the full weight of the federal government to force the South to put these tools into place. As a result of this enforcement, African Americans finally enjoyed a brief period "when they were allowed to vote, actively participate in the political process, acquire the land of former owners, seek their own employment, and use public accommodations."[35]

Even with two arms and a leg tied behind their backs, many Black people began to learn, progress, and succeed. Some even ran for office, and as I've mentioned, in 1868, South Carolina elected a majority Black state senate. For the first time in its young existence, the United States had a Black senator and Black congressmen from across the country. What this shows is that every time even a sliver of advancement has presented itself, Black people have seized the opportunity to leap forward. These leaps, unfortunately, fly in the face of white supremacy, which clings to the fiction of Black intellectual inferiority and the promise that the American Dream was only meant for them. This is why over time, the lies about Black people have morphed into a day-to-day reality where most Americans—regardless of race—have internalized racist beliefs around Black intellectual inferiority. As a result, these leaps forward have been and continue to be met with vicious backlash.

Jim Crow and the terrorism that grew up around it, including the Ku Klux Klan, were the legal and social expressions of that backlash. Black men were physically run out of office. Black people were removed from their jobs, the voter rolls, their homes, and their land. This backlash began to reassert most of the elements of enslavement, if not the actual physical aspects. This is because racial equality was in opposition to what Confederate vice president Alexander H. Stephens said in 1861 was the "cornerstone" idea of America: "that the negro is not equal to the white man."[36] In other words, the advancement of Black people is unfair to white people and undemocratic.

The Red Summer, which historians argue lasted for at least five years beginning in 1919, included violent incidents across the country. The burning of "Black Wall Street" in Tulsa, Oklahoma, and the massacre and destruction of the town of Rosewood, Florida, in 1923 were a response to that "unfairness." This spasm of violence saw hundreds if not thousands of Black

Americans killed, terrorized, and again dislodged from their homes, businesses, and land by white mobs that never faced justice.[37] And what was the crime these communities and individuals had committed? Reaching for things that were, by law, practice, and custom, reserved only for white people: success, opportunity, and advancement. Black men had returned from World War I and expected the same rights as other Americans. Communities like the Greenwood district of Tulsa had done everything possible to achieve the American Dream. They worked together, establishing banks, shops, and widespread industry. They went to school and received higher levels of education, counting among them doctors, lawyers, and bankers. By all rights, there should be wealthy Black families today who could trace their economic start to Greenwood. Greenwood Avenue, the center of Black Wall Street, had "luxury shops, restaurants, grocery stores, hotels, jewelry and clothing stores, movie theaters, barbershops and salons, a library, pool halls, nightclubs, and offices for doctors, lawyers, and dentists . . . its own school system, post office, savings and loan bank, hospital, bus, and taxi service."[38] Michelle Place, executive director of the Tulsa Historical Society and Museum, said, "I think the word *jealousy* is certainly appropriate during this time. If you have particularly poor whites looking at this prosperous community with large homes, fine furniture, China, linens, etc., the reaction is, 'they don't deserve that.'"[39]

Conservative commentators today—particularly at Fox News and similar media outlets—say openly that Black people are undeserving of certain positions or of being in certain places and spaces, especially of power. Over and over, the reason for the terror inflicted on Black communities has been their success. Reaching for that success sparks demands for equal rights and necessitates their own pushback against race-based assumptions about what economic position they, as Black people, should hold in American society. The folks in Greenwood paid the price by having their homes and businesses burned to the ground and seeing women, men, and children shot and killed in their homes and on the streets. Some survivors described, years later, having to endure the indignity of seeing their stolen possessions paraded in front of them by those who had invaded their homes, killed their family members, and tried to kill their dreams. The lack of punishment for this terrorism sent a clear message: any time white people felt things were getting out of balance, they were free to reassert the agreement, the promise, and the dream of their superiority—by any means necessary.

While the tactics may have changed, the language of unfairness persists in the face of Black success, be it Greenwood or the crack in the door of opportunity opened by legislation like affirmative action. The fictions of race and white supremacy are just as tightly woven into our collective mind as they ever were. However, these fictions have adapted to the modern day in the guise of pseudoscience, misinformation, and stereotypes, often repeated and taken as fact not only by white people but also by Black and other people of color. Competency checking then exists *not to disprove* these fictions but as a way, once again, to push back against the "unfairness" of Black advancement and success.

To cover the fact that the true culprit in the pushback to Black advancement is not lack of qualifications but race, white supremacy has deployed the fiction that Black Americans don't value education. But Black Americans created our own educational system from grade school through higher education. Historically Black colleges like Howard University still exist today. Even our current system of public education is directly tied to the work of Black and white abolitionists and free people to educate poor Black and white people in the South.[40]

Yet the fiction persists that Black people have not and do

not value education.[41] And even when we do achieve education, our accomplishments are undermined by pseudoscience, from cranium-measuring to the misuse of IQ testing to the bell-curve theory of racial and class intelligence and allegations of affirmative action or "DEI hires." These ideas are nothing more than branches of a vine shooting off from 1851 and Samuel Cartwright's invented diseases, which conveniently ignored the severe prohibitions on enslaved people learning to read or write in their new language or the penalty of physical torture that prevented them from speaking in their own languages because enslavers feared rebellion.[42]

One can easily see how these fictions worked to affirm pre-existing beliefs. It was done by essentially rigging the game to reverse-engineer a person's existing assumptions while ignoring the tremendous amount of work that went into creating the supposed results. For example, IQ testing was never meant to be a measure of innate intelligence.[43] The misuse of the IQ test, using words and phrases that are unfamiliar to children raised in households without access to the same educational system as the dominant culture, makes it appear that those children lack innate intellectual skills or abilities.[44] If you give the test to children for whom English is their second language without ESL assistance, you will get a similar result. But what if you turned the tables? What if you gave white children an intelligence test using African American Vernacular English? Would the assumption be that they lack innate intelligence or that the test was unfair?

Moving Past the Past

I should stress that, as much as we need to study and understand what has happened historically, in order to move forward as a society, it's also important we shift the focus from the failings—deliberate, coincidental, or otherwise—of individuals to the undeniable injustices of laws, practices, policies, and beliefs that continue to create barriers to success for Black Americans. To stop the destructive impact of competency checking, we must acknowledge it and use intentionality to thwart it.

Returning to the poorly laid foundation analogy, we must work intentionally to fix faulty thinking, erroneous assumptions, and lopsided benefits. The purpose of fixing a house's poorly laid foundation is to ensure the stability and longevity of the structure. A solid foundation is critical because it supports everything above it; the entire house is at risk if it fails. Just as a house cannot exist securely on an unstable base, a society cannot flourish, let alone remain stable, when systemic inequities compromise its foundational principles.

There are several ways to fix a poorly laid foundation. The most extreme is to dismantle the house above it and lay a new one. Repairing a foundation, however, requires the process of underpinning: identifying the weak points, shoring up the existing structure, and reinforcing it with new, stronger materials. This process is not only about immediate fixes but also about ensuring that future problems are prevented. In the same way, addressing foundational issues of racism and inequality in society requires a thorough examination of the existing social structures, policies, and attitudes that perpetuate these beliefs. It necessitates the reinforcement of our social fabric with laws, education, and systems that promote fairness and justice. Just as a house might need to be temporarily propped up to fix its base, a society might need to support those who have been marginalized as it works to rectify the wrongs of the past.

When fixing a foundation, it might tremble as the work begins, dust swirling in the air. As with any renovation, the initial disruption paves the way for a more stable future. Dismantling systemic racism might require a combination of foundational fixes and "tear-downs," and the purpose of this book is to reveal a blueprint for you to follow to help you identify what you should be aware of and lay out the tools you will need as we jointly begin this work toward building a more equitable and just society that doesn't pretend not to see race but acknowledges and accounts for its role as a destabilizing factor.

CHAPTER 3

Color Blinded

Instead of being blind to race, color blindness makes
people blind to racism.

> —Heather McGhee, *The Sum of Us: What Racism
> Costs Everyone and How We Can Prosper Together*

M Y MOTHER'S OLDER brother, Daniel Staples, was among
the 1.2 million Black men who served their country in
World War II. Uncle Daniel once vividly described to the family the moment his unit reached San Francisco following the
end of the war in 1945. Uncle Daniel and the other Black
soldiers were initially filled with a sense of achievement and
anticipation but soon found themselves marginalized and humiliated. Once arrived at the dock, the Black soldiers were
instructed to remain on board until the white soldiers had
all disembarked. Uncle Daniel noted that when they finally
disembarked, the heroes' arch that had been constructed for
the white soldiers to pass through was still set up; the Black
soldiers were explicitly told to walk around, not through it.
This act of exclusion was a deliberate message underscoring
a bitter reality: Black soldiers may have helped "save democracy" abroad, but they weren't allowed to participate in democracy at home. Their wartime exploits—their bravery and

sacrifice—were color-blind, but the country they had fought for and returned to was not.

In his book *Half American*, Matthew Delmont describes a similar scene: "When [Sergeant James Tilman's] unit crossed the Atlantic, they were forced to wait on the dock in Norfolk, Virginia, because local officials did not want Black soldiers marching through town."[1] This wasn't just about exclusion from a parade; it was about enforcing systemic racism. If humiliation didn't work, violence was used to bring home the point. Shortly after his discharge, Sergeant Isaac Woodard boarded a bus in Batesburg, South Carolina, still wearing his uniform. Woodard asked the bus driver not to disrespect him by calling him "boy," and the bus driver called the police. The police beat Woodard so severely he was blinded in both eyes.[2] Some Black veterans met an even worse fate. George W. Dorsey, who had served in the Pacific and North Africa, was among a group of four Black men who were beaten, tortured, shot to death, and hanged from a bridge in Georgia in 1946.[3]

This is the system into which "America's first color-blind social legislation" was launched.[4] Officially known as the Servicemen's Readjustment Act of 1944, the GI Bill was technically considered "race-neutral." According to American political scientist and historian Ira Katznelson, "The GI Bill's remarkable array of advantages for American troops contained not a 'single loophole for different treatment of white and Black veterans.'"[5] And yet, the GI Bill arguably had the single biggest impact on positively transforming only the lives of *white* men in United States history.

According to Professor Suzanne Mettler of Cornell University, who has written extensively about the impact of the GI Bill, "Prior to 1940, colleges were mostly for the privileged, but the G.I. Bill opened doors to many who were Catholic and Jewish, including rural people, first-generation immigrant offspring, and veterans from working and middle-class backgrounds."[6] The rigid prewar class system saw primarily wealthy, Protestant white men accessing higher education and the opportunities that flowed from it.[7] But by 1947, veterans accounted for almost 49 percent of college admissions.[8] This led to a more educated workforce and contributed to the expansion of America's middle class and the overall strengthening of the US economy.[9] The GI Bill also created a housing boom through $33 billion in low-interest home-loan guarantees. This enabled many veterans, including ethnic and working-class white Americans, to become homeowners, often in the new suburbs, which would dramatically alter the country's geographic and economic landscape.[10] The echoes of this boom continue through to today, as wealth gained is often—though not always—wealth inherited: "Over the next decade or so, a massive transfer of wealth and assets [built in part on homeownership] will occur as the silent generation and baby boomers hand over the reins to millennials. The shift will see US$90 trillion of assets move between generations in the US alone, making affluent millennials the richest generation in history."[11]

However, the singularly transformative legislation that was the post–World War II GI Bill did not impact all veterans equally. While it may have been written to be "color-blind," the system administering it was not. Jim Crow in the South was still the law of the land when the war ended and would continue to be practiced well past the 1954 Supreme Court decision in *Brown v. Board of Education.*[12] Jim Crow in the North would continue to be de facto policy culturally, practically, and legally through tools such as redlining, restrictive housing covenants, and racially biased lending from the Federal Housing Administration.[13] Racist and specifically anti-Black bias prevented Black men from either accessing or utilizing the full benefits of the GI Bill. Retired US Air Force lieutenant colonel Robert

Levinson wrote, "In theory, a Black veteran might qualify for a GI Bill loan guarantee to buy a house, but no bank would give him a loan, no realtor would show him a home, and no white owner would sell him one. In New York and northern New Jersey, fewer than 100 of the 67,000 mortgages backed by the GI Bill supported non-whites."[14] So, for the more than 1 million Black men and women who served during the war, there was to be no Levittown, New York, one of the well-known planned communities that sprang up after the war that GIs flocked to. These communities explicitly forbade Black people from purchasing homes and did so with the blessing of the FHA through restrictive covenants and intimidation. As the National Urban League found in 1947, "It was as though the legislation were earmarked For White Veterans Only."[15]

The legislation and the implementation of the GI Bill reveal two critical truths: First, targeted and affirmative action can transform the lives of a specific population or group, in this case veterans. Second, the problem with color-blind solutions is that they can end up being blindingly white.

These narratives—of my uncle, Isaac Woodard, and millions of Black veterans—paint a vivid picture of the struggle for equality and justice. They remind us that while policies may not explicitly discriminate, their implementation within a biased system can and do perpetuate inequality. The experiences of Black soldiers returning from World War II encapsulate the failure of "color-blind" policies in a society where racial biases influence every facet of life both then and now.

Legally Color-Blind

In 2023, the Supreme Court ruled in *Students for Fair Admissions v. Harvard* that race-based admissions programs violate the equal protection clause of the Fourteenth Amendment and

Title VI of the Civil Rights Act of 1964.[16] Chief Justice John Roberts wrote for the majority: "They have wrongly concluded that the touchstone of an individual's identity is not challenges bested, skills built, or lessons learned but the color of their skin. Our constitutional history does not tolerate that choice."[17] This quote from Roberts feels remarkably close intellectually to the majority opinion in *Plessy v. Ferguson*, the 1896 case that ushered in Jim Crow, aka "separate but equal." Justice Henry Billings Brown, writing for the majority in *Plessy*, stated, "We consider the underlying fallacy of the plaintiff's argument to consist in the assumption that the enforced separation of the two races stamps the colored race with a badge of inferiority. If this be so, it is not by reason of anything found in the act but solely because the colored race chooses to put that construction upon it. . . . If the civil and political rights of both races are equal, one cannot be inferior to the other civilly or politically."[18] The critical nexus between the majority in the Roberts Court and the court that decided *Plessy* is this idea of racial neutrality that is "post-racial" or color-blind.[19]

The problem with both these decisions is that we did not and do not live in a color-blind society. Race is still a factor in nearly every area of life, from health outcomes to employment opportunities, because we have never truly addressed some of the foundational fallacies upon which America was built.[20] As Justice Ketanji Brown Jackson highlighted in her dissent to the *Harvard* decision, "[g]iven the lengthy history of state-sponsored race-based preferences in America, to say that anyone is now victimized if a college considers whether that legacy of discrimination has unequally advantaged its applicants fails to acknowledge the well-documented 'intergenerational transmission of inequality' that still plagues our citizenry."[21] What Justice Jackson rightly pointed out is the fact that for three hundred years, every American institution saw race as a negative when directed toward Black people, and thereby provided an opportunity advantage to white people. Pretending that didn't happen and that it has no impact today—as they say in the law—strains credulity.

According to Cedric Merlin Powell, a professor at the University of Louisville's Louis D. Brandeis School of Law, the Roberts Court advances three myths related to race.[22] The first myth is a revisionist version of American history, the second is an unworkably narrow definition of what constitutes discrimination, and the third is what I call the reverse-engineering method of explaining structural inequity: focusing on the results, not the cause, of racial discrimination. In doing so, the Supreme Court does not acknowledge that structural racial inequity exists in any meaningful way. Instead, they see it as the *Plessy* court described: an "underlying fallacy." This was brought home with shocking clarity during the oral arguments over *Harvard* when Roberts said, "We did not fight a Civil War about oboe players. We did fight a Civil War to eliminate racial discrimination, and that's why it's a matter of considerable concern."[23]

As a former practicing attorney, hearing the chief justice of the United States Supreme Court articulate what historian Kevin Levin calls "an overly simplistic view of the past"[24] was shocking. Even a casual observer of history knows that the Civil War was not fought to end racial discrimination. Many antislavery proponents, including President Lincoln, did not believe in equality between the races. In Lincoln's own words: "I will say then that I am not, nor ever have been in favor of bringing about in any way the social and political equality of the white and black races."[25] This, of course, is the exact opposite of Roberts's interpretation. The very idea that an "inferior race" could be discriminated against would have been laughable to most, even those fighting against slavery. While Black Americans were to be freed, there would be no agreement by law, custom, policy, or practice that they should be equal to or superior in any way to white people. "There must be the position of superior and inferior," said Lincoln, "and I, as much as any other man, am in favor of having the superior position assigned to the white race."[26] To hear Roberts use such a faulty premise to dismantle what are still nascent efforts to address hundreds of years of disadvantage based on race felt disingenuous and eerily reminiscent of the *Plessy* court.

The question, then, is, Why are so many of us unable to see or acknowledge the past and present system of systemic racism and its impact on our everyday lives? I see two reasons. First, systemic racism is like the interstitium in our bodies. The interstitium is the network or container that holds our fluids and cells together, connecting them throughout our body. (Researchers now think it might be how cancer spreads.)[27] But for a long time, Western medicine doubted the interstitium was real, let alone essential, and has only recently accepted it.[28] Structural and practical racial discrimination, past and present, becomes the "interstitium" of our society: We deny its presence when, all the while, it is shaping, connecting, and poisoning everything around us. Why is tipping a part of American society? Systemic racism.[29] Why didn't we get universal health care in the 1950s when President Harry Truman fought for it? Systemic racism.[30]

The second reason is what I call "the hidden hand" of those who purposely seek to obscure the true nature of systemic inequity. When the hand of systemic inequity is hidden, the impact can be misidentified as the cause. So the "forced ignorance" laws that prevented the enslaved from learning to read led to illiteracy, which was then held up as evidence of Black intellectual inferiority. Hiding systemic inequality allows for the reinforcing of historical narratives and the creation of an ouroboros, "snake eating its tail"–type logic where Blackness, by its

very nature, is seen by white supremacy as inferior, unqualified, and incompetent. Still, just to be sure, systemic efforts are
implemented to prove it.

Nicholas Confessore, in an investigative piece for the *New
York Times*, uncovered a concerted effort by conservative activists, academics, and political figures to dismantle diversity,
equity, and inclusion (DEI) initiatives across the United States.
Those who wield the hidden hand might look like what Confessore found: a complex network of think tanks, political groups,
and influential donors engaged in a calculated attempt to re-
shape public opinion and education policy. He describes how
Scott Yenor, a fellow at the conservative Claremont Institute,
laid out a strategy for using the term *social justice* in place of *diversity*. *Social justice*, he argued, could be "stigmatized so that
when people hear it, they can act on their suspicions."[31] So this
is how you hide what you're doing: don't let them know you are
in favor of policies and practices that further discrimination;
say you're against "social justice."

Much of the backlash against acknowledging and correcting for anti-Black bias in the United States is rooted in the
historical trope that to do so is considered "unfair" to white
people. While white people have been saying Black inclusion is
"unfair" since emancipation, many today will say it's not fair to
"punish" them for what their ancestors did. The first problem
with that framing is the idea that removing anti-Black bias is
a "punishment." This seems to be a tactical psychological acknowledgment that there are unique benefits to being white,
and allowing Black people full and fair participation would take
away those "unique benefits," which one can assume would
be the punishment. There is also a willful ignorance about the
ways even those whose families came after slavery ended benefited from a society that provided opportunities based on the
color of their skin, such as the ability to utilize the postwar

GI Bill, as we discussed above. Finally, it places white people outside of history, denying their role and even presence, while Black people are held in a type of perpetual limbo encumbered by the vines of race-based assumptions that are seen as simply factual. In the lead-up to the 2022 midterm elections, the advocacy group America First Legal (AFL), founded by Stephen Miller, the former policy adviser in the Trump White House, ran a series of ads that "included inflammatory radio and TV spots demanding an end to 'anti-white bigotry' and accused the Biden White House, businesses, and universities of discriminating against White people."[32]

About 156 years before those ads ran, President Andrew Johnson, in his veto of the Civil Rights Act of 1866, spread almost the same message and maybe the first argument for "reverse discrimination" when he said the act would "establish for the security of the colored race safeguards which go infinitely beyond any that the General Government has ever provided for the white race. In fact, the distinction of race and color is by the bill to operate in favor of the colored and against the white race."[33]

Notably, this first claim of "reverse discrimination" came only two years after the Emancipation Proclamation was signed. The state of the newly freed was dire, as noted historian Eric Foner makes clear: "After the Civil War, freed slaves faced a world of freedom without resources. They were 'free to starve,' as one former slave put it, lacking land, tools, and basic necessities."[34] President Johnson's words, so close on the heels of the end of slavery, seem to imply that the very nature of Black freedom was itself "unfair," a reversal of fortune so egregious as to be discriminatory to whiteness itself. It projects the notion that the cessation of outright oppression is an *overcorrection* rather than a first step toward rectifying centuries of injustice.

Claims of reverse discrimination today continue to rely on a misunderstanding because of the "hidden hand" of the historical and systemic advantages that have been afforded to white people. The hidden hand keeps the power of systemic racism out of sight and places prejudice, which anyone can have about a variety of things, including race, on the same playing field. As Dr. Erica "Ricky" Sherover-Marcuse said in her seminal work on defining racism, "While any form of humans harming other humans is wrong because no one is entitled to mistreat anyone, we should not confuse the occasional mistreatment experienced by whites at the hands of people of color with the systematic and institutionalized mistreatment experienced by people of color at the hands of whites."[35]

It's not just AFL pushing this narrative. It's people like Christopher Rufo, the conservative activist central to the critical race theory hysteria and the 2024 ouster of Harvard president Dr. Claudine Gay. That Rufo has also been reported to be associated with and influenced by groups that espouse scientific racism is not surprising.[36] Race science, also known as scientific racism, refers to the pseudoscientific belief that empirical evidence exists to support or justify racism (racial discrimination), racial inferiority, or, conversely, racial superiority. Scientific racism began in Europe with the slave trade to legitimize colonialism, slavery, and segregation by suggesting that there were natural, biological differences between races that made some superior and others inferior. It is a fiction that has always been playing in the background but that has now made a loud and regrettable comeback in modern-day discourse.[37]

It's also thirteen Republican state attorneys general who have sent letters to Amazon, Microsoft, and other Fortune 100 companies to inject themselves into these private corporations' hiring decisions based on the idea that by introducing DEI initiatives to their workplaces, hiring diversely, or requiring things like antibias and antiracism training, those organizations are discriminating against white people.[38] The fact that eight of the signatories come from former slaveholding states and that the language used so closely resembles Johnson's nineteenth-century complaints proves that everything old is indeed new again.

The ridiculousness of this framing is highlighted by AFL demanding that the Equal Employment Opportunity Commission investigate NASCAR's alleged discrimination against white male Americans. NASCAR is historically very white; it currently boasts one Black driver, one native of Mexico, no women in its Cup Series, and 5 Black pit crew professionals out of over 300.[39] This might seem laughable but claiming reverse discrimination because of attempts to remedy the harm done to what is now a minuscule group of Black people has worked in the courts. Black farmers make up 1.4 percent of farmers. That number is so low because for decades the United States government unfairly denied Black farmers critical loans and grants that were afforded to their white counterparts.[40] In 2021 the Biden administration sought to rectify this systemic discrimination against Black farmers with $4 billion in aid. However, AFL challenged the aid using President Johnson's framing—and won.

While AFL has not won every lawsuit or challenge issued, it should raise the alarm for everyone, especially Black people and others in the workplace and businesses seeking to employ a diverse workforce and serve a diverse consumer base. David Hinojosa, an attorney with the Lawyers' Committee for Civil Rights Under Law, said in an interview in 2022, "Many of these lawsuits are centered on making sure that white people remain in control . . . and on maintaining the systemic discriminatory policies that have harmed Black people and other people of color for generations."[41]

Change for Me but Not for Thee

A great irony of all this pushback and attempts to undermine targeted affirmative action programs to address systemic inequity and anti-Black bias is that these very programs have helped millions of white people in the United States access opportunities that otherwise would have been difficult, if not impossible, to get. Some of the loudest anti-DEI and systemic racism deniers owe their own success to the same policies they now decry. Nimarata Randhawa, now known as Nikki Haley, was born just an hour from Batesburg, South Carolina, where Isaac Woodard was blinded for having the audacity to ask for respect upon returning as a veteran from World War II. Many say it was the blinding of Woodard that helped launch the fight for civil rights in the United States, a fight that Nikki Haley's parents would directly benefit from. The Randhawas immigrated to the United States in 1969, four years after the passage of the Immigration and Nationality Act of 1965, which removed de facto discrimination against Asians and others. As a woman and person of color, their daughter benefited from the opportunity expansion, not special treatment, that affirmative action afforded women. Yet Haley opted to Americanize her name to avoid the xenophobia and racism that she now downplays and the systemic racism that she says doesn't exist.

Texas governor Greg Abbott, tragically paralyzed from the waist down at the age of twenty-six in 1984, lives in a world where the Americans with Disabilities Act paved a path of opportunity for people with disabilities. Yet in 2023, Governor Abbott signed into law a ban on diversity, equity, and inclusion (DEI) offices at government agencies, public colleges, and universities across the state.[42] According to CBS News, the governor's office said, "DEI initiatives illegally discriminate against certain demographic groups—though he did not specify which ones he was talking about."[43] In the article, Andrew Eckhous, an Austin-based employment lawyer, says, "The governor's office is 'completely mischaracterizing DEI's role in employment decisions' in an apparent attempt to block initiatives that improve diversity."[44]

Florida governor Ron DeSantis, the great- and great-great-grandchild of immigrants from southern Italy, has benefited from a world in which what he calls "woke" policies and laws changed the perception of and wholesale discrimination against Italians, primarily those of southern origin. That discrimination was unquestioned in the United States until antidiscrimination laws, revised historical education (such as the establishment of Columbus Day after the murder of eleven Italian Americans in Louisiana), and the civil rights laws, including anti–housing discrimination, gave people like his family a type of legal passage into "whiteness."[45]

The truth is that color-blind policies, while seemingly equitable on their face, do not exist in a historical vacuum. Rather than act as a complete course correction, they instead often serve to perpetuate a status quo that upholds systemic racial barriers. The stories of Black soldiers facing discrimination starkly illustrate how race-neutral laws and policies like the post–World War II GI Bill cannot withstand the impact of a system that is fundamentally race-based. However, these policies also make clear that you can change circumstances through intentionality; their impact has already proven transformative for white Americans.

All this hypocrisy further exposes the fallacy of arguments against race-based solutions to correct historical and current barriers. The stark contrast in outcomes highlights the potential of such policies to foster genuine equity when applied with intentionality that acknowledges racial realities in their design and implementation. It's clear what we need to do to transform the lives of Black Americans and other people of color, namely, use the same intentionality and focus that helped white veterans after World War II. We do this by acknowledging that Black Americans have been and continue to be blocked by systemic racism and targeting those things blocking Black Americans' path to access, opportunity, and success, things like competency checking.

White people should be just as invested as Black people because they have deeply benefited from targeted solutions that have provided for them expansion of opportunity that has only ever helped our country. But we must use targeted intentionality and let go of the idea that we are simply a meritocracy. To do that we must therefore explode the myth of qualification.

CHAPTER 4

The Myth of Qualifications

The able-bodied C man! He sails swimmingly along. . . .
The light of his ambition is respectably to pass and to
hold a firm position in the middle of his class.[1]

—1909 verse by Harvard alumnus
Robert Grant, LLB, 1879

The Gentleman's C

One of the things I most enjoy in my work as a consultant is coaching both individuals and teams on DEI. These sessions allow me to listen to people's concerns and questions about these topics in a space where they can be heard and, crucially, not judged. My role is to provide my clients, specifically my white clients, something very few of us really get to experience: cross-racial dialogue with someone who can speak on these issues from a place of personal experience. The education in these sessions isn't one-sided—because of my coaching, I have learned firsthand what some white people never knew about race, that it is made up, and what some people were taught, that Black people have a different type of blood.

I also get some insight into white people's fears. In one coaching session, I was working with someone who was incredibly frustrated with a recent meme they had seen on Facebook, a visual representation of the difference between equity and equality. The three-paneled picture shows kids of different heights in front of a wood fence, watching a baseball game. Under Equality, each kid is standing on an identical box, but the fence is too high for the smaller children to see over. Under Equity, the kids are standing on the exact number of boxes they would need to be able to see over the fence, or, in the case of the tallest child, no box at all, since they can already see over it. Under Justice, the wood fence is replaced with no fence, removing the need for boxes entirely.

At first, my client couldn't articulate what exactly about the picture upset them; finally, they said emphatically, "It's unfair." I was baffled and asked them to walk me through what, exactly, was unfair. After a minute or so and with some emotion, they said, "Well, it took away the tall kid's advantage; that kid had an advantage, and now it's gone."

This person was articulating the fear of losing what I call "accidental advantage." I explained to the client that the tall kid didn't do anything special; they were tall as an accident of genetics. Conversely, the shorter kids didn't do anything wrong and, to my mind, weren't asking for anything special, just for the ability to watch the game. Those explanations, unfortunately, did not assuage my client's fear. A fear that, however unfounded, didn't come from nowhere. The upset they experienced when confronted with the image was about loss, a loss they couldn't fully articulate but could feel acutely as fear. And to them, that fear was real. I believe that fear is a major driver of one of the major myths created by systemic racism: the myth of qualifications.

In my coaching work and in casual conversations, I often hear people parroting some version of CNN commentator Fareed Zakaria's take on diversity, that workplaces and universities are "neglecting excellence to pursue a variety of agendas—many of them clustered around diversity and inclusion."[2] The folks equating diversity with a lack of excellence also use that false equivalency to cry out for a return to the halcyon days when only the "most qualified" people got ahead. It was a time when, according to them, universities were rigorous institutions where only As and few Bs would do, and when workplaces were full of only the best and the brightest who deserved their roles because of their hard work.

Spoiler alert: There were no halcyon days before diversity when being "qualified" was the only thing that mattered. Rather, what we see again and again from education to employment is the "tall kids" shifting what it means to be qualified to keep—and maintain—their "accidental advantage." According to an article in the *Harvard Crimson* titled "The First Harvard Graduate," Harvard graduated its first class of nine white, Christian men in 1642. Their degrees were given to them "not according to age, or scholarship, or the alphabet, but according to the rank their families held in society."[3] They were the tall kids. "For the next 121 years, Harvard continued to classify its graduates by their family status."[4] While there was a small amount of space made for poor white Protestant boys, institutions of higher learning were generally seen as places for the superior elite, and that was the primary qualification. "[G]aining entry was not overwhelmingly difficult for those who had completed the required course work [and] had the money."[5]

Robert Grant, the Harvard alumnus, jurist, and satirist who wrote about the "gentleman's C," is recognized for his contribution to understanding the academic culture of his time.[6] He wrote his little ditty in 1909, "The able-bodied C man! He sails swimmingly along . . . The light of his ambition is respectably to pass and to hold a firm position in the middle of his class," as a funny way to highlight the fact that chasing an A grade was seen as déclassé; you didn't want to be seen as "on the grind."[7] If you think this was an exaggeration, we must only turn our attention to two members of Harvard's class of 1904: Lathrop Brown, a congressman, and Franklin Delano Roosevelt, a soon-to-be president, to see the "able-bodied" C men in action. The Franklin Delano Roosevelt Foundation's website has both men's original entrance examination results and their grades for each semester they were at Harvard. According to today's pundits, neither man was qualified for admission to Harvard, nor qualified for the significant positions they eventually held based on their grades at graduation. Both Lathrop and Roosevelt scored mostly Cs and Ds on their entrance exams, and both averaged about a C-minus their entire time at Harvard, with neither man ever obtaining an A and both with a substantial amount of Ds and even a few Es.

This has nothing to do with grade inflation, as Robert Grant's writings reveal; it's simply that it was seen as tacky to work hard for good grades. But then, in a society run by men like Lathrop and Roosevelt, there wasn't really any need to be a good student; theirs was a society of "tall boys."

That being said, I believe two contradictory things can be true: First, grades are not always an indicator of intelligence or a person's propensity for success. Second, grades became an indicator of intelligence and a propensity for success when those in the "out-group" sought admission to the tall kid's clubs. Once the short kids started to infiltrate "tall" spaces, the rules changed, and now the shorter person must find a way to reach the same height as someone who is born tall.

In his book *The Chosen: The Hidden History of Admission and Exclusion at Harvard, Yale, and Princeton,* author Jerome Karabel examines how these most esteemed tall-boy institutions reacted to what they saw as an influx of the "other." A. Lawrence Lowell presided over Harvard from 1909 to 1923 when he and other university presidents, including those at Columbia, Yale, and Princeton, were facing their institutions being "'overrun' with politically undesirable and socially inferior students who showed little evidence that they would ever appreciate American institutions and life."[8] And who were these "undesirables"? Jewish students.

Research has shown that what constituted "qualified" began to shift after 1918, when Jewish students started to gain admission and increase their numbers at what many had long referred to as "gentlemen's finishing schools."[9] These schools started to erect figurative fences to block access to Jewish students by creating higher and harder hurdles for admission. "[T]he desire to restrict access of Jewish students led to drastic changes in the way that students gained admission to college. Selective admissions, psychological tests, the lengthy application (including a 2" x 2" photograph), and many other mechanisms now in general use."[10] In fact, the entire standard college admissions process as we know it today, including the SAT, has its roots in anti-Semitism and a desire to keep the accidental advantage held by those born rich, white, and Protestant.

The SAT, LSAT, MCAT, and Bar Exam

Aptitude and standardized tests have a specious history at best and eugenic/scientific racist foundations at worst.[11] Each of these tests, including the Scholastic Aptitude Test (SAT), the Law School Admission Test (LSAT), the Medical College Admission Test (MCAT), and the bar exam, are, on the one hand, hailed as bringing "professionalism" and providing for "merit" based access to the institutions they were designed to protect.[12] But there's something else: each of these tests happens to coincide with moments in history when those from the "outside" start to seek entry into the tall kids' clubs.[13] The SAT came online in the late 1920s as even more Jewish students started to seek access to higher education. The bar exam follows a similar track, and its modern incarnation is contemporaneous with the SAT. For most of the United States' history, lawyers apprenticed with a more senior attorney, and then the apprentice took an oral bar exam. Eventually, that oral exam fell out of favor, and "[after] the 1870s, many states began granting diploma privileges to graduates of local law schools, making bar examinations unnecessary."[14]

However, something began to change in the legal profession starting near the end of the 1800s and picking up steam in the mid-1900s: a desire to "professionalize" the bar. So, "in 1921, the American Bar Association (ABA) declared that it preferred licensing lawyers based on their performance on written bar exams rather than on receiving a diploma." What was changing? Ethnic, religious, and racial minorities who had a hard time getting access to apprenticeships based on discrimination saw another route open and "obtained entry to the bar by virtue of open admissions law schools."[15] This was not well received, "When an ambitious Italian, Jew or Black vaulted the bar into the legislature, he often carried his group identity with him . . . [and] any movement to limit access to the bar might easily become (or indeed originate as) a device to deny political power to specific ethnic or religious groups."[16]

The fact that the written bar exam was formalized in 1921 and the Medical College Admission Test (MCAT) was first administered in 1928 cannot simply be a coincidence: Both came hot on the heels of Carl C. Brigham, PhD, adapting his military intelligence test into what would eventually become the SAT. Brigham designed the test to prove the superior intelligence of the "Nordic" race: "there is only one other possible escape from the conclusion that our test results indicate a genuine intellectual superiority of the Nordic group over the Alpine and Mediterranean groups."[17] Brigham separated the white race into subsections: the Nordic Race, supposedly originating from Northern Europe; the Mediterranean Race, for people from what he called the Mediterranean region, including Italians;

and the Alpine Race, for people believed to be native to the central and eastern European mountain regions, which he described as having a shorter and stockier build, round heads, and intermediate skin and hair color. Jewish people were put in the Alpine group.[18] While Brigham set about "proving" the Nordic Race was superior to all groups, there was a specific focus on proving the inferiority of the Alpine group. Brigham admitted the "Nordic" designed the test to favor themselves, and then he pulled the curtain back and revealed an essential truth that "our educational institutions are themselves a part of our [the Nordic's] own race heritage."[19] This test then becomes the basis for the SAT, with an emphasis on race and class heritage remaining prominent features—not bugs. "For years, the SAT included an analogy question that asked test-takers to identify 'oarsman: regatta' . . . the correct answer to 'runner: marathon.'" White students answered correctly at a higher rate than students of color—not because of innate knowledge, but because they were more likely to know the word *regatta*.[20]

The Law School Admission Test (LSAT) came about in the 1940s and picked up steam after World War II, when ethnic, religious, and racial minorities, as well as working-class and lower-income white men, returned home and started to take advantage of the GI Bill. Though some believe that "the primary consideration appears to have been providing a neutral benchmark to assess potential applicants," there is at the same time an acknowledgment that "the LSAT, though labeled an 'admissions' test, was from the very beginning a test of 'aptitude' . . . [and] this choice was very much one of its times."[21]

That time was one of calculated racism—the military itself was still segregated—when the tall boys set about creating obstacles for those seeking inclusion to their clubs. What it meant to be qualified began to shift at an unprecedented rate and scale. It was a time when the roots of our modern system of vetting qualifications became entrenched in the soil of American life. Those deep roots have never been excavated, and the vines that have grown from them are woven into our modern world.

Beyond the Elites

For most of our history, people, even doctors and lawyers, learned to do their jobs by *doing* them. They apprenticed with someone in the field, learned on the job, and in time passed the knowledge on to their apprentice. But that process was notoriously discriminatory toward initially ethnic whites and religious minorities like Jewish people and largely remains so toward Black people. While the history of Black workers in apprenticeships and unions is complicated, there were some successes, like the Reconstruction-era Colored National Labor Union and the Southern Tenant Farmers' Union (STFU), which played a crucial role in advocating for tenant farmers and sharecroppers.[22] But the overwhelming theme when it comes to unions and apprenticeships has been one of shifting definitions of qualification and access to exclude Black workers. The impact of licensing laws on the ability of Black workers across a variety of trade industries is analogous to the impact of the SAT, LSAT, bar exam, and MCAT on higher education.[23]

In response to the pressure to allow more Black people into the trades, licensing laws were used in both the North and the South to prevent Black people from competing with established white workers. Just like with the college admissions and certification testing, these licenses were couched in terms of quality and public health. But as the author David E. Bernstein points out, this government-sponsored exclusion has had an impact in the past and the present: "Because unions did not admit Blacks into their apprenticeship training programs . . . Black workers generally had little formal training in their professions and therefore often could not satisfy certain licensing requirements despite their practical experience."[24] Bernstein also cites relatively recent data showing that Black cosmetologists were passing the practical portion of the cosmetology exam at the same rates as whites but failing the written exam at a higher rate because "they could not answer questions [in the written exams] that were tangentially related to their jobs." This is where language usage, culture, and context, "oarsman and regatta," come into play.[25] Bernstein showcases how physician licensing laws led to the closure of Black medical schools, and plumber licensing laws gave control of the field to unions that were de facto for white's only. From a system-wide perspective, Bernstein argues that the legacy of governmental support for occupational licensing laws "has been underestimated as a factor in the plight of black Americans."[26]

Bernstein illustrates that the vines of licensure testing were grown in the soil of scientific racism and nurtured by the "in-group" decades ago and are still impacting Black people today. In an article for the *Stanford Social Innovation Review* titled "Union Construction's Racial Equity and Inclusion Charade," Travis Watson, a construction and workforce expert, lays out the ways the "tall boys" in construction still work to keep Black people and women out. He states that despite claims of inclusivity in 2021, Boston's union construction workers remain overwhelmingly white, with zero Black senior leaders, barely 2–3 percent Black membership, and a negligible number of Black-owned union-signatory companies, which is in stark contrast to Boston's 25 percent Black population.[27] Watson documents the environment Black workers face on construction sites in the city: "From being called racist names to being administered tests designed to ensure their failure, a gamut of discriminatory practices make it difficult for Black workers to enter, remain, and grow in the industry."[28] Again we see those "tests" not designed to assess ability or practical skills but "designed to favor the in-group."[29]

Watson goes on to lay out six key strategies he says white union members employ to maintain their dominance. First, there is the Catch-22: requiring prior job experience for union membership when you can only get the experience through union jobs or apprenticeships. Second is Stonewalling: ignoring or refusing communication with Black applicants to discourage them from pursuing union membership. Third is Biased Gatekeepers: the people who control job access, intentionally refusing to send Black workers to jobs. Fourth is that Discriminatory Testing we've talked about, and Fifth is Explicit Racism: language, intimidation tactics, and even threats or actual physical harm to deter Black workers. The sixth method he identifies is Voter Suppression: keeping Black membership low through restrictive voting practices and ensuring white control over union elections and policies.[30]

What Watson describes sounds like something from 1877, when Reconstruction ended, and in many ways it is. The vines of discrimination and anti-Blackness continue to wind their way through time and gum up our systems with their historically deep roots. How do we manage it, then? The first step is acknowledging that things are broken, and the next step is to start digging downward. It will require pulling up the roots of this, which means getting rid of the wink-and-nod mentality and those gatekeepers that allow this to go on while rewarding those who move swiftly and urgently to correct what's wrong and do more of what's right.

Who's Qualified in the Modern Workforce?

You now have some historical and current context that you can use to challenge and excavate the ways in which our systems—in particular hiring, retention, and promotion—are corrupted by inequity. Now we turn our attention to how competency check-ing manifests in your workplace today.

As we have seen, the fictions of Black intellectual inferior-ity and incompetence are much older than any of the programs designed to address them and the harm they have caused. Un-fortunately, these fictions appear to be evergreen. That's how we get Wells Fargo CEO Charles Scharf implying that there is not a single Black person in all of America qualified and possessing the competency to work as a senior executive at his company. And that's why we have people unabashedly conflating diversity with a lack of qualifications, for the most part unchallenged, to fight against any programs designed to address systemic ineq-uity and simply provide access to opportunity in American life.

The narrative is so strong that it would almost be comical if it weren't so dangerous. Fareed Zakaria used his platform on CNN to bemoan all the "unqualified" people who have flooded the workplace, thanks to affirmative action, and taken so many jobs that, according to him, "a white man studying the US pres-idency does not have a prayer of getting tenure at a major his-tory department in America."[31] Despite being an oddly specific statement (maybe a friend of his didn't get a job), the numbers don't add up: the most recent statistics show that in 2021 na-tionwide, 73 percent of university faculty were white.[32] Accord-ing to the career planning website Zippia, 68 percent of history professors are men, and 66 percent are white as of 2021.[33] When it comes to tenure specifically, according to the National Center for Education Statistics (NCES), "in 2021 . . . 40 percent of tenure-track faculty were White males."[34] So, is the idea that it should be 100 percent? That would be strange, considering the total non-Hispanic white population in the United States is 58 percent; this includes women and men.[35]

So representation is skewed, just not in the way some people claim it is. In 2016, Georgetown University's McCourt School of Public Policy Center on Education and the Workforce high-lighted significant racial differences in the distribution of what they called "good" jobs among white, Black, and Latino work-ers. At the time, the study defined good jobs as paying at least $35,000 annually, or $45,000 for those forty-five and older. What the study found was that white workers are more likely to secure "good" jobs compared to equally educated Black or Latino workers; note, too, that it says this holds true across different educational levels.[36] In fact, it found that white workers held a disproportionate amount of "good jobs" relative to their over-all employment numbers. So 77 percent of "good jobs" are held by white people, who hold only 68 percent of all jobs.[37] Finally, there's this fact: "Black men have the highest unemployment rates among all race/gender groups, with the lowest labor force participation and employment rates among men."[38] Brookings Institution senior fellow Harry J. Holzer found that while there were what he calls proximate causes, education, and work ex-perience, mediating factors, health and family structures, and reinforcing factors, such as incarceration and other financial burdens, there is only one ultimate factor—discrimination.[39]

One of the first things you can do to dispel the notion that workplaces have been "overrun" by "unqualified" Black people and other people of color is to use your eyes and look around. What do you see? Do you see a C-suite full of Black people in your workplace? Do you see the VPs and directors overflowing with Black people? Do you see managers and decision-makers in your company who are made up of more than 50 percent Black people? If not, then where are all these unqualified people?

The Illusion

I was at my church one day when a fellow congregant said something interesting to me about another church: "Well, our diverse group is different than the one in the suburbs; they don't have a multiracial group like we do." I was genuinely perplexed by this statement, and I began to wonder what this person saw when they looked at our group. We have about two hundred members; fewer than ten are Black, and five or fewer of them are present at any given time. And based on visuals alone, maybe four other people are people of color. Somehow, this person saw 0.07 percent diversity as very diverse and multiracial.

According to a research paper published in the *Proceedings of the National Academy of Sciences*, the most-cited peer-reviewed journal in the world, this kind of phenomenon is a result of our mind playing tricks on us. Our brains are "tuned toward spotting the uncommon and unexpected [and they] propose that individuals coming from minority groups are, by definition, just that—uncommon and often unexpected." As a result of this, white people tend to "overestimate the prevalence of minorities, leading to an erroneous picture of our social environments—an illusion of diversity."[40] The report goes on to show that this isn't just some people: "[a]cross all of these studies, 82.6 percent of the participants overestimated the proportion of minority group members."[41] And there's something particular about seeing the faces of Black people, "[w]hen 25 percent of the images in the grids were of Black people, white participants estimated the proportion of Black faces to be 43.22 percent."[42] The study's authors say this can lead to white people feeling threatened by a perceived influx of Black people that doesn't exist and reduce support for efforts to improve and increase Black people's presence in the workplace.

This means that Black people seeking employment or who are already in the workforce are dealing with three contradictory assumptions. First, that there are already "too many" of them, when it's really few to none. Second, because of their race, they face widespread assumptions that they are unqualified or incompetent and were "given" jobs because of their race. And finally, because of all of this, they must meet a higher bar when competing for jobs and for advancement once in the workplace. That higher bar brings us back to the Shifting Standards Model (SSM), which "can help explain . . . [why Black employees must meet a higher standard]. Simply put, you shift the requirements or 'standards' based on who it is."[43] Because white employers frequently assume Black people are unqualified or incompetent, they competency-check them by paying more attention to any mistake made during the interview (or on the job) in writing samples, conversations, etc. The SSM could be one factor as to why employers consciously or unconsciously set the bar higher when reviewing the background and qualifications of Black and other candidates of color.[44]

Writing for the *Atlantic* in 2014, Margaret Barthel tackles why "Black Men Need More Education Than White Men to Get Jobs." Using research and data from a policy brief for the Young Invincibles program on closing the race gap in employment, Barthel discusses how African American men face systematic disadvantages in the job market: "African American millennial men need two or more levels of education to have the same employment prospects as their white peers."[45] Even as the research shows that while "the African American man is much, much more likely to be employed now . . . a white man with a bachelor's degree *still* has slightly better employment prospects than a black man who *has gone to graduate school.*"[46]

As a consultant I have witnessed this arbitrarily higher standard being upheld repeatedly at companies. It's not uncommon for me to see Black people with master's degrees, JDs, and PhDs combined with skills and experience "stuck" in midtier positions while white colleagues, some of whom may have more time in the industry but possess less education and/or applicable skills, populate more senior positions and roles. Black people, as well as other people of color, are frequently castigated for not applying for jobs they are not 100 percent qualified for; however, based on what I know about competency checking, they are rational actors. They know from experience that they will be subjected to a much more rigorous check of their competency as part of the hiring process if they even make it past the initial screening. Experience has shown them that their odds of securing a job without meeting all the qualifications are extremely low. I couldn't find a better example than the one Leniece F. Brissett, the founder of the recruitment firm Compass Talent Group, shared in her Vox article titled "I Help Organizations Hire People—and Watch White Candidates Get Favored Again and Again."[47] In it, Brissett gives a stark example of how pernicious the fiction of diversity equaling a lack of qualification really is. When presenting two candidates, Naima (a highly qualified candidate of color) and Matt (a less qualified white male candidate), to a national nonprofit for an open position, Brissett explains how the nonprofit saw Naima differently from the jump. Brissett quotes the client as parroting a variation of the oldest racialized trope in the book: "I noticed the pool is very diverse, *and I want you to know diversity is important, but quality matters most.*"[48]

Having heard variations of this exact sentiment for years from clients, including C-suite executives and HR managers, I wasn't surprised to read Brissett's example. People with influence or direct decision-making power over hiring often express subtle and direct concerns about the "quality" of an applicant if they open their process to include more people of color, and uncertainty about how even to evaluate candidates of color. Brissett goes on to write that despite the candidate Naima being more qualified, she underwent a far more rigorous and extended interview process, while Matt advanced to the final interview stage with significantly less scrutiny.[49] Naima was subjected to this because of race-based assumptions. In a word, she was competency-checked.

In the workplace, heightened scrutiny and undefinable "uncertainty" about the candidate or promotion is a clear sign that competency checking is happening. This, again, is a likely explanation of why Black people tend to be "underemployed" based on their level of education and experience in the workplace.[50] Combine this with the shadow hiring pipeline and de facto race-based referrals that overwhelmingly favor white employees, and you have a perfect storm of exclusionary and racist hiring practices. Black employees face higher expectations, need more qualifications, and face a narrower and more formal path of entry. All of this combines to put Black people in the position of needing to, in fact, be twice as good to get half as much.

But that is not what most people *believe* is happening. They hear of and "see" an illusion of diversity that leads them to believe they live in a world in which Black people are perpetually whining about things being unfair while getting "all the good jobs" and having to meet little to no qualifications to get any job they desire—a world that quite literally doesn't exist.

Busting Myths and Making Real Change

To be clear, I am not suggesting you pull a random Black or brown person off the street and sit them behind a desk. *That* would be tokenism, "the practice of making only a perfunctory or symbolic effort to be inclusive to members of minority groups, especially by recruiting people from underrepresented groups in order to give the appearance of racial or gender equality."[51] The fact that I need to say that out loud is because some white people, so rooted in the idea that Black people are incompetent, seem to approach hiring in this manner, unable to distinguish between highly qualified, average, and below-average Black candidates. I have often wondered if the mere sight of Black skin and the stereotyping attached to it is so overwhelming that it renders some white people simply unable to hear, see, and discern the qualifications, or lack thereof, of the person sitting right in front of them. So when I have had clients say they don't want to be seen as "performative" or bringing in "tokens," I'll tell you what I told them: this mindset is still placing the emphasis in the wrong place.

Instead, the mindset should be, "I don't want to competency-check employees of color, and I want to remove hidden blockages that are preventing the natural flow of diverse people from entering, succeeding, and staying in this workplace." But if none of your systems, assumptions, or culture has changed or is actively in the process of changing, then the odds are high that the experience a Black person or other person of color may have in your workplace is that of being a token.

I speak from experience and understand why employers are small-c conservative when it comes to hiring. No one wants to get burned by a bad employee. Employers believe that all their vetting is a means of preventing just that. But here's the problem: white employees may be good or bad, and no one says, "Well, I hired one, and it didn't work out, so I am not sure what to do." In fact, part of what is happening in competency checking is that white people are not being held to the same standards as Black people. Because of competency checking, they are given an "assumption" of qualification when that may not be the case. But in my work, I have heard this sentiment about Black employees from more than one employer. There is so much packed into that statement, but at its core is the denial of the humanity of Black people. One person does not represent all Black people; an individual's success or failure cannot be the standard by which all Black employees are measured.

Dr. Alisha Moreland-Capuia, or Dr. AMC, as she is affectionately known, is a practicing community psychiatrist and the author of three books. In 2020 she founded the Institute for Trauma-Informed Systems Change at McLean Hospital/Harvard Medical School, where she trains hundreds of organizations and leaders. As we discussed what it meant to be Black in the medical profession, especially during residency, when a doctor is initially practicing their craft, something Dr. AMC said stopped me in my tracks: "You are constantly subject to the questioning and the surveying of others. Residency training means that you should be able to make mistakes, right? Because that's how you learn and grow. Imagine a world where you're in training, which is when you should be able to kind of fail, learn again; you're not allowed to fail; you're not to make a mistake." Dr. AMC went on to explain that even the medical apprenticeship model used by doctors for hundreds of years has been warped by anti-Blackness and competency checking, thus putting Black people in a position where they are expected to know the job before they've done it.

This is not just true of the medical profession; ask and, to the extent possible, evaluate who can make mistakes in your organization and still succeed and who can't. Understand that as you reexamine *how* you think about who is qualified, what those qualifications look like, and how to assess those qualifications, you will hire Black people who might not be good at their jobs. Not because they are inherently intellectually inferior or because they are Black or because of diversity but because *they* are not good at *their* job—the same as with any white employee. You are going to hire Black and other people of color who are superstars; they are not the standard by which every other Black employee should be measured, just as the white superstar employee should not represent the universal standard at your workplace. If you are not asking Rebecca, who is white, why she isn't like John, who is white and works in a different department, then why are you asking Lisa, who is Black, why she isn't more like Mary, who is Black and who worked there five years ago?

When you expand your view on qualifications and mitigate competency checking, you might hire a diverse group of diverse people. By this I mean Black people and other people of color who are also neurodiverse, disabled, or otherwise unique from each other. This is called the natural variance of human ability and presentation and is not confirmation that diversity equals a lack of excellence and competence.

With this in mind, let's look at some concrete ways that you, as a CEO, HR director, manager, or employee, can advocate for and bring real change to your workplace when it comes to competency checking and the myth of qualifications:

1. **Audit Your Instruments**

   Is your company using some type of preemployment testing? Bring together a group of HR managers and employees to review and evaluate these instruments. Make sure this is a diverse group, even if you must engage a consultant to represent the diversity that you don't currently have in your workplace. Are your preemployment and/or advancement assessments aptitude tests, job knowledge skills tests, or a combination of both? Given what we now know about aptitude tests, your company should be wary, as these tests inevitably tend to be based on white people's "own race heritage" and frequently use language that enforces that (see: "oarsman: regatta"). But is that what's necessary to do the job you are recruiting for? Where possible, try to move toward job skills–based testing and consider the language being used in their design. If you don't know the answers to these questions, ask your vendor or whoever designed the instrument. Require that they walk you through how they have thought about and are inclusive of multiracial, gendered, and diverse test takers. Don't accept "we have a diversity lens." Ask specifically how they have done this. Did they use AI or consultants to evaluate the language and the analogies they use, and how much of this test is based on and rooted in white cultural assumptions?

If your vendors or training department cannot answer these questions clearly and with examples, you should find a different vendor. If you are uncertain about the instruments that you are using, you can bring in consultants, educators, and trainers who can provide an assessment of the inclusivity and accessibility of your preemployment and advancement tests. Your company can then use that assessment to instruct your current or future vendors on what you will need from them. The more your preemployment and advancement testing moves away from job skills testing and goes into general aptitude, personality, and other areas, the more room there is for different types of biases, such as confirmation and similarity/familiarity bias, to infiltrate and dominate.

2. **Personality Testing**

I do not like personality tests; I do not believe they are accurate, helpful, or inclusive. There is no way a personality test that is rooted in white normative behavior and is therefore a tool of white supremacist thought can give us an adequate assessment of the personality or potential of a first-generation immigrant, a

Black woman from the South, or even a white man from Indiana. I realize I'm talking about what has become a billion-dollar industry, but according to researchers, academics, and those negatively impacted by it, personality tests are a bunch of pseudoscience masquerading as fact. According to Adam Grant, an organizational psychologist at Wharton, research shows that Myers-Briggs Type Indicator (MBTI) scores are unreliable, and there is no scientific evidence to support the validity of the MBTI or its ability to predict job performance or team effectiveness.[52] According to an article in the *Guardian* about the 2021 documentary *Persona*, filmmaker Tim Travers Hawkins takes a deep dive into the history of MBTI and touches on other tests,[53] revealing that the MBTI was, in fact, created by a mother-daughter team that reflected their biases against race, gender, class, and mental health.[54]

From my vantage point as a consultant, this is simply another tool of the "tall boys." And it's not just the MBTI. Scholars and advocates have raised similar questions about other tests. In an article for Business Insider, organizational psychologist Dr. Benjamin Hardy says, "Type-based personality tests like Myers-Briggs, DISC, and Enneagram are junk science. There is no such thing as a personality 'type.' That's a gross oversimplification and stereotype that leads to mindlessness, both about yourself and other people."[55] Personally, I think a company is better off spending money learning how to communicate across things we know exist, such as race, gender, class, etc. Understanding *those* differences and how they appear in the workplace would be far more beneficial to everyone and the company's bottom line.

I once had a client who ran a program where employees could apply for more training as a precursor to advancement. The client found that their Hispanic/Latinx[56] employees rarely applied for the program. The client was perplexed as to why these employees were not applying for this opportunity. Employers normally see this through the lens of motivation or ability. They think, "This group either isn't interested or isn't ambitious as a whole." We eventually learned that the client had a high number of first-generation and second-generation Hispanic/Latinx employees, which turned out to be the core issue at play, not their perceived lack of interest or ambition. Upon speaking to individuals on this client's staff, we learned that these employees felt that if they did a good job, they would be asked to apply; according to them, it was a cultural difference in approach to management and advancement and had nothing to do with ability or interest. Once the client understood that there was a communication gap across differences, they could do proper outreach to all employees with similar cultural or "personality traits." Understanding *that* type of difference matters much more than a made-up personality type.

3. **360: The Drive-By Evaluation**

The other instrument that I encourage you to reconsider using is the somewhat infamous 360 evaluation. Beyond the wide-open door 360s allow for bias, unconscious or otherwise, the 360 is frequently used improperly. People who have little to no insight into what they are being asked to evaluate generally provide imprecise "feelings" about someone or their work, not tangible, actionable items for the employee to address. According to Katica Roy, CEO of Pipeline and gender economist,

"Women not only receive more critical, more negative, and more useless feedback than men, they also receive more feedback on their communication style."[57] Researchers like Alison T. Wynn and Shelley J. Correll have found that the vines-through-time of sexism and gendered expectations are still tightly woven into our current evaluation processes: "Stereotypic expectations [about women] like these can lead to bias in how information is processed, ultimately influencing the evaluations, opportunities, and influence."[58]

The fact that there is little available research on the impact of 360s on Black people speaks to the general lack of consideration on the impact these evaluation instruments have on Black and other people of color. In my own work, I have coached Black employees and other employees of color who find themselves on the losing end of what is often a vague process that allows people who may not like them to enact a workplace "drive-by" that could have a significant impact on their career. I had one such client, a Black leader, who was frustrated by the 360 they'd received that said they were not "leading," with no clear discussion about what that meant. This person was new to the job and trying to be collaborative and cooperative. However, their intention was at odds with how their work was evaluated. Or there was the Asian American client who was being perceived through the lens of the "model minority myth" that boxes Asian Americans into the role of perfect, robotic, unassuming worker bees. The client was told they were too focused on their goals and the business, which was odd because the client worked in a field where being business-focused and goal-driven was usually seen as a desirable trait.

Rather than jumping straight to conclusions—which are often, as we've seen, the result of bias, miscommunication, ignorance, or some combination of the three—and writing it in a review that impacts the employee's overall ability to progress in their career, there is an opportunity to change this problematic review system for the better.

- Collaboratively set the goals and what they will be judged on for the coming year.
- Conduct more "real-time" monthly or quarterly feedback sessions with those direct reports based on job-specific accomplishments or deficits. Use these to roll up to the end of the year and ditch that once-yearly evaluation process.
- Do not ask people who have no direct line of sight into the person's work to evaluate them.
- When asking people who are supervised by the person for an evaluation, restrict or eliminate open-ended questions to limit bias. Instead, ask clearly defined questions, seek examples, and follow up to clarify what is being said.

I once had an employee tell me a coworker had "yelled" at them. I was naturally alarmed; after investigating the issue, I found that the person who reported the "yelling" was using the term in the colloquial way some younger people use it, meaning the person was "telling them what to do," not literally raising their voice and shouting.

When it comes to Black people in the workplace, many historical stereotypes are at play, those old vines woven through our conscious and unconscious processing. Research has shown that "Black employees who rated themselves highly on self-promotion received lower ratings of their job performance and assessments of their fit with the organization." This also happens to Black people when they are applying for jobs. The response to them promoting themselves in interviews can almost seem visceral and feels connected through time to the "uppity" trope. "The 1952 edition of The Oxford English Dictionary listed the term uppity (N-word) with this definition: "Above oneself, self-important, 'jumped up, haughty, pert, putting on airs." If you hear or sense that a Black person is being criticized or penalized for being confident in themselves during a job interview, for example, the question should be, "Isn't a job interview the time to sell yourself?" and "Did we penalize anyone else for that?" It's amazing what can happen because of a simple mindset shift.

4. **Evaluate the Evaluators: External**

Third-party leadership assessment firms claim they can help you figure out who in your company is ready to ascend to upper management and beyond. In coaching a Black woman who had been sent by her employer to one of these firms, I heard how the process can be stacked against Black people. From the start, the process was "off." She reported having an older, all-white male panel that was supposed to evaluate her. During a portion of the evaluation, one of the men fell asleep. She did not feel, obviously, that these people were invested in understanding her or fairly assessing her potential for leadership. Sure enough, they did not rate her highly for advancement and gave a puzzling coda to their evaluation that she might be more concerned with home and family. This woman has years of experience in the workforce, is unmarried, and does not have children. The process was an insult, but the firm is well-known and recognized and is given way too much authority to decide who gets ahead. Even though this was reported to the company that referred her for this evaluation, it is unclear what was done to address the issue. Further, this puts this employee and any Black employee in a catch-22 where their choice is to accept this biased evaluation and be deemed unqualified for advancement or complain and be seen as unwilling to take "constructive" feedback as well as unqualified for advancement.

Many of these executive recruiting/leadership assessment businesses are using some variation of aptitude testing, personality testing, supposed learning ability assessment, and "culture" fit assessment, all tools that have historically favored the "tall boys." As Rita May Brown, the civil rights campaigner and feminist writer, said, "Insanity is doing the same thing over and over again and expecting different results."[59] As a practice, this *is* insane. Research in the *Journal of Management* on the impact of gender and race and executive search firms found that "executive search firms contribut[ed] to existing gender and racial pay inequalities in the managerial and professional labor markets. It calls for theoretical and practical considerations to address these issues and promote fairer career mobility opportunities for all."[60]

Because these particular companies are so deeply enmeshed within corporate America, I am going to suggest two alternative approaches. First, if you get a report like the one above, stop, listen, and follow up with both the firm and the employee. The firm should be put on notice that this conduct is unacceptable and may impact their continued business relationship with you; this is not a small thing. Prior to sending employees to these firms, meet with them and have them walk you through what all their assessments are based on. Are they based on aptitude testing, job skills tests, or pseudoscientific personality tests? To what extent have they factored in the vast diversity of the human species? Their answers must be more substantive than "We have a racial equity lens" or "We've thought about it." You must demand specifics as to how exactly they factor in differences in communication styles and differences in the reception of said communication styles (remember, Black people and women aren't well received when they openly take pride in themselves and their work, speak colloquially, or otherwise fall outside white standards of behavior and presentation).[61] Demand diverse panels to evaluate all your employees, not just people of color or other minoritized folks. If a company cannot provide that, *that's* a problem. A recruitment or leadership assessment firm that can't find a way to hire a diverse workforce is unlikely to help you find or advance one either.

5. **Evaluate the Evaluators: Internal**

In addition to evaluating your external evaluators, you must also evaluate and support those who do this work in your company. Consider developing a core group of in-house evaluators that rotate on an annual or biannual schedule. Train these folks on spotting issues such as competency checking, confirmation, and other types of bias. Also, train them on "communicating across differences." Provide "case studies" or examples for these folks to work through as part of their training so they can spot, interrupt, challenge, and mitigate these factors during the hiring and advancement process. This should happen concurrently with your EEOC training, which everyone who participates in hiring must be required to attend, to ensure that interviews and assessments do not violate any existing laws. And this can't be a series of "one-offs." Rather, this should be a best practice seen as part of continuous improvement. Make sure your interviewing panels are diverse across positions, race, age, ability, gender, and so on.

6. **Basing It on Skills**

It's not enough to say you do "skills-based hiring." Learn how to do it. Skills-based hiring focuses on evaluating job candidates primarily on their skills, abilities, and knowledge rather than on traditional credentials such as degrees, job titles, or professional backgrounds. This approach aims to match individuals with jobs more effectively based on their actual ability to perform specific tasks or roles.[62]

So, how do you do actual skills-based hiring? Clearly define the skills and competencies required for each role. Use a test to assess the skills required for that job—a practical test. You must train hiring managers and recruiters to focus on skills and competencies rather than traditional credentials and outline what that means for your company/industry. You can use AI and other software but recognize these tools are not "neutral" and can have bias built in. So, providers of AI skills-based evaluations must still walk you through how they are accounting for that bias in language, analogies, etc. Finally, continuously update the skills framework to reflect evolving job requirements. In an article on the Society for Human Resource Management (SHRM) website, two critical elements of skills-based hiring are highlighted. The first is evaluating for skill, not personality, and the second is leaning into up-skilling people on the job. Both are excellent suggestions, but part of implementing them must include a continuous evaluation and acknowledgment of the impact of competency checking. While many hail skills-based hiring as a way to increase workforce diversity and open opportunities for people from non-traditional backgrounds, it won't work if we ignore the ways Black people, because of historical and current anti-Black bias, and other minoritized groups are held to a higher standard through competency checking.[63] Any legitimate attempt at skills-based hiring must include internal audits to check who gets the benefit of the doubt and who doesn't. How are we comparing people with the same or equal skills? What are we penalizing some for and not others? A perfect example comes from research revealing that "Both Black and Hispanic men [with a criminal record] were less likely to receive a positive response from employers—including a callback or email for an interview or a job offer—compared with white men."[64] And here is the flashing neon sign: "White men with a criminal record had more positive responses than Black men with no criminal record."[65]

While skills-based employment can open the door to a more diverse workforce, if we use the same competency-checking framework and shift our standards when it comes to who is qualified, we will only continue to get the same results.

Check, Check, and Check Again, and Then ACT!

We must dismantle the myth of qualifications while immediately mitigating and working to eradicate competency checking in the workplace. It is only through acknowledging the unique impact of anti-Black racism that we can create workplaces where Black people and all workers can truly flourish. We each have a role to play, and the road to meaningful change lies in revising systems and assessments, confronting our biases, and holding ourselves accountable.

Every interaction, every evaluation, and every decision are opportunities to bridge the gap and dismantle competency checking and anti-Black bias. These concrete steps can move you beyond hollow promises of diversity and embrace a deeper understanding of what it means to create a just and equitable space for all. Ask yourself: Are you evaluating potential or perpetuating outdated norms? Are you empowering advancement or holding people back with biased tools? The answers to these questions lie not only in your hearts and minds, but in your algorithms, assessments, and beliefs.

CHAPTER 5

Unmasking Imposter Syndrome

It's like you got to be careful what life you live cause it
may not be your own!

—J. California Cooper, *Some Soul to Keep*

Misdirection

The impact of competency checking, as expressed through the
myth of qualifications that shifts what it means to be qualified
based on who is seeking admission, can't be understated. Feelings of uncertainty and anxiety, among other, more strenuous
feelings, can occur due to being competency checked. But what
is especially clear is that there has been a weaponization of
what is colloquially known as "imposter syndrome," which mis-
identifies the natural and logical responses to the mistreatment
women and people of color experience in the workplace.

This misidentification was never clearer to me than when I
spoke with a prospective client, a white woman, who reached out
to me about giving a keynote speech on imposter syndrome. In
the course of our conversation, I gave her my take on it: namely,
that *imposter syndrome* is a catch-all term that effectively ob-
scures the impact of sexism, patriarchy, and white supremacy
on a specific subset of women in the workplace that is now being applied well beyond its original meaning. I explained to her
that this misidentification has set up white women to blame

themselves for their response to what is, in fact, constant and persistent competency checking.

The woman I was speaking with was "shook," for lack of a better word. She looked confused and concerned, and I quickly found out why. After regaining her composure, she told me that none of the consultants she had spoken with had given her this framing and that one consultant had even told her, "Everyone has imposter syndrome, and anyone who says they don't is a liar or a narcissist." It was my turn to be rendered speechless. Imposter syndrome is not a recognized psychiatric disorder in the American Psychiatric Association's *Diagnostic and Statistical Manual of Mental Disorders, Fifth Edition* (*DSM-5*). It is also not listed as a diagnosis in the International Classification of Diseases. So the idea that a consultant would make such a sweeping generalization, let alone one that makes assumptions about a person's mental health, should tell you how far down the rabbit hole we've gone.

Once I recovered my bearings, I explained to this prospective client that everyone feels insecure and uncertain; that's part of being human. But while we may doubt ourselves, that doesn't mean we have a disorder. She seemed reticent to agree or perhaps was still struggling to understand. I pointed out that the research the concept is based on was conducted in 1978 and was limited to upper-class white women. I tried to show her how this misidentification was putting Black women and other women of color in a difficult position in the workplace. This is because they tend to identify the *factors* that are *causing* them harm as having the biggest impact on their feelings of uncertainty or distress in the workplace.[1] When that didn't work, I told her about an article in the *Harvard Business Review* by Ruchika Malhotra (née Tulshyan), a South Asian woman, and Jodi-Ann Burey, a Black woman, titled "Stop Telling Women They Have Imposter Syndrome." That Burey and

Malhotra are both women of color is not an accident. I can tell you that every Black woman I interviewed for this book and every Black woman in my network rolls their eyes and gives a *tsk* under their breath when imposter syndrome is brought up. Not because they are "liars or narcissists" but because, as corporate event professional Talisa Lavarry, whose experience is highlighted in the *HBR* article, discovered, "It wasn't a lack of self-confidence that held her back. It was repeatedly facing systemic racism and bias."[2]

Burey and Malhotra explain that women of color often experience heightened feelings of self-doubt and a sense of not fitting into corporate environments, not due to any inherent lack, but because of the complex interplay of their racial and gender identities in historically white spaces, which frequently puts them in challenging situations in the workplace.[3] Finally, I told the client that imposter syndrome is not an illness; if it is anything, it is a symptom of systemic illnesses that are sexism, racism, and white supremacy. I also gave her the excellent framing that Burey and Malhotra use in their study about the cause-and-effect problem: "Impostor syndrome directs our view toward fixing women at work instead of fixing the places where women work."[4]

After I finished explaining my position to this woman, which I admit is not a common framework used when discussing this topic, I was asked to prove that what I was saying was true by sending the client the articles I had cited, along with any additional research that could be considered relevant to my argument. There was no indication that the previous consultant she had met with, who had improperly ascribed *DSM*-level pathologies to anyone who dared to say that they don't "suffer" from imposter syndrome, was asked to prove their faulty framework. This incident showcases not only a recent moment of competency checking in my own life, but perfectly illustrates the chasm that can and often does separate white women and women of color in the workplace. On the one side, white women, generally of a certain class, are unaware or unconcerned about the ways they filter what it means to be a woman through a white normative lens, rendering them unable to incorporate the reality of the intersection of race and gender into their understanding. On the other side are women of color, unable to fathom how white women cannot understand the intersection of race and gender and be able to point out the "real" culprits that are causing them harm.

Unmasking

In the wake of this experience, I now explain the act of unmasking "imposter syndrome" as competency checking, like Scooby-Doo and the gang unmasking the villainous "ghost" in each episode. This boogeyman inevitably turns out to be some guy trying to scare people away from impeding on his schemes. The real issue for us, of course, is not a ghostly apparition but a tangible, systemic problem that requires a grounded, comprehensive approach. Once the mask is off, the question then becomes, How did we get here, and why do so many people, specifically white women, think the ghost is real?

In 1978, psychologists Pauline Rose Clance and Suzanne Imes introduced a theory, originally called "impostor phenomenon," described as "an internal experience of intellectual phonies, which appears to be particularly prevalent and intense among a select sample of high achieving women."[5] The group that Clance and Imes followed for five years was made up of 178 primarily white, highly educated upper-class to middle-class women. The women included undergraduates, PhD candidates, faculty members, medical students, and other professionals. The women ranged in age from twenty to forty-five years old;

about one-third of these women were already in psychotherapy for issues unrelated to imposter syndrome, and the remaining two-thirds participated in classes taught by Clance and Imes.[6]

According to Clance and Imes, the women in the study expressed persistent beliefs of intellectual inadequacy despite objective evidence of their achievements and abilities. Of note, the discussion of perfection throughout the article is critical to understanding the so-called imposter phenomenon. The authors detail how the women's fear of not meeting their or others' expectations of themselves led them to believe they were not genuinely intelligent or capable. This belief system was supported and maintained by various behaviors to avoid failure or exposure, including overpreparation, hard work, and a reluctance to accept or internalize success.[7]

In my work as a consultant, one of the first things I ask a prospective client is, Who is missing? Who is missing from the discussion, the decision, the approach, and the impact? In the case of the Clance and Imes study, Black and other women of color and low-income white women's voices are missing because they were deliberately excluded. Because the vast majority of LGBTQIA+ women were closeted at that time, it is impossible to know if their voices were present in this small study, let alone excluded. And we can infer women living with visible disabilities were missing because that information is not called out. Also missing is the impact of the volatile times in which these women lived, as well as the culture of patriarchy and white supremacy that surrounded them.

Because this was a study of white women in particular, I want to first look at those missing from the study: lower-income and working-class white women. If this study had included women like Crystal Lee Sutton, the real-life inspiration for the film *Norma Rae*, about a poor working-class woman fighting to unionize her workplace, she could have told the researchers what was really going on in blue-collar workplaces across the country. Sutton *knew* what was causing her and the other women at the J. P. Stevens textile plant in Roanoke Rapids, North Carolina: stress, uncertainty, anxiety, and feelings of insecurity—rampant, unchecked capitalism, poor working conditions, low wages, and racial and gender discrimination. Sutton was doing her union organizing work in the 1970s, and the Academy Award–winning movie came out in 1979. When Sutton stopped her work and famously stood up on a table in the mill, she didn't hold up a sign saying she felt like an imposter; she held up a sign that said "UNION."

There must have been days when Sutton felt uncertain and maybe even like a fraud, not because of a clinical disorder, but because she was human, and that's how we sometimes feel. She, however, was able to go beyond that and identify the real culprit, the ways in which she and other working poor women were being exploited. This ability led to her understanding that the only way to bring change for women in a place where, "in truth, we don't belong because we were never supposed to belong"[8] was to build a coalition of white and Black women at the plant to challenge the status quo together. Sutton identified the correct source of the illness—external factors—and then fought back with the correct medicine: solidarity.

There is something about the self-flagellation that imposter syndrome imposes on white women that feels like punishment for not fitting into the status quo. I can't help but wonder, if the study had been more inclusive, could it have helped change how women of color and white women understand and support each other in the workplace today? If those women had been able to identify the real culprits working against them, would they be more invested in upending the status quo of white supremacy? And would women of color be allowed to take up space and express their thoughts and opinions without the risk of being tone-policed or competency-checked at work?

Beyond not being a diverse study, the Clance and Imes study seems to have been performed in a kind of bubble, again with only a glancing mention of "societal issues," leaving out an incredible wealth of factors that would have had an undeniable effect on women in the workplace. When the study began in 1973, women were undergoing the biggest cultural, political, and economic changes since the Industrial Revolution. Affirmative action, legislation that would have the single biggest impact on professional white women in the workforce, was only six years old, as amended to include gender. In 1974, the second year of the Clance and Imes study, it took an act of Congress and the signing of the Equal Credit Opportunity Act by President Gerald Ford for women to be able to open their own bank accounts without a male cosigner. Other legislative and cultural changes were occurring, including the Equal Rights Amendment, Title IX, and *Roe v. Wade*. Additionally, there was an intellectual framework that could have opened the door to a more inclusive study. "Second-wave feminism," which tried to incorporate critiques of patriarchy, gender norms, and the intersectionality of race, class, and gender inequalities, was at its apex.[9] Yet none of this is seen as impacting the women's "internalized self-evaluations."[10]

Most egregious to me is how the study homes in on the devastating impact perfectionism has on a person and how it is critical to understanding the so-called imposter phenomenon but then doesn't take the next logical step toward pinpointing the source of that perfectionism. The knowledge that patriarchy and white supremacy have and continue to enforce unrealistic standards of perfection on white women is not new. From writings dating back to the antebellum South to the writings of suffragettes seeking the right to vote, white women have wrestled with societally imposed standards on what white womanhood should look like, sound like, and act like.[11]

Deconstructing society's need for perfection from white women has been central to the work of Saira Rao and Regina Jackson. Rao and Jackson are the founders of race2dinner and are the authors of *White Women: Everything You Already Know About Your Own Racism and How to Do Better.* The authors, through a series of conversations over meals, walk white women through the ways in which perfectionism harms them and how to be better antiracist allies. "If white womanhood (as defined by patriarchy and white supremacy) is a house, your need to be perfect is the foundation. The con, of course, is there is no actual recipe for perfection, as there is no such thing as perfection."[12] Rao and Jackson see perfectionism as the trap it is: no one is ever going to meet a white patriarchal society's impossible standards of physical, mental, familial, and sexual perfection. It's a setup designed to keep people—especially women, especially white women—in an inescapable place of shame and self-disappointment. That white women were and continue to be shaped by these notions of perfection and by a society that seeks to "infantilize" them in a type of perpetual girlhood would no doubt have an impact on their sense of self-esteem and self-worth. In her article "The Infantilization of Women in Mainstream Media and Society," Tavisha Sood deconstructs the ways in which society infantilizes women physically, sexually, emotionally, and mentally: "The infantilization of femininity has led to a stereotype of women being vulnerable, weak and childlike: thus, undermining them as adults and altering their position in relation to power in society."[13]

While Sood uses women universally in her article, I make the argument that this is primarily society's view of white women, and a certain class of white women at that. Black women were not even seen as humans for most of our history in this country. Society's view of us did not ascribe feminine qualities; these were reserved for white women. During Jim Crow, which only fully ended in my lifetime, Black women in the South were not allowed to use honorifics such as Ms. or Mrs.; those were reserved for white women. Working-class white women and immigrant women "worked like men" and also had their femininity stripped from them by society. Of course, this leads to the other gap when discussing "women." We have and are currently having very different experiences of what it means to be a woman in this world. When we "whitewash" womanhood, we devalue our myriad of experiences, and we leave white women searching in vain for the perfect amount of self-talk to counter the impact of sexism and white supremacy—when only direct action can accomplish that.

The Impact of the Misidentification of Imposter Syndrome

The misidentification of competency checking as imposter syndrome is having a devastating impact on white women in the workplace because, once again, when we misidentify the illness, we use the wrong medicine to treat it. In a study paralleling the legal memo evaluation—in which law partners judged the identical memo more critically when they believed a Black associate wrote it versus a white associate—a similar experiment was conducted with science faculty from research-intensive universities. These faculty members were asked to evaluate a student's application materials for a laboratory manager position, with the student's name randomly assigned to be male or female. Despite the applications being identical in content, the male-named applicant was consistently rated as more competent and hirable and was offered a higher starting salary and more career mentoring than the female-named applicant.[14] One of the study's most unsurprising findings, to me, was that "the gender of the faculty did not affect responses, such that female and male faculty were equally likely to exhibit bias against the female student."[15] This finding underscores the deep-seated nature of sexism and patriarchy. The internalization of patriarchy, sexism, and racism and the expression of these ideologies through competency checking by women against other women is a tangible result of the consequences of misidentifying the illness.

So, in the real world, the white female research assistant with the same qualifications might feel "unsteady" once she is rejected for a position or learns she is receiving less mentoring and less pay than her male colleague. She may question her success and become uncertain about her abilities, unaware of the hidden hand of competency checking that has her in its grip. Because she has been "misdirected toward seeking individual solutions for issues disproportionately caused by systems of discrimination and abuses of power,"[16] she may be unwilling or unable to connect with Black and other women of color to work together toward collective solutions to change the status quo in the workplace. In fact, she may competency-check those same women if they try to talk to her about the intersection of racism and sexism and how it is impacting them. The white research assistant may even feel that the women of color are simply "not taking responsibility" for their own failings or shortcomings. If this conversation is with a Black woman and she pushes back and proclaims her knowledge and competency, she may be seen by the white research assistant as a "narcissist" or somehow "overconfident." This will then prevent the white research assistant and the women of color in her workplace from exploring, let alone launching, collective action.

So how do we achieve that collective action, and how do we overcome this fever dream that is imposter syndrome? First and foremost, we must stop pathologizing normalcy and cease framing self-doubt and uncertainty as a "syndrome" that solely requires individual correction. We also must start shifting the blame to those issues rooted in systemic discrimination and power imbalances. Here are a few suggestions for how we can do that:

- REIMAGINE THE WORKPLACE: Champion systemic reforms within organizations that aim to identify and eliminate microaggressions, identify and eliminate competency checking, and address implicit biases to ensure equal opportunities for all women in the workplace. This involves developing comprehensive policies that address not only the symptoms but also the root causes of discrimination. Implement training programs that educate employees at all levels about the interplay of race, sexual orientation, ethnicity, disability, and gender so they can identify these biases in order to challenge and change them.
- EMPOWER BEYOND DOUBT: Shift the focus from personal inadequacies to systemic injustices by empowering employees to recognize and call out competency checking. Create workshops and support systems that help individuals understand how systemic biases affect their work environment and personal growth within the company. Develop resilience training that emphasizes strength in diversity and encourages employees to support each other in facing these systemic challenges.
- BUILD COMMUNITY AND SUPPORT: Foster a culture of inclusivity and solidarity among all marginalized groups within and outside of the workplace to combat feelings of isolation and self-blame. Create

intersectional networking groups. Ensure these groups include and actively engage with varied expressions of womanhood that do not center on white womanhood as the standard—to expand opportunity for all. This should involve collaborative efforts to design interventions that address the specific needs of different groups, promoting a holistic approach to inclusivity.

- **CHALLENGE THE STATUS QUO**: In HR roles, critically evaluate and question existing hiring and promotion practices. Investigate whether these practices inadvertently perpetuate gender and racial biases. How are candidates being assessed for positions, including hiring and promotions? Are there ways in which white women and women of color are being inadvertently excluded similarly or differently? Collaborate with your colleagues to remove the blockages discussed in this book, which prevent qualified individuals from entering the workplace. Conduct an audit to evaluate who is being hired, their compensation, and who receives mentorship. Use the findings to implement targeted strategies that ensure fairness and equality in career opportunities, particularly for women and people of color. Collaborate with impacted groups to develop and refine these strategies, ensuring that the changes are meaningful and effective.

Moving Toward a New Understanding

To prevail over inequality at work, we must look to a future beyond imposter syndrome, where we stop punishing ourselves and others for being human. We need to scale a world where women of all races are aware of the ways in which competency checking, rooted in patriarchy, white supremacy, sexism, *and* racism, is impacting them and their work and actively inhibiting their collective ability to create change. We must encourage an understanding that allows for normal self-doubt that doesn't hinder potential and where women who stand ready and able to lead are not pathologized or punished for their competency and confidence.

White women especially must broaden their perspectives to understand that their successes and burdens are intertwined and inseparable from those of Black women and women of color, a crucial element of the larger story of the fight for civil rights and the fight against anti-Blackness. And because white women make up the lion's share of HR professionals in the United States, they are often the first and last line of defense, so they must work diligently to learn what they have been missing about the ways racial and gender bias are expressed through competency checking in their workplaces.[17]

White women can no longer afford to see themselves standing alone in a mirror, seeking to correct what they believe is solely some internal error in their thinking or self-image. They must work with women of color to turn their gaze and action toward the real villains: the systems of oppression that continue to undermine and destabilize all women in the workplace. In the wake of the great DEI surge of 2020–21 and its ensuing collapse, women of color, and Black women in particular, find themselves under attack and out on a ledge, desperately needing support from a true sisterhood, one that is grounded in our shared struggles and looks toward a truly equitable future.

CHAPTER 6

For Black Girls Who've Considered Quitting When Sisterhood Would've Been Enough

Life for me ain't been no crystal stair. It had tacks in it . . . and splinters and places with no carpet on the floor—bare.

—Langston Hughes, "Mother to Son"

BECAUSE THE PROBLEMS and issues Black women are experiencing and reporting in the workplace are, as I have previously said, the canary in the coal mine signifying that something is terribly wrong, I want to now turn my focus to them.

Every Black woman I have worked with—either one-on-one in coaching, during my consulting work, or in interviews for this book—has reported receiving one or more of the exact same critiques: too direct, too aggressive, too results-orientated, too intimidating. And it doesn't matter if they are those things or not; one young woman I coached was painfully shy and quiet, but her law school classmates told her they didn't want her on their mock trial team because she might "dominate everything." This is why I want to take this chapter to speak specifically to and for Black women and those white women who truly seek to be allies, conspirators, and true sisters. Black men and other people of color navigate competency checking in white workplaces. But Black women sit at the unique intersection of anti-Black racism, sexism, and, because it can frequently take so long for Black people to be promoted, ageism. In my consulting work and interviews for this book, I have heard the frustration, confusion, and exhaustion of Black women who are ready, willing, and able to lead in the workplace but find their path obstructed by relentless competency checks, pushback, and hostility from men, women, and other people of color.

How could it be that a government employee on the West Coast, an East Coast academic, and a manager from the Midwest hear the same critiques and report almost identical experiences? Experiences and critiques that were summed up by Atlanta-based serial entrepreneur and marketing executive Ekaette Kern during my interview with her for this book. "You know, it's so interesting when I first came into this team, where there were literally all white women, and they were so excited to have me. But things started to change because I had expectations for my team. When I first came in, I was almost everyone's therapist; they brought me all their personal problems, 'You're the new Iyanla Vanzant, you're the next Oprah,' it was always comparing me to [the few Black] women that they know . . . and I found that to be exhausting. As I started establishing boundaries and setting expectations, it changed. I never yelled; I never used foul language; I was always very pleasant, but I was very direct. But my directness was very offensive; I was told I was unapproachable and aggressive."[1]

Ekaette Kern's experience illuminates a common challenge I have seen faced by Black women no matter what role they have in the workplace. Still, it becomes even more pronounced once they reach leadership positions. They are celebrated early in their career but then find things start to sour the moment they begin enforcing professional boundaries, exercising authority, and establishing expectations. Paradoxically, they often find themselves "tone-policed" by white women who simultaneously promote "leaning in" while shutting others down. As a result, many Black women find themselves in a confusing double bind within the workplace. Rather than being seen as leadership qualities, their competence and assertiveness are often interpreted through that historical "racial screen of contempt" that warps their actions into stereotypes. This leads to characterizations of being "too direct" or aggressive. This misinterpretation is less a reflection of their behavior and more an indication of systemic bias and white discomfort with Black authority—specifically, Black female authority.

Two Roads

I frequently do keynotes and trainings for women in leadership. During these presentations, I talk about how society responds to the different (actual and perceived) communication styles that Black and white women bring into the workplace. Societal expectations and enforcements have unfairly impacted both groups, but we need to have an honest and hard conversation here if we are ever to support each other.

White women live in a dual reality. They live as both the oppressed and the oppressor. From owning slaves to becoming "Karens," white women have always been participants in white supremacy, willing or otherwise. At the same time, they too have been victimized by white supremacy and the patriarchy. White women function in a world that has historically minimized, undermined, trivialized, and excluded them. A world that can frustrate and anger them, or worse. But white women can inflict those same things on others; frequently, in the workplace, that historic anger and frustration can be targeted at Black women and other women of color. As we discussed in the previous chapter, American society and culture has expressly "infantilized" white women, which looks like enforcing the pressure of perfection, overvaluing their youth and beauty, and requiring childish expressions of femininity that literally steal their voices. During one of my training sessions, I had a white woman tell me she'd been taught as a child not to speak too loudly because it was considered rude for a woman to do so.

As Deborah Tannen writes in her book *You Just Don't Understand*, "Even if they grow up in the same neighborhood, on the same block, or in the same house, girls and boys grow up in different worlds."[2] These gender differences in ways of talking have been "observed in children as young as three years of age, about the time language is developed. While little girls talk to be liked, boys often talk to boast. . . . Little girls talk more indirectly; little boys talk directly."[3] Tannen argues that men and women use language differently due to differing socialization experiences; I would argue that white women and Black women also use language differently because of their respective socialization experiences. However, in the workplace, white women's ways of communicating—often indirect, low-volume "upspeak"—are seen as the norm. Some Black women can, by doing what is known as code-switching, change how they talk in specific environments and adapt to it; others cannot.

The irony here is that for so long, the white women's liberation and empowerment movement has been about rejecting these enforced gender norms and allowing space for white women to step into "adulthood." In my training, I have had white women who will sometimes dispute this and tell me that they are direct and assertive because of, say, their sexual orientation or family situation. For example, a white woman who, as a child, had to deal with a parent with addiction might say, "I, too, was treated as an adult." That is true, but this treatment is not simply based on how you present internally or even externally but on how society interprets and responds to that presentation. We live in a system that values white women's tears and well-being above all others; the existence of the so-called "missing white woman syndrome," where a disproportionate amount of media attention is given to missing white women while little attention is paid to missing Black, Indigenous, and other women of color reinforces that fact.[4]

That white women's fear and discomfort, no matter their socioeconomic status, have historically meant punishment and even death for Black men, women, and children heightens the stakes of everyday incidents that naturally occur in the workplace. "I was a young girl who got fired from my first job because a white girl cursed *me* out. By the time the boss came out, she was crying, and he let me go. I didn't know how to defend or protect myself when I was seen as the aggressor. . . . I think somehow, they convinced me that my posture or something made her cry." That was one of the comments posted online after the social media influencer, author, and educator Luvvie Ajayi Jones posted an interactive article on her blog, *Awesomely Luvvie*, titled "About the Weary Weaponizing of White Women's Tears."[5] I have personally seen white women yell at the boss of a workplace, slam doors, and then, instead of being punished, people attend to *them*. A Black woman executive I know found herself going over a workplace issue with a young white woman who began to cry. The Black woman became concerned as they were in a conference room where people walking by could see inside. She told the white woman that she must understand that people would see the scene and decide that she, the Black woman, had made the white woman cry by being "mean" to her. That it was simply the young white woman's own anxiety wouldn't matter to anyone not in the room with them. There is nothing inherently wrong with crying or emotions; we should all be able to express ourselves and have it matter, but we can't, and it doesn't. The threat her tears posed to her Black superior hadn't occurred to the white woman.

This disconnect between the Black manager and the white supervisee about the impact of her tears has to do with the fact that the road Black women walk to enter the fray of adulthood is very different. Because of that walk, who we are colors how society perceives and responds to us. Not because that is who we are born to be or who we want to be; Black women are shy, we cry, have anxieties, and are messy, but the world makes it clear that it most definitely does not care about our tears and has always seen us as adults.

The adultification of Black children refers to the ways they are treated as older and more mature than their actual age by society, but especially by those in authority, teachers, and law enforcement. Adultified children are held to higher standards of behavior and expected to act more responsibly and maturely than others their age; for Black girls and children, these standards are even higher, even when engaging in typical childhood activities. They are subjected to harsher punishments; Black girls are disproportionately disciplined in schools and the juvenile justice system, even for minor infractions. They are sexualized at a younger age, and ultimately, they are denied the innocence of their own childhoods.[6] While Georgetown Law School is credited with bringing the issue to the forefront, Georgetown Law didn't create the concept of the adultified child; authors like Dr. Monique Morris, Dr. Kimberly Seals Allers, Dr. Yolanda Williams, and others laid the groundwork for the research. Of course, like everything in our collective story, this is part of a vine from slavery that has wound its way through time and into our modern day. Enslaved women were not seen as feminine; they worked, were beaten, and were sold like men. There was no childhood for enslaved children, so adultification is simply another iteration of that historical fact. While many

Black families work very hard to mitigate this from happening to their children, building homes that reinforce their child's inherent value and worth, once a Black child enters the world, from preschool on, they are confronted by the world outside of their home and all the ways in which they are wrongly perceived and treated. I call it a racial distortion filter, where it seems a Black person can say "I feel upset" and be perceived as yelling, screaming, and threatening. It truly is bewildering and can show up anywhere. As a Black woman, I know that if I barely raise my voice in frustration or anger—normal human emotions—I might be fired or have the police called on me. While watching a game show on TV, I noted that a young white man and a Black woman were deciding how to proceed with the game. The young Black woman stated what she wanted; she did not raise her voice or even seem angry, but the young white man immediately told her to "stop yelling at me."

This tracks with a study published by the American Psychological Association on how people read emotions differently in children based on race.[7] Of all the differences seen, the difference between Black and white girls was most dramatic. Adults had higher odds of mistakenly attributing anger to Black, as opposed to white, girls.[8] Researchers believed that one reason for the gap was that most adults participating in this study were white women. But there was also the fact that Black adults were just as likely as white adults to mistakenly attribute anger to Black girls. I emphasize mistaken here because previous research cited found that Black adults making neutral or ambiguous facial expressions were also at greater risk of being misperceived as angry.[9]

Being subjected to adultification and the racial distortion filter from childhood to actual adulthood is going to shape a very different adult than one who has been subjected to infantilization. The communication style will be more direct and less vague because it is vitally necessary that you be clear in your intentions. This is because adultification means facing much more severe consequences over any misinterpretation or confusion about what you've said and what you mean. So, as I say in my presentations, "When infantilization meets adultification in the workplace, what could possibly go wrong with communication except for everything."

Black women face constant competency checking specifically related to their communication style in the workplace. This puts them in a position where they must navigate their work life while constantly worrying about hitting an unseen tripwire with white women, white men, or even other people of color who traffic in stereotyping. This type of constant vigilance against the idea that Black women are angry, bossy, or threatening is a huge distraction from a person's actual job, and it's exhausting too. Black women frequently find themselves awkwardly supporting vague notions of "women's" empowerment that don't really include them because when Black women "lean in" decisively, they often find themselves forced back. Deena Pierott, the visionary leader of the national nonprofit iUrban Teen, and I discussed this when I interviewed her. Deena reflected on the nature of philanthropy, generational wealth frequently wielded by white women, and how some use their power. Deena spoke about how this power requires you to modulate yourself to access their wealth: "If you're not dancing to the beat of their drum, they will get their little circle against you. [There are] four of them up there that control pretty much a whole lot of purse strings, and this is sad because I'm not doing the soft shoe [dance] for you."[10]

From *The Help* to "Pet-to-Threat"

Beyond the different societal pressures that impact the communication styles of white and Black women, there is the historical positionality of our relationship with each other. Dr. Kecia M. Thomas, a renowned industrial/organizational psychology scholar focusing on workplace diversity, racism, and sexism, is credited with identifying the concept of "pet-to-threat." The concept highlights how Black women might, like Ekaette Kern, be initially viewed as nonthreatening, even favored ("pets"). However, once they begin to assert themselves, become more visible, or in any way challenge the status quo, the dominant group can quickly shift its perceptions to see them as a threat.

Dr. Thomas's research focuses on how this shift can impact the careers and psychological well-being of minority employees, particularly Black women.[11] Management Leadership for Tomorrow (MLT), a national nonprofit working on diversifying leadership pipelines, surveyed eight thousand alumni about racism and pet-to-threat experiences in the workplace. MLT found that 50 percent felt that their white mentors or sponsors who had initially supported them later tried to undermine them. One respondent wrote: "[My manager] refused to let me participate in conferences, saying they were 'above my pay grade,' even though colleagues of my level on other teams were encouraged to go. Eventually, I had to leave the organization because I was afraid that she would try to sabotage my relationships and hard-earned reputation."[12]

The dynamics behind pet-to-threat are much older than the modern workforce. The relationship between enslaved Black women and white women on plantations and in domestic servitude was complex and fraught with power imbalances rooted in the institution of slavery and gendered racial hierarchies. Black women found themselves having to appease white women for the sake of their own survival. In her book *Ar'n't I a Woman? Female Slaves in the Plantation South*, Deborah Gray White explores this historically unequal power dynamic: "The slave woman was forced into submission to white society because her labor was needed. Unlike the white woman, the slave woman was seen as a worker and as property, not to be pampered or protected."[13] As a result, enslaved Black women were forced to be a pleasant mirror reflecting only what white women wanted to see. This dynamic comes up in critiques of the movie *The Help*. The Black women in the movie are there to help the white women feel better about themselves, to listen to and sacrifice for them. They are the "pets" of their white employers, valued for their service and loyalty, but become "threats" when they choose to tell their own stories or push back against their oppressive conditions. The film has been critiqued for reducing Black domestic workers to background characters in their own story and elevating the narrative of a white character who "helps" them find their voice—an iteration of the "white savior" trope.

Whether we want to acknowledge it or not, this dynamic is behind what plays out in the workplace as an exhausting expectation that Black women are there to support, listen to, and elevate white women but not challenge them. As Kern found out, "I was almost everyone's therapist; they brought me all their personal problems."[14] Some Black women try to meet these expectations, always friendly, always "on" in the workplace while making themselves smaller or their voices higher to be treated as less of a "threat." It is, to be sure, a survival technique, but it puts Black women who can't or won't meet these expectations at odds with white women who expect this type of deferential treatment. You become different, difficult, unapproachable, or just too "you." When I worked in the news, a young white woman I worked with literally yelled that at me apropos of nothing one day. I could only assume she meant I was too confident, too adult, too knowledgeable, and a good decade older than her, so maybe too old? I thought I was the only one who had such a bizarre critique lobbed at them, until I heard a similar story from a Black woman attorney: "My assistant didn't want to be managed by me and got so upset with me correcting her. When I asked what was wrong, she said, 'It's just you, you know how you are!'" The attorney, a partner at a law firm, wondered if the assistant would have said the same thing to a white woman or man in the same position.

In my interview with Dr. Tina Opie, associate professor of management at Babson College and a coauthor of *Shared Sisterhood*, we talked about why women of color don't feel supported in the workplace. Dr. Opie shared, "What we found was that specifically in an environment where we were working in a team, and my work was interdependent with yours, Black women and Latinx/Hispanic women were less likely to trust or engage in these authentic connections with white women." Dr. Opie also said that her research found that Black and Latinx/Hispanic women worry that "if I reveal something to you that I'm struggling with at work, or that it's bothering me, or if I talk about something in a way that is not polite, according to you, you can affect my ability to be productive to be promoted and to enjoy the workspace." As we were wrapping up our chat, Dr. Opie shared that her research also found that even when Black women and white women are in a relationship with each other, they see that relationship very differently: "white women often perceive Black women as being closer friends than the Black woman perceives the white woman."[15]

To be clear, there is nothing wrong with friendship, sharing, and getting to know each other, but it must be mutual. Currently, in the workplace, when it comes to Black women and other women of color and white women, it is not. Black women tend to keep their relationships with white women in the workplace superficial because what happens if I share with you what is bothering me and causing me problems, and it's you or women like you? Can white women hear criticism and not be threatened, upset, or even cry, thus minimizing Black women's experience and pushing the burden of assuring them back onto Black women? This is not to say that no authentic relationships or conversations are happening between white and Black women in the workplace. Nor am I saying that the only pushback Black women receive is from white women. In fact, both from the experiences reported by the women I've worked with and my own observations, I've noticed instances where some Black women and other women of color have acted in ways that hinder the progress of their peers. Power perpetuates itself through the strategic use of scarcity to pit minoritized groups against each other—this is how things like racism, patriarchy, and injustice survive.

Unexpected Allies

The function of both patriarchy and white supremacy is to convince those of us who aren't white and male that there are only a few "slots" available in society, so we must fight it out among each other to be the winner of patriarchal and white supremacist largess. While the above is true, it is also true that white women have more power in the workplace than Black and other women of color, if only by sheer numbers, and even then only marginally. So, who has the "real" power in this scenario? White men. Because they have an outsize portion of the balance of power, they emerge as unexpected allies in many of the stories I have heard in my coaching and interviews. As a Black woman tech executive said to me, "If I am honest, it has been white men who have told me, 'Let me tell you about this opportunity,' or gave me insight into 'the game.'" The story that Juatise Gathings, a former regional operations director at Discover Financial Services, told me during our interview provides a case study of this phenomenon.

I first heard Gathings and Discover CEO Roger Hochschild on NPR talking about opening a call center in Chicago's predominately Black Chatham neighborhood. It was the first call center outside the suburbs, providing one thousand full-time jobs to neighborhood residents. I was impressed by what I heard: low employee attrition, a motivated workforce that had already seen promotions, and the start of a community-wide transformation. But I was most impressed by this Black woman, who had worked at Discover for eleven years, being featured with the CEO, openly crediting her and her hard work with getting this project off the ground. I had to find a way to connect with her, talk more about her experiences, and find out what could be learned from them. Little did I know that by the time I reached Gathings, she would be leaving Discover, with her situation mirroring what I was hearing from Black women across the country. Gathings provided substantial insights into the duality of her role there, juxtaposing her public representation of the company's racial equity initiatives against her actual experiences and challenges within the corporate structure. "You have this Black chick that, two years ago, no one at Discover even knew who I was other than the people I work directly with, and there I was sitting side by side on an NPR podcast with our CEO."[16]

But Gathings and other Black Discover employees found her external portrayal—pivotal to Discover's good PR around its commitment to social justice—at odds with the internal struggle Gathings faced when it came to actually advancing her career. "I have influence without the appropriate authority," she explained. She went on to say that this created an authority gap that was tricky to navigate, "and that's where the rub is, for a lot of the day-to-day challenges." This influence-without-authority is a theme that I have heard from other Black women. They become what I call "shadow elevated," doing elevated work but not given an elevated title or pay.

Things came to a head for Gathings when a new slate of VPs was being chosen; two older white men with years of combined experience at Discover tried to advocate for her and found that even their efforts were insufficient in the face of the system. Gathings recounted how the executives responded to the pushback they received when advocating for her: "When advocating for my promotion or policies benefiting Black employees, their influence suddenly seems ineffective. They're left bewildered, questioning why they can't achieve what they set out to do. It's new territory for them."[17] Their support was ineffective because of the large, small, formal, and informal ways competency checking based on race can come together to make up the blockage that is systemic racism.

What also surfaced during our conversation was the truth about where Gathings's superiors said some of the strongest pushback to their efforts came from: "Interestingly, they've noticed that resistance often doesn't come from white men in leadership but rather from white women." As Gathings reflected on the situation, she theorized that the white women saw the advocacy on her behalf as encroaching on their territory, an insult to their own success. "This discomfort arises because there's now a Black woman receiving the level of support they've traditionally seen as reserved for themselves."[18] We must remember that this was reported to Gathings by those same white male sponsors. In truth, it seems that someone at Discover, possibly the CEO or someone(s) on the executive team, had enough juice to make a promotion happen for Gathings, but ultimately, no one did. Black women know that the cards are stacked against us at work, almost as a rule. That doesn't stop us from trying or hurting when we are let down, whether for the first time or the twentieth.

So, is the fact that it was two white men who were trying to advocate for Gathings proof that there is no white supremacy or patriarchy and that white men are just misunderstood secret allies? Unfortunately, no. Rather, it's a reflection of another fact: White men are the ones who have the most relational capital to spend. If we think of capital in the workplace like an arcade game where your energy pack starts at a certain charge, and when you reach the end, you're out, white men's capital starts charged at 100 percent, and if they spend some of their capital on promoting someone and it doesn't work out, they lose maybe 2 percent. But let's say a white woman's capital starts at 50 percent; now she's worried that if she uses some of her capital on elevating anyone, especially a Black person, and it doesn't work out, she might lose 15 percent of her already limited capital. Now, a Black person at work, male or female, no matter their role, starts with, let's say, a 25 percent charge of work capital. If they use some of their capital on another Black person and it doesn't work out, they might end up with zero. In fact, Ekaette Kern has an example of this playing out with a Black woman in leadership whom she went to for help and guidance while at a previous job. Rather than intercede on Ekaette's behalf, the woman told her to keep her head down. Years later, Ekaette spoke to the executive after both left the company and found out that she was just as scared for her job as Ekaette was, even though the woman was "in power" at the company. "A decision maker for sure," she says. "But when you talk about power, she was powerless to help me. I saw her making moves for other people. But she was not comfortable or confident enough to decide to help me. And she said that she had too much at stake to help me."

In my experience, authority without real "juice" and leadership without a full charge of working capital renders many Black and other leaders of color unable or unwilling to take a "risk" or even a sure bet on another Black person or other person of color. This is because if things go wrong, they may find themselves with zero capital and out of the game. From this viewpoint, we can see that white men can be supportive when they choose to be because, generally speaking, they have less to lose.

There's another strange phenomenon that might also be at play when it comes to white men and Black women in the workplace. During research on the impact of Black women as "agentic" leaders, meaning assertive, competitive, independent, and courageous, it was found that Black women did not face the same backlash that white women and Black men did when displaying dominance and leadership.[19] A couple of things to add here: the study was small, comprising 84 people, and most participants were non-Black men. This is relevant for two reasons. First, white men's historical fear of Black men and their physical presence and perceived dominance is well documented and at the root of many of the incidents of police brutality that we see today.[20] Researchers frame this dynamic in the workplace as what they call out-group males being seen as more of a threat in power dynamics, leading to a penalization of Black men for agentic, dominant, and leadership behaviors in favor of more communal or deferential ones.[21] The second reason the makeup of the group as predominately non-Black males matters is that, as we already discussed, patriarchy and white supremacy demand a certain type of presentation from white women, one that it does not from Black women. In other words, it would make "sense" if a pool of white men reacted negatively to a white woman exerting authority and power based on preconceived gendered notions of *white* femininity. But because Black women have not been seen in the same light and are adultified from childhood, the idea that a white man might be more "comfortable" with a Black woman displaying these skills makes some perverted sense.

Where Are They Now?

Today, Black women face an almost constant barrage of competency checking in the workplace, from tone policing to constant "challenging" of their knowledge, skills, and even right to be in certain places. It is so pervasive that even award-winning directors and multitalented entertainers deal with it. Beyoncé's recent film, *Renaissance*, moved Ava DuVernay so much that she posted her reaction to the movie on her Instagram story, and the message quickly went viral. While praising Beyoncé's skill as a creative, DuVernay homed in on several interactions captured in the film: "[Beyoncé] talks candidly about having to fight to be heard as a Black woman leader working at a high level of difficulty. We see moments of this happening to her on camera. People directly doubting, shortchanging, gaslighting her." DuVernay then connects this to her own experience: "Though I have lots of practice with this kind of blatant disregard, it never gets easier to stomach. Never easier to watch someone diminish themselves by their downright disregard for you."[22]

What DuVernay is describing happens to Black women every day, both in the workplace and outside of it. What she, Beyoncé, and millions of Black women experience is competency checking, done by people who believe that Black people—and Black women in particular—are incompetent, and who believe it's their duty to verify your competency and correct you, even when you know that what you said, or what you experienced, is true.

Beyond the professional toll all these obstacles have on Black women, there is a very real physical, emotional, and economic toll to competency checking as well. As Nataki Garrett, the former artistic director of the Oregon Shakespeare Festival, described it to me: "I'm stressed in ways that, like—I'm unrecognizable to my mother. Your body is in a state of hypervigilance. And that means your entire body, your inflammation response, your stress response, and everything else is on high alert, right? Everything that happens is a ten-alarm fire." Garrett's tenure at the Oregon Shakespeare Festival was short, complicated by the impact of COVID-19 and the astounding level of pushback her presence received from some staff, donors, board members, and the overwhelmingly white surrounding community. All of it culminated in Garett needing a security detail just to leave her house.

Garrett described to me how the combined impact of a type of professional violence and threats of actual physical violence kept her in a near-constant state of stress, affecting her physical health and necessitating a focus on healing not just from the situation she found herself in but from years of trauma working in American theater. What Garrett endured might sound extreme, but it's not, and science can measure the impact. While people have heard the phrase "Black don't crack" relating to the overall physical appearance of Black women as they age and maintain a youthful visage, the truth is that Black does crack from the *inside*. Researchers have hypothesized that continuous exposure to anti-Black racism and sexism leaves Black women's bodies exposed to the highest possible levels of toxic stress hormones as a result of being in "fight-or-flight" mode on a daily basis.[23] This impacts everything, from the higher risk of premature births, no matter a person's economic status or prenatal care, to internal "weathering" that sees Black women's health indicators, and internal systems, heart, arteries, etc., age faster than white women's.[24] Arline T. Geronimus, one of the primary researchers to identify the concept of "weathering," found that Black women had the highest scores for allostatic load, the cumulative burden of chronic stress. And it wasn't just a class thing; wealth did not shield Black women from the stress of facing racial disparities daily.[25]

It is the impact of having to adapt to the physiological and psychological burden of constant stressors that gave birth to the myth as well as the reality that is the idea of the "strong, independent, long-suffering Black woman." She is someone who can endure "superhuman" pain, humiliation, and burdens without breaking a sweat and without complaint. Adultified from childhood and denied the softness of femininity by a white supremacist society in adulthood, Black womanhood needed to define itself by its ability to **endure**. While some see this as a dangerous myth, others see it as a stark reality. I see it as a combination of the two. The fact is that Black women have and currently do respond to actual environmental stressors and threats that they must navigate to survive. So, unlike imposter syndrome, the strong Black woman has been a natural and valuable adaptation technique to survive big and small battles. A soldier must wear armor during the battle; that is a fact. But the idea that the armor is impenetrable and that the soldier wearing it feels no pain is a myth.

This may be why the suicide of Dr. Antoinette Candia-Bailey, a key administrator at Lincoln University in Missouri, hit many Black women, particularly in academia, so hard. According to reporting by *The Hilltop* at Howard University, Dr. Candia-Bailey's suicide in early 2024 sparked discussions within the HBCU community about the distinct pressures Black women face in higher education and the mental health crises those pressures can induce. Some saw Dr. Candia-Bailey's death as highlighting the severe impact of misogynoir—a term coined by Dr. Moya Bailey (no relation) to address the ways misogyny and anti-Black racism merge in spaces such as hip-hop to target trans and cisgendered Black women.[26]

While we will never know all the factors that led to Dr. Candia-Bailey's death, we do know that constant competency checking and having to face systemic anti-Black racism daily

is harming Black women. And it's having not just a physical impact but a devastating economic impact as well. Black
women are more likely to make more money or be equal economic partners in their relationships and are more likely to be
single heads of households. So, when their financial fortunes
are stunted by competency checking and racism, it directly impacts Black wealth accumulation for generations to come.[27]

Despite their incredible capacity and desire to advance and
lead, Black women in the workplace are tired and frustrated.
This is partly because on those rare occasions when a Black
woman does get into a leadership position, she finds herself
on the jagged edge of a glass cliff that has already cracked.
While interviewing Kyra Kyles, the CEO of YR Media, she expressed the reality of what this has looked like for her during
her twenty-year career: "It is almost like you're handed a mess
and asked to straighten it up. And not only do you need to
straighten up this mess, but you also have to do it fast. You
have to do it with grace, you have to do it with elegance, you
can't complain about it, you can't show any weakness, because
if you do, people will pounce."[28]

What are the alternatives? Many Black women have
started to look beyond the traditional office structure for
work. According to a 2023 report by GoDaddy's Venture Forward research initiative, Black women represent the most
rapidly expanding segment of entrepreneurs in the United
States. From 2014 to 2019, there was a 50 percent surge in
the number of enterprises operated by Black women, marking the most significant increase observed among all groups
of female entrepreneurs.[29] This may seem like a great thing,
and as a Black woman who owns a small business, I think it
generally is, but we still have to be honest about what is driv-
ing this trend as well as what stands in its way. Black women
receive less than 0.35 percent of all venture capital funding,

and "in 2020, less than 100 Black women raised $1 million or more in (Venture Capital) VC funding."[30] As a result of this, Black women are forced to self-fund their startup capital. Of course, outliers exist: there exist amazingly successful Black women entrepreneurs like Fawn Weaver, who created the whiskey brand Uncle Nearest, named after the formerly enslaved man who taught Jack Daniel how to make whiskey. As of this writing, Weaver has reached Unicorn financial status, which means her company is valued at $1 billion, a feat she accomplished through self-funding and strategic investments outside the traditional VC marketplace.

But Weaver's experience can't and won't be the norm for most.[31] Black people, in general, need and deserve the ability to succeed and fail like anyone else. If success for Black individuals hinges on rare lottery wins, while white individuals are provided more opportunities to get access to capital because they are deemed "competent" despite frequently squandering it without results, then we're facing de facto discrimination in access to venture capital. This creates an unjust advantage where whiteness, not qualifications, skills, or creativity, becomes the primary qualifier for financial backing. It is this stark reality that prompted the establishment of the Fearless Fund.

Founded in 2019, the Atlanta-based Fearless Fund is a venture capital firm dedicated to supporting women of color–led businesses. By 2022, the fund had supported thirty-one enterprises founded by women of color. Among these, over five succeeded in securing $1 million each in venture capital funding.[32] In August 2023, the Fearless Fund was sued by the conservative group American Alliance for Equal Rights (AAER), led by Edward Blum, the same man behind the Supreme Court case that upended race-conscious college admissions. Arian Simone, CEO and cofounder of the Fearless Fund, expressed to BET.com that she sees AAER's lawsuit as part of a broader anti-American campaign: "It's like a shirt with a string, *Roe v. Wade*, being pulled. Then, you pull another string, Affirmative Action. And as you keep pulling strings, the shirt is undone—stopping millions and billions of dollars from getting into the hands of people of color."[33] On June 3, the U.S. Court of Appeals for the Eleventh Circuit in Miami issued a 2–1 decision to suspend the Fearless Fund's grant program. The court determined that the conservative group's claim that the program is discriminatory is likely to succeed. Fearless Fund CEO Arian Simone described the ruling as devastating, arguing that it undermines efforts to promote diversity in corporate America and other sectors.[34] It seems that the idea of pulling yourself up either individually or collectively by your own bootstraps is no longer an American ideal now that bootstrapping has been deemed illegal.

A Path Toward Sisterhood

The phrase "dancing backward in high heels" became popular thanks to Bob Thaves's 1982 cartoon in which a woman explains to the protagonists of the strip—Frank and Ernest—that although Fred Astaire was a great dancer, Ginger Rogers could do the same, backward and in high heels. The quote is frequently used to describe the complex nature of what it means to be a woman in the workplace and life. What many Black women need their white sisters to understand is not only are we dancing backward in high heels, but we're also doing it while carrying the weight of anti-Black racism, white supremacy, and patriarchy on our backs. All the while, people are literally trying to remove the tiles from the floor on which we are dancing. Regardless of that difference, no one deserves this treatment. But only together can we challenge the systems that force us to dance to a tune we didn't pick and dance a routine that wasn't choreographed with us in mind, let alone as the lead.

So, what can be done to help create a true sisterhood? First, let's not add this work to the already long list of jobs Black women have. Instead, we need white women in general and allies in particular to choose sisterhood over the false promises and illusions of power that white supremacy and patriarchy offer. While that might sound like a big "ask," I am going to break it down into three concrete steps.

Groups

First, examine the "women's" organizations you belong to. Suppose your women in tech, women in academia, women in entrepreneurial groups, etc., are predominantly white and struggle to include the voices, needs, and concerns of Black and other women of color. In that case, they are white women's groups. These groups, regardless of intention, are not designed to change systems or challenge the status quo but rather to access the privileges of the patriarchy and uphold white supremacy. Real change requires reexamining systems that weren't designed for anyone who is not white and male. The only way to do that is to intentionally shift our collective focus from white women's issues to the issues impacting *all* women. You can do this by requiring that every conversation in your organization be actively intersectional. So, a women's entrepreneurial group is going to stop having white-centric conversations about how "women" only get 2 percent of VC funding and discuss why "the combined share of Latina and Black women founders' access to venture capital is only slightly over 1%, .64% for Latina and .41% for Black women founders, respectively."[35] Then your group will discuss the systems blocking access to women and how those blockages look different depending on the race and gender expression of the woman. From there the policies, programming, and advocacy this group engages in will be expressed as multipronged approaches to address the needs of all women intentionally.

The Best Offense Is a Good Defense

Because HR professionals are overwhelmingly white women, they are advantageously placed to champion genuine inclusion and support for Black women. I say this while acknowledging that this demographic dominance in the HR space is not merely coincidental but reflects broader systemic patterns that have historically "ghettoized" or unfairly relegated white women into HR roles. I believe that by working together, we can scale change to provide more choices for all women when it comes to corporate spaces. White women currently working in HR are in the best position to help dismantle the ingrained biases and barriers that Black women face and can do so by undertaking a comprehensive learning journey about the interplay of race and gender. Doing this would help white women in HR ensure that critical issues around intersectionality are at the heart of HR practices and not merely peripheral concerns.

The Society for Human Resource Management (SHRM), alongside local HR organizations, must pivot to make the understanding of race and gender dynamics central to their training programs; one should not be SHRM-certified without this deep knowledge. This shift is crucial for addressing the nuanced forms of discrimination Black women encounter in the workplace, including competency checking and tone policing. This specific form of control, which scrutinizes and penalizes Black women's communication styles, reinforces stereotypes and actively silences their voices. It's a manifestation of systemic racism and sexism where Black women's expressions are misinterpreted and pathologized, echoing the historical witch hunts that targeted innocent individuals based on unfounded hysteria rather than provable facts.

That's the irony of the phrase "witch hunt": you can't hunt something that doesn't exist. I often tell HR professionals that the odds they have a "witch," in the fairy-tale sense, in the workplace are nonexistent. What they are most likely dealing with is a type of mass hysteria in the form of institutional racism and misogynoir. Very few examples bring this home better than an example that Minda Harts, a Black woman, shares in her book *Right Within: How to Heal from Racial Trauma in the Workplace*. Harts tells the story of her manager informing her that her white male colleague had been reporting false information about her work. "She sat in shock and disbelief as her manager made excuses for him because he was going through a rough time in his personal life. Minda believed that she and her colleague had a good working relationship and mutual respect, even though they were competing for the same promotion. Her manager reassured her that she had not believed his false reports and that Minda should stay focused on the assigned project."[36] In Harts's case, she was lucky that her manager said she believed her. Many Black women find themselves struggling to try to disprove a negative that has already taken root. However, Harts's manager making excuses for the coworker left Harts feeling gaslit about the severity of his actions.

For many Black women, false allegations of "witchcraft"—entitlement, behavioral issues, unprofessional appearance, threatening tone—often lodged by their white sisters are often the reason they end up fleeing the traditional corporate workplace. What I routinely tell HR professionals in my trainings is that when it comes to interracial disputes in the office, they *must not* make assumptions and they *must* ask **more** questions than they normally would. This is vital for understanding context and ensuring fairness. I understand that we are talking about these deeply rooted power structures that have been growing between the cracks of this country for centuries and that trimming them back, let alone doing away with them completely, won't be easy. But white women in the HR space must navigate these challenges with sensitivity and depth.

White women can also step up to help break a significant block to women's progress by addressing the unique impact of ageism on Black women. For Black women, ageism is exacerbated by anti-Black racism and the resulting professional challenges they face. In 2020, Lean In and McKinsey & Company reported on "The State of Black Women in Corporate America." They found an "alarming" gap between how long it took Black women versus their white male counterparts to receive a promotion.[37] This is something that Nataki Garrett touched on during our conversation as she reflected on the stark contrast of her career progression due to racial and gender biases versus that of white men in the theater. "I started [that] job when I was forty-eight. . . . I am ten years older than when most of the white men in my field started [as an artistic director]. In some instances, I'm fifteen years older." This highlights the compounded effect of ageism and racism. By the time a Black woman gets promoted or even finds herself up for promotion, she may be older than her white counterparts, male or female.

So, white women in HR must be a first line of defense. These women must interrogate, raise the alarm, and demand an examination of the ways patriarchy and white supremacy have socialized all of society, including white women, to value youth over experience. Ways that might inadvertently lead to denying promotions to or undermining older Black women, thereby perpetuating ageism against all women, who statistically bear the brunt of it in the workforce.[38]

To confront and transform these entrenched dynamics, HR professionals must develop a profound understanding of the interconnectedness of racism, sexism, and ageism. This requires more than mere compliance with EEOC guidelines. Again, the certification process for SHRM professionals should incorporate rigorous training on these intersections, ensuring HR professionals are well equipped to foster environments in which Black women can thrive without the threat of tone policing or any form of competency checking. By prioritizing education on these issues, white HR professionals can evolve from mere participants in a gendered corporate structure to active allies and change agents.

Humanity

Everyone can help Black women in the workplace by allowing them the space to put down the armor they are forced to wear. Black women don't always want to be soldiers—they want softness, support, and help. In the journey toward fostering a genuine sisterhood within the workplace, white women can, through authentic communication and trust building, allow Black women to unburden themselves.

This need for vulnerability and support was poignantly illustrated in my work with a birthing center that sought guidance on enhancing support for Black women and other women of color. Through examining the center's existing practices, I found that they commendably coached patients to lean into their strength and resilience as women. However, I suggested that when working with Black women, they also cultivate an environment that welcomes fear, expressions of concern, and the open expression of emotions, including crying, without judgment. This approach is not merely about adjusting services but is deeply rooted in understanding the systemic pressures Black women face, pressures that demand constant resilience and strength. By allowing Black women the space to be vulnerable—to cry, to curse, to be a mess—we acknowledge their humanity beyond the confines of societal expectations and stereotypes.

For white women seeking to extend true sisterhood to Black colleagues, it is essential to move beyond superficial archetypes and strive for authentic understanding and connection. It's about seeing the individual in their entirety, beyond the shadow of powerful figures with dehumanizing phrases such as "you're like Oprah Winfrey or Michelle Obama," and recognizing the unique experiences and challenges the Black woman sitting next to you navigates daily. Building mutually beneficial relationships with Black women and other women of color means committing to listen without judgment, to support without dominating, and to help without overshadowing. It requires a willingness to confront and dismantle the structures of white supremacy and patriarchy that not only segregate us but also hierarchize our struggles.

True sisterhood in the workplace transcends mere solidarity in words; it embodies solidarity in actions, fostering an inclusive environment where Black women can be supported in their vulnerability and celebrated in their strength. By collectively committing to these principles, white women can help foster true sisterhood. A sisterhood where none of us need to dance backward, wear the armor of long-suffering, or bear the weight of systemic barriers alone. Instead we can together pave the way for a world in which all women are valued, supported, and empowered to thrive at work and in life.

CHAPTER 7

It's Not Just Black and White
(or American)

The curse of anyone nonwhite is that you are so busy
arguing what you're not that you never arrive at what
you are.

—Cathy Park Hong, *Minor Feelings:*
An Asian American Reckoning

WHILE COMPETENCY CHECKING in the United States grows
out of the fertile soil that is anti-Black bias, it doesn't
just impact Black people. It also expresses itself anywhere in
the world that colonialism or occupation has left its mark. The
architects of white supremacy, such as the British and French
empires, spread racial hierarchies and white supremacist ideologies across their vast colonial domains in North America,
Australia, Africa, Southeast Asia, and the Caribbean, instill-
ing a sense of European superiority. Similarly, Spain, Portugal,
the Netherlands, Germany, and Belgium implemented racial
categorizations and stratifications in their colonies—from Latin
America to Africa and Asia—reinforcing white dominance and
often with brutal consequences for indigenous populations.[1]
These colonial powers understood that to entrench their power
fully, they needed to denigrate the intellectual abilities of those

they sought to dominate. By propagating damaging stereotypes and promoting biased narratives, they effectively shaped a story that portrayed formerly colonized people as intellectually inferior. This tactic served multiple purposes: it justified the exploitation of resources, masked the true motivations behind colonial endeavors, and reinforced the myth of whiteness and, as a result, white supremacy. Those efforts created a shock wave that continues to have a global impact in the form of competency checking.

In a multiracial population such as ours in the United States, the phenomenon of competency checking, due to the diverse backgrounds of our people, takes many forms of expression. People of color, regardless of their origin, experience competency checking to varying degrees, and they also engage in competency checking among themselves. This practice can serve as a form of asserting power and establishing social hierarchies, or in extreme cases, as a means of assimilating into white culture. Engaging in such practices may stem from a desire to reinforce a sense of intragroup superiority or a sense of competition for seemingly limited opportunities or resources. These divisions place people of color in the role of foot soldiers for white supremacy by helping to reinforce discrimination in hiring practices, unequal access to education, and subtle biases in the workplace.

I recently gave a Black History Month presentation titled "Black History, Past, Present, and Future" for a local company here in Portland, Oregon. The presentation was about how Black Americans' struggle for freedom, respect, and inclusion, from emancipation to Black Lives Matter, has influenced liberation movements in the US and globally. After the presentation, one of the employees, who did not disclose her ethnicity but spoke with a South American accent, came up to speak with me. She had a look of wonder on her face, and she said to me,

"I didn't know any of that; I never heard any of that before. I am not from the United States originally, and I didn't know all of this." Her comments hit home for me because, as a consultant, I know there is so much we as people of color don't know about each other, and much of what we do know has come to us through, if not a white supremacist lens, then a white normative one. By way of example, let's take a look at what Black soldiers said was happening to them during the Vietnam War. Black soldiers reported to their superiors that white soldiers were slandering them to Vietnamese civilians. Gerald Goodwin, writing about an incident Ronald Lewis—an African American stationed in Vietnam—described in *Ebony* magazine, says, "He [Lewis] recalled an incident in which a Vietnamese proprietor who happened to be reading a copy of *Ebony* informed him that the information in the magazine contradicted everything whites had told him about African Americans, which was that 'our race were the peasants of the United States and were inclined to cut you with a razor (which we all carry) almost any time.' Whites had told the man that blacks were only capable of working menial jobs and were not intelligent enough to attend school . . . or take on meaningful jobs."[2]

In the example above, we see how white supremacy positions itself between people of color in the same way Iago in Shakespeare's *Othello* positions himself between Cassio, who is white, and Othello, who is a "Moor" or Black man. Iago is a master manipulator who deceives nearly every other character to achieve his ends, telling each person different things to incite jealousy, mistrust, and, ultimately, tragedy. This is why, even as a person of color, I must acknowledge that when discussing the experiences of other people of color, I am an outsider. I can only speak from my perspective, which is impacted by the racial filters we are all exposed to. As a result, I must rely on trusted voices from within the community to guide and inform my understanding while recognizing that those voices don't represent the collective because no one person, or even a handful of people, is a monolith. So, as I move through this chapter, examining the ways competency checking has impacted Asian Americans in particular, how and why all people of color competency check each other, and how competency checking shows up worldwide, you may notice a bit of a tonal shift as I try to do so with respect while acknowledging the limits of my understanding.

"Asian"

Given the complexity of how competency checking varies across racial and ethnic groups, it's challenging to thoroughly address every aspect of the issue without omitting important details. Therefore, to provide a more detailed analysis, I'll focus specifically on how competency checking affects Asian Americans.

During a DEI training session I was conducting for a large multinational company, one of the employees told me, "I didn't know I was Asian until I came to the United States; for my entire life, I've been Chinese." In that one comment, the man, a Chinese national working in the United States, encapsulated the limitation of using one word, *Asian*, to describe billions of different people from forty-eight countries and three territories on the largest continent on the planet.

The term *Asian American* was born in the late 1960s, inspired significantly by the Black Power movement. The banner of *Asian* in the United States was to be a solid front against racial discrimination and social injustices.[3] Pioneered by figures like Yuji Ichioka and Emma Gee, who established the Asian American Political Alliance (AAPA) at the University of California, Berkeley, in 1968, the term marked a pivotal moment in political activism among Asian communities.[4] This alliance, which rallied Asian students from various backgrounds, represented a collective stance against the Vietnam War and racial discrimination, and "a rejection of slurs that had been imposed on people of Asian origin and of stereotypes that painted them as passive."[5]

While it's true that *Asian American* served as a banner for unity and collective action, it also blended the complexities and diversities within the Asian diaspora, overshadowing the distinct narratives and challenges faced by different Asian communities. For example, it merges the experiences and histories of East Asians, Southeast Asians, and South Asians, who each have unique stories of migration and life in the United States.

Model Minority/White Adjacent/Tiger Mom

In the workplace, the competency checking of Asian Americans is deeply influenced by the perception of what it means to be "Asian." One of the central tenets of Asianness, as prescribed by white supremacy, is compliance. The term *model minority* was introduced by sociologist William Petersen in his 1966 article in the *New York Times Magazine* about the "success story" of Japanese Americans in the US. In the article, Petersen asserts that Japanese Americans—despite facing intense racism and discrimination (including the mass internment of Japanese Americans after the attack on Pearl Harbor for the duration of the war)—achieved success in a way that other minority groups had not.[6] In her book *Minor Feelings: An Asian American Reckoning*, Cathy Park Hong, a Korean American, critically examines the model-minority myth, which portrays Asian Americans as successful, compliant, and devoid of the challenges faced by other minority groups. According to Hong, this myth is a double-edged sword that makes invisible the struggles of Asian Americans, pits them against other minority groups, and serves the interests of white supremacy by upholding a false narrative of meritocracy.[7] She writes, "The indignity of being Asian in this country has been underreported. We have been cowed by the lie that we have it good. We keep our heads down and work hard, believing that our diligence will reward us with our dignity, but our diligence will only make us disappear."[8]

This leads to the second aspect of competency checking of Asian Americans: the unease or surprise when confronted with leadership capabilities displayed in ways not seen as "prototypically Asian." This reaction underscores a deep-seated belief in racial hierarchies where Asian competence is tied into expectations around Asian passivity and deference, with any deviation from these stereotypes (for example, taking on leadership roles, displaying assertiveness) being met with discomfort and resistance.

All of this is rooted in the idea that Asian Americans are raised to be robotic and accepting of white supremacy. This is seen in the concept of "white adjacency" and the Tiger Mom stereotype popularized by Amy Chua's memoir, *Battle Hymn of the Tiger Mother*, in which she extols the virtues of harsh discipline and rigid expectations when raising children. However, Scarlett Wang, writing in *Applied Psychology Opus*, questions the portrayal of Chinese parenting in Chua's book, which may have inadvertently added to the model-minority stereotype. Wang believes that the portrayal of Chinese parenting as extremely strict and demanding, focusing on success over happiness, is incomplete and inaccurate. Wang points out that while this is now a part of the American idea of how Chinese people raise their children, it differs significantly from the diverse parenting styles practiced by Chinese parents.[9]

In a white supremacist system, both the model minority and the Tiger Mom idea exist in service of whiteness as a type of technical support, and the payment for that support is something many Asian writers and thinkers have called "white adjacency." Jeff Chang, author of the book *We Gon' Be Alright: Notes on Race and Resegregation*, talks about white adjacency as a type of conditional privilege that creates a precarious sense of security for Asian Americans. He also expands on the myriad of ways privilege can be quickly revoked in the face of racial animosity or political tensions, such as the internment of Japanese Americans. Ultimately, Chang argues that Asian Americans cannot rely on proximity to whiteness for social and economic gains.

So, competency checking of Asian Americans in the United States is built on both collective and individual erasure, leaving behind only what white supremacy chooses to see. An example of this would be how the model-minority myth not only disappears the many nuances of Asian American life but also erases whole sections of it. Southeast Asian communities like the Hmong, Cambodian, Laotian, and Bhutanese Americans, many of whom arrived as refugees, face higher levels of poverty and lower educational attainment compared to other groups. These challenges are attributed to a range of factors, including historical trauma, refugee status, language barriers, and limited access to resources before and following their migration to the US.[10]

This erasure can generally be understood in a dual light. On the one hand, stereotyped as inherently intelligent and hardworking, East Asian Americans (Chinese, Korean, and Japanese) specifically face lower expectations and pushback when they seek to move out of their "prescribed roles" and into leadership or displays of assertiveness. This dichotomy was present during a coaching session I had with a young East Asian American woman. The woman had been hired by a large nonprofit out east and was having a lot of trouble with the white women in her workplace. The problem seemed to be that she was forthright and direct and did not apparently perform her

Asianness properly for her coworkers. She reported to me that she was told she was "surprisingly" aggressive and direct and that she was "different" from other Asian people they had met. At some point during the upheaval at her workplace, she had gotten hold of the notes taken during her initial job interview. Her supervisor had written: "She speaks English surprisingly well," and again, a reference to her being surprisingly direct. As the woman I was coaching explained, the supervisor knew she was born in America, so the comment that "she speaks English well" can only be seen through the other key element of competency checking that is cast on Asian Americans: "the perpetual foreigner" stereotype.

This stereotype suggests that regardless of how long they or their families have been in the United States, Asian Americans are outsiders or not fully American.[11] This perception contributes to competency checking in both personal and professional contexts. The perpetual foreigner stereotype underpins the assumption of Asian intellectual superiority while simultaneously serving as a justification for oversight, mistreatment, and marginalization. Asian Americans find their achievements attributed to their foreignness rather than their individual hard work or intelligence, and this can lead to their contributions being undervalued or overlooked, particularly in leadership roles or fields not stereotypically associated with Asians.[12]

Because the model-minority myth is so good at masking the details and nuanced ways in which race impacts those of Asian descent, many reading this book, including some Asian Americans, will be surprised to learn what was found in research and reported on in an article published by the *San Francisco Chronicle* in 2023 regarding the "bamboo ceiling." According to the article, "Asian Americans lag behind all racial, ethnic and gender groups in promotion to managerial and executive ranks in spite of their education, work experience and job performance.

Even in fields in which Asian Americans are overrepresented—including technology, medicine, the natural sciences, engineering, and law—they are rare in leadership."[13] The article goes on to cite research that shows how, despite making up a sizable portion of the workforce in Silicon Valley's top tech firms, Asian Americans are half as likely to reach executive ranks compared to their white counterparts. The cumulative result of these race-based blockages is called the "bamboo ceiling," which limits and prescribes the roles certain Asian Americans can play in professional landscapes.[14]

You might be thinking, Wait, aren't there a lot of Asian people in leadership positions in tech companies? This is where specificity starts to matter. Remember *East Asian* refers to people from China (including Macau and Hong Kong), Korea, Japan, Okinawa, Taiwan, and Mongolia. *South Asian* refers to people from Bangladesh, Bhutan, India, the Maldives, Nepal, Pakistan, and Sri Lanka.[15] This distinction matters—historically, where an Asian person is from has a lot to do with how white supremacy in the United States views their ability to lead. The *Chronicle* article and other research implies that the difference in advancement to leadership positions between East Asians and South Asians may be related to differences in cultural norms around assertiveness. Specifically, it was found that South Asians tend to be more verbally assertive. Because that aligns more closely with Western corporate expectations for leaders, they are more likely to ascend to leadership positions. Conversely, East Asians, are described this way in the research: "Strongly influenced by Confucianism, EA cultures emphasize humility, conformity, and harmony rather than assertiveness in interpersonal communication."[16]

According to research, because East Asians have a harder time accessing leadership positions, companies should reconsider how they see a "leader." Does a leader need to be traditionally assertive to be able to succeed in the role? It is also suggested that companies invest in cultural understanding/ training as well as support and training for East Asians seeking leadership roles.[17] While I don't disagree with any of those suggestions, this conclusion by the researchers gave me pause when I read it: "East Asians hit the bamboo ceiling because their low assertiveness is incongruent with American norms concerning how leaders should communicate. The bamboo ceiling is not an Asian issue, but an issue of cultural fit."[18]

I worry that this conclusion ignores an additional factor related to archetypical stereotypes and East Asian Americans. Based on my work with them and my own research around leadership in nonprofit spaces, it appears that when East Asians display assertiveness and "traditional" leadership qualities, they may face pushback in a way that South Asians do not.[19] Now, why might that be? First, the research on the bamboo ceiling asserts that East Asians face less prejudice than South Asians. But I believe if we contextualize the impact of the model-minority myth and white adjacency, it might reveal that the prejudice is there; it just shows up differently.

Disaggregation

The complex histories of East Asian and South Asian communities in the United States have significantly shaped their experiences within the country. These experiences are distinct yet undeniably influenced by the pervasiveness of white supremacy and systemic racism. East Asian communities, particularly those with Chinese and Japanese roots, have a long history in the United States, marked by both significant contributions and brutal discrimination. Chinese immigrants, among the first Asians to arrive on the continent, faced intense racism culminating in the Chinese Exclusion Act of 1882, the first federal law restricting immigration based on nationality. Japanese Americans, meanwhile, experienced a complex shift during World War II. Their perceived "white adjacency" dissolved into open discrimination, property restrictions, and mass internment. The use of atomic bombs in Japan further solidified the violation of their human and civil rights based solely on ancestry. Korean Americans grapple with the legacy of post-imperialism, as poignantly described by Cathy Park Hong: "I am here because you vivisected my ancestral country in two."[20]

These historical encounters with occupation, racism, exclusion, and internment have profoundly impacted how both white Americans perceive East Asians and how these communities view themselves. A peculiar result of these historical traumas has been that white supremacy has demanded and expects deference and gratitude from East and Southeast Asians, those from countries touched by wars such as Vietnam, Cambodia, and Laos. Hong also sums up the peculiarity of this dichotomy, saying: "In our efforts to belong in America, we act grateful as if we've been given a second chance at life. But our shared root is not the opportunity this nation has given us but how the capitalist accumulation of white supremacy has enriched itself off the blood of our countries. We cannot forget this."[21]

On the other hand, South Asian immigration to the United States, particularly from countries like India, Pakistan, Bangladesh, and Sri Lanka, follows a different historical narrative. South Asian immigration increased significantly after the passage of civil rights legislation in 1965, the Immigration and Nationality Act, that overturned immigration laws favoring western and northern Europeans. This wave of immigrants often came as professionals or students. The more recent history of South Asian immigration means these communities have had different initial encounters with American society, including opportunities in higher education and professional sectors. However, South Asians have faced racial discrimination and violence, particularly in the aftermath of 9/11, when anti-Muslim sentiment surged, affecting many South Asian Muslims and those perceived as Muslim. Both East and South Asian Americans experience the perpetual foreigner stereotype, regardless of theirs or their ancestors' time in the US. But from what I have seen and read, there is something about the historical backdrop of East Asian communities in the US versus the relatively recent large-scale immigration of South Asians that impacts how white people see and relate to these groups. White supremacy has systemically marginalized both groups, but most of how it has impacted South Asians occurred in either their countries of origin or in Europe and the United Kingdom. There may be a qualitative difference in how white supremacy expects and will *accept* the performance of Asianness from East Asians versus from South Asians, which is a significant factor in competency checking for those in leadership positions.

However, white supremacy can still competency-check South Asians around leadership. A stark reminder of this was the conversation the conservative commentator Ann Coulter had with former Republican presidential candidate Vivek Ramaswamy on his own podcast, *The Truth*, on May 8, 2024. During a conversation on nationalism and Ramaswamy's run for the presidency, Coulter said, "But I still would not have voted for you . . . because you're an Indian. There is a core identity that is the identity of the WASP [White Anglo-Saxon Protestant] . . . the core around which the nation's values are formed is the WASP."[22] Ramaswamy is extremely "conservative" and has denied the existence of white supremacy.[23] He was born in the United States to two noncitizen Hindu American parents, who came after the 1965 Immigration and Nationality Act. He is a citizen because of the Fourteenth Amendment to the US Constitution, which guaranteed citizenship to the formerly enslaved, aka birthright citizenship. However, when faced directly with blatant systemic racism and identified as a "perpetual foreigner" by Coulter, Ramaswamy chose to keep his white adjacency and simply smiled as she insulted him.

As we address how competency checking impacts Asian Americans, we must lean toward specificity *and* universality. Specifically, Southeast Asian Americans need support to help overcome the education and economic attainment gaps that the model-minority myth would have you believe do not exist. East Asian Americans need an end to being competency-checked on their ability to lead; such competency checking is based either on a misunderstanding of their cultural norms or their lack of desire to "perform Asianness" as demanded by whiteness. South Asian Americans need support along various lines, including religious discrimination, cultural discrimination, and the impact of Islamophobia on those who are either Muslim or perceived as Muslim. More broadly, all Asian Americans need an end to, as was described above, the perpetual-foreigner stereotype, and that will require all of us to interact with the people in front of us and not the stereotypes we've built up in our minds. All Asian Americans need an end to the debasement that is white adjacency and the model-minority myth, which demands gratitude and wipes away individual accomplishments while simultaneously restricting individual expressions that may not align with the expectations of "model minorities."

Cathy Park Hong also calls on Asian Americans to reexamine the role they play, either by default or with the intention of advancing white supremacy, "I have to address whiteness because Asian Americans have yet to truly reckon with where we stand in the capitalist white supremacist hierarchy of this country. We are so far from reckoning with it that some Asians think that race has no bearing on their lives, that it doesn't 'come up,' which is as misguided as white people saying the same thing about themselves . . ."[24]

Hurt People, Hurt People

Competency checking within communities of color may sound paradoxical, but it's not. It is the natural result of breathing the air, eating food from the soil, and being bathed in the waters of white supremacy. In some sense, how could we not competency-check each other? We've been led to believe there are limited resources for which we must compete against each other. We also have our own historical biases, including caste in South Asian communities and colorism in communities impacted by colonialism and slavery.

Fractured Solidarity: Competency Checking Among Asian Americans

The University of California caste discrimination lawsuit filed in 2022 by two Hindu professors who oppose the addition of caste to an antidiscrimination policy exposed historical fault lines within the South Asian community[25] that were not left in their countries of origin. The lawsuit opposing the inclusion of caste seems to fly in the face of the experience of those from "lower" castes who live in the United States. "Dr. Promila Dhanuka said that once word got around more than 15 years ago in Redding, Calif., that she had Dalit roots, some Indian American doctors stopped referring patients to her oncology practice."[26] In India, the concept of caste "is a comprehensive, systematized, and institutionalized form of oppression of members of the lower castes, particularly the Dalits. Formalized during the British colonial period, the caste system brings together two related Indian concepts of *varna* and *jāti* to create four social orders and multiple subunits."[27] South Asians in the US, particularly those of higher castes, may engage in competency checking against those perceived as lower caste, hindering solidarity and progress.

Beyond caste, Asian Americans can also exhibit competency checking toward other Asian ethnicities. Historical tensions between East Asian (Chinese, Japanese, Korean) and South Asian (Indian, Pakistani) communities can lead to assumptions about intelligence or cultural superiority. The legacy of Japanese ethnocentrism and Chinese imperialism could subconsciously influence these dynamics. Additionally, some Asian Americans may view proximity to whiteness as a marker of success, leading them to distance themselves from other groups perceived as further away, such as newer Southeast Asian immigrants.

White supremacy continues to try to use the model-minority myth of Asianness as a cudgel against Black Americans, as seen in the rationale behind the *Harvard v. SFFA* case, which pitted a minuscule Black and Hispanic/Latinx presence on campus under affirmative action as unfair to Asian Americans. In 2016, Edward Blum, who seems to have made it his life's mission to unravel and roll back protections for African Americans and Hispanic/Latinx people in the United States, first tried to undo affirmative action in college admissions with a white woman plaintiff, Abigail Fisher.[28] While the Fisher case was unsuccessful, Blum finally found success in 2023 using Asian Americans to advance his case; Blum said that Harvard was letting in "unqualified Black and Hispanic students, while 'intentionally discriminating' against deserving Asian American applicants."[29] Blum claimed to be representing Asian Americans while failing "to present a single Asian American student at trial."[30] Blum also engaged in erasure when it came to applicants who identify as Cambodian, Hmong, Laotian, or Vietnamese, for whom affirmative action is critical in leveling the playing field in college admissions. According to an article in the *Nation*, "Blum tries to hide [the impact of affirmative action on these groups] by denying the existence of affirmative action's many AAPI [Asian American and Pacific Islander] beneficiaries." In his complaint, he states that "references to Asian applicants will exclude racially-favored Asian applicants," meaning those who benefit from affirmative action."[31] This all signaled that this case was never about Asian Americans as real people but as useful shields to hide behind to advance white supremacy. Janelle Wong, a professor of American studies at the University of Maryland, College Park, said, "This is an old tactic in white supremacy's playbook and should not be allowed to succeed."[32]

Colorism's Shadow: Competency Checking in Hispanic and Black Communities

The concept of colorism, or prejudice based on a person's skin tone, plays a significant role in competency checking within Hispanic/Latinx and Black communities. Because of Latin America's history of being both the colonized and the colonizer, a hierarchy developed in which lighter skin was associated with European ancestry and higher social status. This legacy can manifest in competency checking, where lighter-skinned Hispanic/Latinx people are seen as more competent than their darker-skinned counterparts. This issue burst out into the open when Tenoch Huerta Mejía, who played Namor in Marvel's *Black Panther: Wakanda Forever*, called out racism and colorism in modern Mexican society in the *New York Times*: "The prevalent racism in Mexican society, Huerta said, is the living consequence of the cultural genocide that European colonizers perpetrated against Indigenous peoples in the Americas. Through intercultural mixing, they tried to sever the population's ties to their Indigenous forebears. They taught us to be ashamed of our brown skin, to despise brown-skinned people, to mistreat Indigenous people, to feel ashamed of our ancestors, and I can no longer tolerate that."[33]

Black Americans also grapple with colorism. While the "one-drop rule," meaning one drop of Black blood makes you Black, was meant to harm us, it ultimately led to fostering a sense of shared, if imperfect, identity that allowed Black Americans to work together to scale historic change on the national level. But it did not erase colorism in the Black community. Lighter-skinned Black people might be perceived as more intelligent or "closer to white" than those who are darker-skinned by both white and Black people because of the value white supremacy places on whiteness. While colorism and classism have led to hierarchies within the Black community, colorism in the United States did not lead to whole-scale acceptance by the white community as it has done in other countries touched by slavery and colonization. To fully access whiteness, light-skinned Black people in the United States needed to "pass" as white and disavow any connection to Blackness. In other countries, however, levels of privilege and access were meted out based on the amount of whiteness present *with* the full knowledge that racial mixing had occurred.

Competency checking based on skin tone persists, with phrases like "light-skinned privilege" within the Black community highlighting the complexities of racial identity in America. Black Americans also question the ability of other Black people and other people of color because a white supremacist society has either explicitly or implicitly communicated to us since childhood that people who look like us are incompetent. It is a hard thing for us to admit that we do this, so I appreciated it when one of the Black folks I interviewed for this book opened up to me about how it happens. "I remember talking to a Black dude who owns a CPA business, and I remember wondering, 'Does he actually know what he's talking about?' I literally found myself asking that question, which is not the question I asked about the white guys who didn't know what they were talking about, who did a terrible job." As we talked more about this, they revealed the impact of realizing that they were, in fact, competency-checking another Black person: "I remember sitting there, exposed to myself, and saying 'this happens to me every day.' So how do you interrupt it when you yourself are a part of the engine of inequality that disproportionately impacts Black people?"

Breaking the Grip of White Supremacy: Moving Beyond Competency Checking

I believe there are some key ways we can break this cycle among ourselves. First, we, as people of color, must face the fact that the practice of competency checking ultimately only benefits white supremacy.

But before we do that, we have to figure out, who "is" we? And what exactly do we mean when we say "us"?

For some, the terms *people of color* (*POC*) and *Black, Indigenous, and people of color* (*BIPOC*) are powerful organizing banners, and for others they represent tools of erasure. In their modern incarnations, these terms grew from the term *women of color* (*WOC*). WOC emerged in the 1970s from the activism and organizing efforts of Black, Native, Asian, and Latinx/Hispanic women. Scholars trace the origins of *women of color* to the work of the 1977 Combahee River Collective Statement and a group of activists who convened at the 1977 Women's Conference in Houston.[34] Four years ago, I was lucky enough to interview activist, academic, and intersectional feminist Loretta Ross, who was present at the Houston conference and is widely regarded as one of the activists who helped coin the term. During our conversation, Ross, a Black woman, emphasized several points.

First, Black women have always used collective action and emphasized solidarity with other oppressed groups to achieve group liberation. Second, the term came about because Native, Asian, and Hispanic/Latinx women wanted a way to signal solidarity, remove barriers, acknowledge shared oppression, and foster collective action.[35]

While the modern meaning is relatively new, the term *people of color* is a very old one, likely going back to the earliest days of colonialism to describe mixed-race people.[36] In the American South, Black people were referred to as *colored people*; the NAACP is the National Association for the Advancement of Colored People. My grandparents preferred *colored* as a better descriptor of the many hues that those now identified as Black come in. Of course, *colored* fell out of usage after the struggle for civil rights and became emblematic of segregation with its "whites only" versus "colored only" drinking fountain signs. But *POC* as a term made a comeback in the wake of *WOC* and reached its most recent apex over the last decade and a half, spurred by activists looking to organize and respond to racial violence against Black people as well as a desire to move away from terms such as *minority* or *marginalized*.[37] And just like other Black-led movements, the use of *POC* has spread around the world.[38]

BIPOC, on the other hand, is the newest entry into the racial identifier pool. The earliest usage of *BIPOC*, standing for "Black, Indigenous, and people of color," can be traced to a 2013 tweet from an account based in Canada.[39] The article, "Where Did BIPOC Come From," further discusses including Black and Indigenous within the BIPOC acronym to ensure representation and acknowledgment of these communities' unique histories and experiences. In the article, a Missouri School of Journalism professor, Cynthia Frisby, says the BIPOC designation allows for "voices that hadn't originally been heard."[40] But Sylvia Obell, podcaster and social activist, voiced concerns that *BIPOC* and

POC could cause more problems, rather than remove them: "When you blend us all together like this, it's erasure. It allows people to get away with not knowing people of color and the separate set of issues that we all face."[41]

As one of the people who helped coin the term *WOC*, Loretta Ross is sympathetic to the concerns about erasure. She says, "When we're calling specific attention to the negative impacts of white supremacy on Black folks, we need to say 'Black.'" And that is the issue here for many Black people who dislike these terms. First, there is the fear that these terms might be used to "brown-wash" anti-Blackness, allowing those who engage in it an "out" where they do not even have to say the word *Black*. Then there is the concern expressed by the author Damon Young, who explains, "Doing this has a way of flattening unique cultures and the unique battles each racial group faces in America."[42]

Personally, I don't think the usage of terms like *WOC/POC/BIPOC* is a black-or-white issue. There's a compelling argument to be made that the very concept of "whiteness" is itself a form of erasure, blending diverse ethnic backgrounds into a singular power dynamic. James Baldwin insightfully remarked on the transformation individuals undergo in embracing whiteness, describing it as a "terrifying witness to what happened to everyone who got here and paid the price of the ticket."[43] According to Baldwin, this process involved not just assimilation but a profound loss of identity, as "no one was white before he/she came to America."[44]

Baldwin further critiques the construct of whiteness as simply a mechanism to control and diminish other racial identities. "It is a vision as remarkable for what it pretends to include as for what it remorselessly diminishes or leaves totally out."[45] This leads to concerns that using terms like *POC/BIPOC/WOC* may inadvertently replicate the erasure that is whiteness, echoing Audrey Lorde's warning against using "the master's tools" to dismantle the master's house.[46] Lorde was skeptical that adopting the oppressor's strategies could lead to true change, fearing it might only yield temporary victories.

However, I see the adoption of the terms *POC* and *BIPOC* as marking a significant moment in US history, as it represents a shift away from assimilation into whiteness and toward a more intentional connection to Blackness. This shift carries the potential for deeper understanding and solidarity among minoritized groups. This allows us to speak directly to each other, and both remove whiteness, like Iago, from our conversations and expose its role as an unreliable narrator of what we know about each other.

But I do understand that the concerns over Black erasure are valid. Historical instances of alliances, such as those between Black people and immigrant groups like the Irish and Italians, underscore the complexities of these relationships.[47] These groups, once aligned to varying degrees with Black Americans, ultimately chose to pursue whiteness, often at the cost of their own self-interests. Baldwin again helps us understand this choice as one motivated by the violent realities of white supremacy, which saw some Irish and Italian people hanged for their association with Black people.[48] In choosing, they not only shut the door between us, but became some of the fiercest guards of white supremacy in the process. Art McDonald writes in "How the Irish Became White": "And so, we have the tragic story of how one oppressed 'race,' Irish Catholics, learned how to collaborate in the oppression of another 'race,' Africans in America, in order to secure their place in the white republic. Becoming white meant losing their greenness, i.e., their Irish cultural heritage and the legacy of oppression and discrimination back home. Imagine if the Irish had remained green after their arrival and formed an alliance with their fellow oppressed co-workers, the free Blacks of the North."[49]

Yes, imagining how different our world could be if the Irish had chosen collaboration and collective liberation with Black Americans might seem like a dream to some, but what we do know is that it would have been a nightmare for white supremacy. This is why I don't want to abandon terms like *POC/WOC/ BIPOC*. Instead, I want to find a balance between universality and specificity. These terms can have a crucial role to play when communicating with each other in collaborative efforts and organizing for change. However, it is important that we assert our individual identities and address our specific issues too. We cannot allow whiteness to hide behind *POC/BIPOC* when addressing issues like white supremacy and anti-Blackness. In our language, we must be clear and direct to confront these issues head-on.

In order to build true solidarity we must understand that white supremacy seeks to undermine collective efforts for social justice by pitting us against each other. So, to dismantle this system, we need to:

- **PROMOTE EDUCATION:** Open dialogues about the history of racism, colorism, and caste within our communities are crucial. Understanding the roots of these biases empowers us to challenge them.
- **CELEBRATE OUR DIVERSITY:** Highlight the rich tapestry of experiences and backgrounds within racial and ethnic groups. This dismantles the notion of a monolithic "Black," "Asian," or "Hispanic/ Latinx" identity and fosters appreciation for internal differences.
- **BUILD COALITIONS AND BRIDGES:** By recognizing our shared struggles against white supremacy,

communities of color can build strong alliances. Collective action is far more effective than fragmented efforts.

- **MOVE BEYOND:** To overcome intragroup and intergroup competency checking, we must actively weaken the grip of white supremacy, even—and perhaps especially—when it manifests in us.

Reclamation

While the terms *BIPOC* and *POC* represent opportunity and controversy among the communities they seek to connect, they also, along with other linguistic changes, are upsetting to those who have launched the so-called "war against *woke.*" As I understand it, a cardinal sin of "wokeness" is that those who until very recently have been excluded from participating in the evolution of how language refers to them now assert their right to name themselves and demand a reexamination of the language imposed upon them. George Packer made a big splash in 2023 with his *Atlantic* article, "The Moral Case Against Equity Language." In it, Packer—in a very "old man yells at cloud" fashion—confidently states that "although the [equity] guides refer to language 'evolving,' these changes are a revolution from above. They haven't emerged organically from the shifting linguistic habits of large numbers of people. They are handed down in communiqués written by obscure 'experts' who purport to speak for vaguely defined 'communities,' remaining unanswerable to a public that's being morally coerced."[50]

This is deeply flawed reasoning, and it ignores several salient facts. First, there was no "organic" development of language, as Packer calls it, when it came to those who saw themselves as empowered to rename others, places, and things. The apex of this was the creation, naming, and designation of "Black" and "white" out of whole cloth to further a political agenda—the consolidation of white supremacy—without input from those most grievously impacted by it. Colonizers renamed Indigenous territories, landscapes, and people, defining social categories to entrench white supremacy. All this "woke" language really is, is an assertion of identity and the right to self-name; it's not merely a matter of semantics but a profound act of self-definition and resistance.

I think this struggle for self-naming and the reclamation of identity is akin to the characters in Luigi Pirandello's play *Six Characters in Search of an Author*, who seek to break free from the confines of their scripted roles to tell their own stories. It underscores a broader narrative of resistance against imposed identities and the fight for self-definition. Black Americans have transitioned through various identifiers—Colored, Black, Afro-American, African American—reflecting the long journey taken by those attempting to reclaim stolen identities and resist monolithic labels that fail to capture the breadth of their experiences and aspirations. Similarly, the term *Asian American* was coined not just as a demographic marker but as a political identity, aiming to unify diverse Asian communities under a collective struggle against racism and for civil rights in the United States. The *Latino/a/x*, *Hispanic*, and *Chicano* identifiers encompass various cultural, national, and racial identities within the Latin American diaspora—each with distinct historical and political connotations. The LGBTQIA+ community's adoption and promotion of inclusive pronouns like *they/them* and the broader queer nomenclature are pivotal in challenging binary notions of gender and sexuality.

These efforts emphasize the right to self-identify and demand recognition and respect. The evolution and debate around these terms signify a desire to articulate identities that resonate more closely with a given community's self-perception, history, and aspirations than what white supremacy imposed upon us.

International Coda

When I started posting about competency checking on social media, I received many responses, but one of the most interesting was from a woman of color in France, who wrote:

> Dear Shari, thank you for highlighting what we are also seeing as a growing phenomenon on this end in Europe. They are targeting the narrative within private networks—first building up the profiles of people of colour, then colluding to block our progress with carefully crafted narratives, which are then used to justify their actions within these groups.

I was not surprised by this message, because my experience as a consultant with international companies revealed a common denial of racial issues in countries like the UK, France, and Canada. These countries often depict race as a minor issue and instead highlight class-based problems. However, conversations with local people of color and further reading confirmed the presence of significant racial challenges in these nations, contradicting the common narrative that racism and the resulting competency checking isn't as much of an issue abroad as it is here at home.

The Long Shadow: Competency Checking and Race in Former Colonial Powers

The insidious practice of competency-checking the abilities, skills, knowledge, and competency of people of color plagues former colonial powers like France, the UK, and the settler-colonial nation of Canada.[51] And this legacy of colonialism shapes contemporary attitudes, where these nations view themselves as superior and their former colonies' populations as inferior. In the 1950s, Martinican philosopher Aimé Césaire captured this dynamic in *Discourse on Colonialism*: "I am talking of millions of men who have been skillfully injected with fear, inferiority complexes, trepidation, servility, despair, abasement."[52]

In Canada, while it was not itself a colonial power, it is a nation where settlers were encouraged to take land from Indigenous people on behalf of colonial powers. This fact means there is a history of marginalizing Indigenous populations that continues to impact race relations today. Indigenous families were not seen as "competent" to raise their own children, thus setting in motion a horrific system of abuse and attempted cultural genocide that manifested as "residential schools."[53] At these "schools," Indigenous children were forced to disavow their own culture and learn Euro-Canada culture. In Canada, the Truth and Reconciliation Commission documented current systemic racism within institutions like education and health care, a direct result of colonial policies.

Competency checking in Canada extends far beyond historical policies, with Canadians of color often facing skepticism about their qualifications despite demonstrable skills and experience.[54] Black and Indigenous Canadians often face microaggressions, subtle yet demeaning comments, or actions that communicate their supposed inadequacy. In fact, according to a research project by York University's Institute for Social Research, Black Canadians see workplaces as the epicenter of racial discrimination and unfairness.[55] That our brothers and sisters in Canada face similar levels of anti-Black bias is driven home by these statistics: "The [research] found seventy-five percent of Black Canadians experience racism in the workplace and think it's a problem. Seventy percent of other non-white people also see workplace racism as a serious or very serious problem. . . . In addition, forty-seven percent of Black people surveyed believe they have been treated unfairly by an employer in hiring, pay, or promotion in the last year."[56]

France's colonial past casts a long shadow on its present-day relationship with people of color. Competency-checking people of color is a deeply ingrained practice that disproportionately affects Black and African immigrant communities. As seen in the quote above from the Martinican philosopher Aimé Césaire, France portrayed itself as a civilizing force during colonization, implicitly positioning its former colonies' populations as inferior. French sociologist Pierre Bourdieu captures this dynamic in his concept of "habitus," unconscious dispositions shaped by social structures. Here the colonial habitus can lead to unconscious biases against Black and African people, hindering their perceived competence.[57]

This is likely why the global Black Lives Matter movement resonated so deeply in France, with protests raising the awareness of police brutality against Black people and systemic issues like underrepresentation in leadership positions. Even before the protest, in 2019, a report by the French National Consultative Commission on Human Rights (CNCDH) found Black and African-descent individuals were significantly underrepresented in leadership roles across various sectors.[58] This persistent underclass status highlights the entrenched nature of competency checking, creating a cycle where Black and African immigrants struggle to find advancement due to constant questioning of their abilities and their "Frenchness." In fact, according to a shocking report in the French newspaper *Le Monde*, 9 out of 10 Black people in France report being victims of racial discrimination. "The discrimination occurs largely in the public space and at work, according to the report. More than half of the people surveyed have experienced difficulty in getting a job interview because of the color of their skin."[59]

The United Kingdom (UK) is a former colonial power and the place that outlawed slavery before the United States. As a result, there has always been tension in the UK between discrimination as race-based versus class-based. To be sure, the UK has a complex system of class that finds expression in discrimination, such as "accentism," where Britons with "lower-class" accents can find it hard to advance in their careers.[60] And even though the UK saw its first prime minister of color, Rishi Sunak voted in in 2022, his presence did not fundamentally change the conditions of many Black and Brown Britons, tracking a similar reality in the United States after electing our first Black president. But what the Black Lives Matter movement confirmed is that racial prejudice is also a significant factor in British life. Thousands turned out to protest police interaction, statutes, workplace discrimination, and the basic quality of life affecting Black Britons. In an article for CNN titled "The Greatest Trick Racism Ever Pulled Was Convincing England It Doesn't Exist," the authors say that "nearly two in three Black people say the UK has not done enough to address historical racial injustice, twice the proportion of White people who say that."[61] Most troubling and telling is that when it comes to the workplace, Black and Brown women in Britain and Black women in the United States have almost the exact same complaints and statistics. A report called "Broken Ladders" paints a stark picture of racism faced by women of color in British workplaces. A staggering 75 percent of these women reported experiencing racism at work. Half of Pakistani and Bangladeshi women and nearly half of Black African women reported that they faced criticism for behaviors tolerated by colleagues, suggesting a clear bias in how women of color are perceived and treated in the workplace.[62] Another report by Coqual Research found that 52 percent of Black-heritage women in the UK are considering leaving their current jobs due to racial issues in the workplace.[63] This trend mirrors the survey by Working Mother Media in the United States that found "50 percent of multicultural women are considering leaving their companies within the next two years."[64] In the UK, Black, East Asian, and Muslim women report that workplace culture presents a daily battleground blocking their ability to thrive.

Moving Beyond the Past: Dismantling Competency Checking Around the World

Breaking free from the shackles of competency checking worldwide will require a multipronged approach and will inevitably look different in different countries. However, those most impacted should share data, statistics, and universal demands for the ability not just to survive but thrive in the workplace. The fact of the matter is that Black and Brown women in the UK and the US are signaling a catastrophic problem in the workplace. We must find ways to connect and, from a universal human rights perspective, work together to set a global agenda that unmasks those who seek to divert our economic inclusion and advancement and develop shared tactics when possible. This looks like:

- **COLLECTIVE ACTION:** As the global majority, "a collective term for people of Indigenous, African, Asian, Latin American descent who constitute approximately 85 percent of the global population,"[65] people of color must use their combined economic power to signal that they will not continue to be excluded or marginalized in the workplace.

- **BUILDING BRIDGES:** I believe there needs to be an annual conference on the state of Black, Asians both East, South and South East, Hispanic/ Latinx, and other people of color in the workplace worldwide. A time when we discuss the differences and similarities and set an agenda for change.

As for the former colonial powers, they can't just turn around and be the heroes of the story, but they definitely have a crucial part to play. It's time for these countries to face their postcolonial wrongdoings head-on and start tearing down the outdated systems that are still holding us back. We must pave the way for a future where everyone has a fair shot, where diverse and dynamic teams drive progress, open new opportunities, and boost economies and stability worldwide. It's time for all of us to step up and make a real difference, wherever—and whoever—we are.

CHAPTER 8

Leading in Living Color

The function of racism . . . is distraction. It keeps you
from doing your work. It keeps you explaining, over and
over and over again, your reason for being.[1]

—Toni Morrison

Through the Looking-Glass

To be a leader of color in the United States is to embark on
a journey that can, at times, be so perplexing, confusing, and
nonsensical that it can only be compared to a combination of
Lewis Carroll's *Alice's Adventures in Wonderland* and *Through
the Looking-Glass*. "'I can't explain myself, I'm afraid, sir,' said
Alice, 'because I'm not myself, you see.'"[2] There is the Black
woman attorney who had her young, white, female paralegal
yell *at her* and say, "I've had male bosses yell and scream at
me, and they weren't as intimidating as you are!" The attorney
was not yelling or screaming; her mere presence was considered
more intimidating than being yelled at or screamed at. There's
the curious case of a Black business leader, Kyra, being quizzed
on her name: "I'm often told how to spell my own name, which
has been both amusing and frustrating."[3] Frustrating because
the pushback, questions, and situations that Black people and
other people of color in leadership find themselves in can be so
nonsensical as to be unbelievable, like being told that you are
running a business too much like a business, which happened

to me. Or being turned down for a promotion not because you're not qualified, but because of other people's perceptions of you.

That's the looking-glass situation Chantel Adams, a senior marketing executive in Durham, North Carolina, found herself in as she watched white coworkers with less education or experience be promoted above her. Adams, in an article for the *Grio*, reported that she took on extra work and responsibilities and was given high marks for her performance. But when she asked her supervisor why she was turned down for a promotion, she was told that "[she] was so articulate and sharp that it was intimidating to some people."[4] Even if Adams had been promoted, she would have still been in a place where up is down and down is up.

In some of the most extensive research on the intersection of race and leadership, the Building Movement Project, a nonprofit research and consulting firm that supports the nonprofit sector, has surveyed and interviewed more than twelve thousand nonprofit leaders of all races over the last eight years. One of their key findings is that "people of color do not reap the advantages of leadership to the same extent as their white peers."[5] Those "advantages" that white leaders receive include being respected and believed, being accepted as the leader, and not having their authority openly and constantly challenged or being constantly competency-checked. While the Building Movement Project's research focuses on nonprofit leadership, it directly applies to leaders of color across sectors.

The cross-sector nature of this is confirmed by research from Coqual, formerly the Center for Talent and Innovation, which indicates that Black people face more challenges and frustrations in corporate America compared to their white colleagues.[6] Personal experiences aside, I can confirm this based on what Black and other leaders of color have told me across industries—that obtaining a leadership position doesn't change things much. While leadership is difficult and complex for any-one, there are some advantages to it: The Building Movement Project found that white executives report once they leave staff positions, they are less likely to experience common workplace frustrations and challenges. Meanwhile, people of color in ex-ecutive roles report facing the same or higher levels of chal-lenges and frustrations as the people of color who are in staff positions.[7] So, executives of color find themselves dealing with all the issues they had before they assumed leadership *and* the heightened scrutiny and expectations that come with lead-ership for anyone. In the nonprofit space, CEOs of color deal with the complex racial and power dynamics of boards that seem to require more from leaders of color than they did from the white leaders who had the jobs before them.[8] They also must assuage the fears of funders who routinely underfund Black-led or -run nonprofits[9] and manage staff who, though comfortable working with communities of color in need, may bristle at the idea of being led or managed by a person of color. This lack of comfortability with leadership of color can turn into open disrespect, which I have dealt with personally, from having keys thrown at me to being openly undermined. As an Asian American CEO interviewed by the Building Movement Project explains, "Some have characterized what I've faced as insubordination at times, and have made comments that cer-tain attitudes, behaviors, words would not have been conveyed to a director who was a white man or woman."[10]

In addition to all of that, leaders of color face a combina-tion of overwhelming expectations from and occasionally com-petency checking by other people of color in the workplace. As we discussed in the previous chapter, competency checking by people of color against people of color is rooted in the white su-premacist notion of the "scarcity mindset," that instead of there being room at the top for everyone, there is only room enough for a few people of color, at best. This means white supremacy acts as a gatekeeper, limiting the number of people of color in a particular space; this is artificial, and as a result, some people of color become fearful and invested in maintaining what has been called the "only" position. There is also the "crabs in a barrel" phenomenon that Black folks discuss when it comes to the ways we can undermine each other, again under the tutelage of white supremacy that tells us we must fight it out to emerge as the "chosen" or "only" one.

Vu Le, a Vietnamese American nonprofit director, speaker, and writer of the blog *Nonprofit AF*, tackled this issue in a post titled "'There Can Only Be One' Syndrome." In it, he highlights the contradiction of people of color upholding white supremacy, either by distancing themselves—like the Italians and the Irish before them—from their racial or ethnic identity to gain proximity to whiteness and its associated privileges, or by acting as gatekeepers to prevent others within their community from getting access in spaces where there are few to no other people of color. This behavior is not only a survival mechanism but also a reflection of the divisive tactics employed by systemic racism to maintain itself.[11]

Ultimately, it promotes a mindset that fosters competition over collaboration among minoritized groups who fear that there is only room for a limited number of them in positions of power, success, or recognition. It reminds me of the "racial screen of contempt" that historian Edmund Morgan identified as created by white supremacy to break what had been a natural alliance between poor whites and enslaved and free Blacks. But it's not just about competition; it's also about expectations. Leaders of color who come into positions that are often cracked "glass cliffs" with little to no support or real authority are held to higher standards by other people of color. This means there is very little room to make mistakes or to put a "bad foot forward." Ironically,

I have seen this situation in real life, where the staff or employees of color place unrealistic expectations on leaders of color that they did not and would not place on white leaders. They also expect leaders of color to align with their vision of what it means to be that ethnicity, and if that isn't met, the consequences can be severe. I have seen Black employees turn on Black leaders in truly vicious ways, which I can only believe are rooted in hurt. I think of how, sometimes, children can treat their mothers more cruelly than their fathers; perhaps because we have higher expectations of our mothers, and we believe they will accept our cruel behavior.

So it seems to be for leaders of color in the workplace. They find themselves caught between some employees of color who have high and often unrealistic expectations of them and others who because of a "scarcity" mindset withhold resources, and mentorship while allying with problematic colleagues seeking to sabotage the leader of color. What employees of color who engage in this don't realize is that these actions not only hinder collective advancement, but also reinforce the artificial barriers erected by systemic racism.

So, the situation that Black and other leaders of color find themselves in is dizzying in complexity. "The Red Queen shook her head. 'You may call it "nonsense" if you like,' she said, 'but I've heard nonsense, compared with which that would be as sensible as a dictionary!'"[12] These *Through the Looking-Glass* scenarios include being asked if you *really* know what your job title is. Kyra Kyles, who had the spelling of her name questioned, is the CEO of a large nonprofit. When talking with Kyles, she shared with me the story of how she was challenged about her title during a meeting. "I had a white woman put her hand up and say, 'I have a girlfriend who runs a nonprofit and is an executive director. Are you an executive director?'"[13] Kyles said she was taken aback, restated her title, and went on to the next introduction. Later, Kyles saw that the woman still wasn't satisfied. "Next thing I know, I see that this person went on LinkedIn to double-check my title."[14]

Black and other leaders of color in the nonprofit sector find themselves regularly needing to prove themselves or being held to higher levels of skill and competency than their white predecessors for leadership positions. In their report on "Trading the Glass Ceiling for the Glass Cliff," the Building Movement Project found something I have seen across industries: that leaders of color who replace outgoing white leaders in organizations tend to have higher education than their peers. Specifically, the study found that "70% of these leaders of color have a master's or terminal degree. . . . In contrast, white executive directors and CEOs show minimal variance in educational levels regardless of their predecessor's race."[15] What this data confirms for me is that there is an overemphasis on formal educational credentials in these transitions when the applicant is a leader of color succeeding a white person. This is textbook competency checking.

The passage of time hasn't really improved things. From 2016 to 2022, there has been a drop in the number of people of color currently in nonprofits who want leadership positions.[16] However, it has also been found that those who still want to lead want to do so for reasons you might not expect.[17] The nonprofit professionals of color who still want to lead tend to be those who have had adverse experiences in the sector; what motivates them is a desire to make things better, "a necessary step to initiate change and address the inequalities and challenges they've faced."[18] While this desire is strong and noble, it can wilt under the relentless pressure of race-based competency checking, which creates an impact gap for leaders of color that has only gotten more pronounced over the last eight years, as "BIPOC respondents reporting *negative* impacts [on their careers because of their race] increased by 14 percentage points."[19]

This same type of "impact gap" related to leadership and race is seen in academia, which is so full of arcana, intrigue, mystery, and office politics that it's no wonder Lewis Carroll was a professor. In her work examining the career trajectories of senior-level Black women in higher education, Dr. Candice Staples found that "as Black women transition from faculty to administrators, their experiences do not improve."[20] These experiences, according to Dr. Staples, include isolation, scant mentorship, and a "cold climate," in addition to issues women of all races cite, such as salary inequities, the fight for academic legitimacy, and family responsibilities. The impact of competency checking was seen in the drive to achieve the highest credentials possible to prove legitimacy and mitigate the inevitable questioning of their competence. "As Black women, they would have faculty and administrators assuming they did not deserve or earn their role and . . . would be questioned more than their white or male counterparts."[21]

Dr. Staples's focus on Black women in academia is supported by data that finds, as of fall 2019, only 2 percent of tenured associate and full professors are Black women.[22] For those few who do make it through, they describe a road as strange as any imagined by Lewis Carroll. According to Dr. Karsonya Whitehead, a professor of communication at Loyola University Maryland, "The path from associate to full is, in some cases, almost insurmountable. I was watching my white male colleagues and white female colleagues around the country receive the support they needed. . . . I wasn't receiving the same type of support."[23]

In the same article, Dr. Psyche Williams-Forson mentions the waiting game Black people must endure before they are even able to advance, an unwinnable game that, once again, lands Black women squarely at the intersection of racism, ageism, and sexism. "I finished my doctorate in 2002, and I was hired in 2005. I have written two award-winning books, and in 2022, was awarded a full professorship."[24] In the article, Dr. Williams-Forson, reflecting on Nikole Hannah-Jones being denied tenure by the University of North Carolina, expressed her frustration with the looking-glass nature of all this: "No matter that it has earned you a MacArthur 'genius grant,' or no matter that it has earned you a Pulitzer, it's still not good enough. That is galling, to say the least. And it's enough to drive some people into a state, into a fit, of sheer exasperation."

It's that exasperation, not the pipeline, that is the problem in academia, medicine, law, and any other area in which Black people and other people of color seek to lead or even work. Yet there is an almost comical focus on the "pipeline" to ignore the very real and pressing issues impacting Black people and other people of color right now, today, in the workforce. But if it's not just the pipeline, then what is it? Researchers dismantle the idea that a lack of what they describe as qualified, underrepresented minority (URM) candidates is the main reason for the low number of URM faculty in science departments at medical schools. Some key findings include that despite the increasing number of URM PhD graduates in science fields, hiring practices do not reflect this growth. The researchers posit that the real problem is what I see as an example, once again, of the intersection of the myth of qualifications and competency checking, an overemphasis on hiring PhD candidates in general and URM candidates specifically from "prestigious" doctoral programs.[25] So, the data indicates that the primary obstacle to URM faculty representation is not a lack of qualified candidates but rather systemic issues in hiring practices. It was even found that if there were focused efforts to remove those barriers and hire just one URM PhD a year, "URM faculty members . . .

at most medical schools for the next six years could achieve parity with the URM Ph.D. pool."[26]

These same systemic issues are present in the technology field. While no one would argue that the pipeline of Black and Hispanic/Latinx people in the technology sector is overflowing, data tells us that there are more people in that pipeline than end up employed in the field. Over a decade ago an analysis by *USA Today* found that "top universities turn out Black and Hispanic computer science and computer engineering graduates at twice the rate that leading technology companies hire them."[27] And in a striking parallel to the findings on whether it is the pipeline or the blockages holding URM PhD candidates back in medicine, these findings show that technology companies blaming an empty pipeline for the severe shortage of Black and Hispanic people in Silicon Valley "doesn't hold water" according to Darrick Hamilton, professor of economics and urban policy at the New School in New York. Hamilton goes on to explain, "What do dominant groups say? 'We tried, we searched, but there was nobody qualified.' If you look at the empirical evidence, that is not the case."[28] According to the data from The National Center for Education Statistics (NCES) in 2014, "4.5% of all new recipients of bachelor's degrees in computer science or computer engineering were African American, and 6.5% were Hispanic."[29] In 2022, NCES reported that the percentages had doubled, with 9 percent Black and 12 percent Hispanic/Latinx people securing a bachelor's degree in computer science.[30] Yet, for all the increase in numbers, people are not making it out of the pipeline.

Think of competency checking and race-based biases as fine-grade wire mesh within the pipeline. Black, Hispanic/Latinx, and other people of color, even those more represented, encounter these blockages in the pipeline. These competency-checking-based blockages create a type of extruding force. So, by the time you reach the end of the pipeline it might seem like there were very few people in there at the start, but the reality is that there are people stuck in there, blocked from passing through. In the *USA Today* article, computer and information science professor Juan Gilbert at the University of Florida said, "The premise that if you want diversity, you have to sacrifice quality is false." The article says that at that time in 2014, his department had twenty-five African American PhD candidates and that Rice University in Houston has a large number of Hispanic/Latinx students in computer science. But just as in the URM PhD candidate scenario above, we see again a wire mesh of prestige blocking Black and Hispanic/Latinx people from jobs.

Justin Edmund, a Black man in STEM who went to a prestigious university, told the researchers/journalists, "If you go to the same prestigious universities every single time and every single year to recruit people . . . then you are going to get the same people over and over again."[31] But that is not what most people believe is going on; they believe it is simply that there are no qualified Black or Hispanic/Latinx people specifically in STEM. When it comes to Black and other people of color in the workplace, it's that gap between what is real and what is imagined that has us repeating an unfounded story about an empty pipeline while not acknowledging that the pipeline is full of wire mesh filters—called competency checking, cultural assumptions, and "prestige bias," which are designed to block what could and should be a natural flow of diversity.

Things aren't making much more sense over in corporate America. In 2019, the global consulting firm Korn Ferry and the Executive Leadership Council (ELC), a national organization of over eight hundred current and former Black CEOs, senior executives, and entrepreneurs, released a report on the state of Black leadership in corporate America. It's "an alarming reality"[32]: Black CEOs make up less than 1 percent of Fortune 500 leaders, with a projection for zero percent in the next few years. The report, like those previous, found that the under-representation of Black CEOs in Fortune 500 companies is not due to a lack of competence or availability, but because of competency checking.[33] It revealed that Black executives are among the most driven in corporate America, actively taking strategic approaches to their professional development, seeking out challenging projects, working twice as hard as their peers, and relying on sponsors for career progression. Of those surveyed, 35 percent reported being given difficult projects with a high risk of failure that no one else wanted, which, when it happens enough times, can be taken as an attempt to force someone to prove their competency.

"What we've found," the Korn Ferry study states, "is that all roads lead to bias against Black leaders' readiness. Unlike their counterparts, Black executives are often perceived by the majority as not having the intellectual rigor or leadership ability to manage large, highly complex P&L positions. But, as the research in this report shows, Black leaders are as capable and as prepared—if not more so—to meet the demands of those roles."[34] So, it's not an issue of ability or the pipeline: "Despite the wealth of talent featured in the study, Black executives are underrepresented in the C-suite."[35] And no amount of mentoring or sponsoring (which can quickly devolve into a "pet-to-threat" scenario) can address this. So how do we get Black and other leaders of color out of this wonderland?

Curiouser and Curiouser

If where you want to go is around in circles that maintain systemic inequity, then you will keep placing the blame on the pipeline and the responsibility for fixing it on those stuck inside. But if where you want to go is a place where there is a free flow of diversity that includes leaders with amazing talent, normal talent, and some not-so-great talent (otherwise known as the average American office), then you will aggressively work to remove all that wire mesh.

Those who oppose even discussing these issues, however, take a different stance. "Well, if you're qualified, you'll get the job." Or "I only look at merit and qualifications!" However, experience and data tell us that that is not what happens. In fact, those situations seem to be the exception, not the rule. To illustrate this point, in 2022, Brian Flores, the former head coach of the Miami Dolphins, accused the National Football League and its thirty-two teams of discriminating against African Americans in their hiring practices; later that year, two other Black coaches, Steve Wilks and Ray Horton, joined Flores's lawsuit. All three have extensive coaching backgrounds at various levels of the sport, including the NFL. The coaches allege that bogus interviews are a regular part of discriminatory hiring practices and limited advancement opportunities.[36] Specifically, they point to what they call a "sham" application of the Rooney Rule, which mandates that NFL teams consider minority candidates for head-coaching vacancies. The Rooney Rule is not designed to provide opportunities for "unqualified" Black candidates. Rather, it exists to force white team owners to consider extremely qualified Black candidates. Regardless, many believe Black coaches are either unqualified or lack the leadership skills necessary to coach a team.[37] "[R]ace remains a fundamental determinant in the opportunities of prospective head coaches," according to research from the *Journal of Sports and Social Issues*, based on "a careful examination of the experiences of every NFL head coach hired in the last nine years—prior credentials, win-loss records, job prospects if they are fired, among other factors."[38]

That line, "race remains a fundamental determinant," is almost a mantra at this point, repeated and repeated across industries and experiences, and yet we ignore it. Instead we blame the pipeline for being faulty and accuse those stuck in it of not existing. A few months after Brian Flores filed a suit alleging race-based discrimination, the Indianapolis Colts hired a white former player with no prior NFL coaching experience; he had coached high school football, as their interim head coach. The owner of the Colts gave an interview that seemed to prove that the perception of qualifications, experience, and merit is only relevant for Black leaders in the NFL (and beyond). Jim Irsay defended his choice, implying that experienced coaches are "afraid" and lack the "necessary qualities."[39] And what are those necessary qualities? It would seem across industries that whiteness is at least one of them.[40]

Examining the experience of college football quarterbacks, Andrew M. Carton and Ashleigh Shelby Rosette sought to explain bias against Black leaders. Together, they identified the concept of "goal-based stereotyping," finding that Black leaders score lower in evaluations even when they excel, a fact we have already heard confirmed from attorney Adam Levitt whose firm litigates these types of cases.[41] Evaluators, Carton and Rosette found, tend to adjust their application of stereotypes based on the performance outcomes of leaders. Specifically, Black leaders, unlike white leaders, are subjected to a dual mode of stereotyping: if they fail or make a mistake, they are deemed inherently incompetent; if they succeed, their achievements are attributed to external stereotypes, such as being "naturally athletic," not because of skill or knowledge. This combination of stereotypes ensures that misperceptions about Black leaders persist regardless of their actual performance on the job.

How does this happen? Specifically, it is a combination of inference (how we interpret the facts we see), recognition

(how we interpret what we believe, preexisting mental categories), and goal-based stereotyping (how we reconcile the mis-
match between the two). The study suggests that those doing
the evaluation apply different stereotypes based on the race of
the leader and the context of their performance.[42] In theory,
inference-based processing would mean a Black leader or someone seeking to be a leader would be evaluated positively after
success and seen as competent and capable. That is straightfor-
ward and matches our foundational beliefs around meritocracy,
competency, and hard work—the "bootstraps" mentality. But
in practice, that's not exactly what happens. Instead, research
found that evaluators attributed the successes of Black leaders
to factors other than leadership ability, such as luck.

Once again we are confronted with the critical state of our
country's foundations when it comes to race. Because of stereotyping and bias, there are strong preconceived notions about
Black intelligence and ability, so evaluators seem to shift their
reasoning when confronted with people they can't reconcile
against their conscious or unconscious ideas about Black intellectual inferiority. When it comes to failure, it was found that
evaluators attributed failures of Black leaders to inherent flaws
in their leadership skills, or stereotypes, the most pernicious
of which is that "Black [people] are incompetent."[43] Because
attributes such as intelligence or strong decision-making skills
were not seen as "prototypically" Black, the failure of Black
leaders was seen as related to an *inherent lack* of these skills
or, more broadly, competence. Carton and Rosette point out
that this is a big issue for Black leaders because "competence is
the most important drive of perceptions of leadership."[44] When
it comes to white leaders, they found that evaluators often *assume* that white candidates will be effective leaders because
their perceived stereotypical attributes—Intelligence, Knowledge, and Skill—align with the classic leader prototype.

There are implications here, too, for other leaders of color. For Asian Americans, goal-based stereotyping can impact their prospects for advancement because of the stereotype, primarily focused on East Asians, that they are overly submissive and deferential and therefore not leadership material. These results, according to Carton and Rosette, "shed light on these mechanisms by illuminating both how and why such strong bias has been sustained against black leaders."[45]

While this might all sound theoretical, recall the real-world ways in which it shows up across industries as diverse as nonprofit management, computer science, medicine, and corporate leadership. It even shows up in law practices. Diandra "Fu" Debrosse, the managing partner of the Birmingham, Alabama, office of the plaintiff's litigation law firm DiCello Levitt, told me how she is constantly asked to prove her competency. "Despite my legal qualifications, I've been questioned about my qualifications more times than I can count. . . . I recall a client asking if I was 'sure' about my legal analysis, a question I noticed that was not posed to my white male colleague."[46] And again, as Adam Levitt, the cofounder of DiCello Levitt, shared in the introduction to this book, "The types of discrimination we're seeing are not just about being denied opportunities, but about being subjected to a different standard once in those roles."

My dear, here we must run as fast as we can just to stay in place. And if you wish to go anywhere, you must run twice as fast as that.[47] We cannot continue to leave Black and other leaders of color in this nightmarish Wonderland. They can't run any faster than they already are, especially while navigating so many bizarre, confusing, and distressing reactions to their existence. This constant competency checking is a veritable *Groundhog Day* for Black people and people of color in the workplace. Every day, every week, every month, every year; there is no memory of your competency; you are forced to start over again and again like every time is the first time. But if you fail? That memory never goes away.

Waking Up

In order to leave Wonderland, Alice had to wake up. Like her, we—all of us—have to leave behind these outdated, racist ideas around Black intelligence and competency. The first thing we need to do is acknowledge the blockages in the pipeline, expressed through a series of competency checks, which are responsible for slower career advancement, a lower likelihood of promotion, and ultimately, the current widespread underrepresentation of Black and other leaders of color in the workplace.

Then we must find ways to mitigate competency checking and goal-based stereotyping. "'When I use a word,' Humpty Dumpty said, in rather a scornful tone, 'it means just what I choose it to mean—neither more nor less.' 'The question is,' said Alice, 'whether you can make words mean so many different things.'"[48] In the face of all the evidence to the contrary, we must stop equating Blackness with being unqualified, unintelligent, and incompetent. We must allow for Black success as well as Black mediocrity, the same standards by which white people are judged in the workplace and out in the world as individuals. We do this through auditing our reviews, assessments, and ourselves. Carton and Rosette suggest several steps:

1. **Detection of Goal-Based Stereotyping**
   COMPARE EVALUATIONS OF LEADERS WITH SIMILAR PERFORMANCE: Managers should compare evaluations of leaders from different races who've achieved similar performance outcomes.
   - The authors suggest looking for inconsistencies in how these leaders are described, which

could indicate goal-based stereotyping (e.g., attributing a Black leader's success to luck and
a White leader's success to strong leadership
skills).

LEADERSHIP EVALUATION INSTRUMENTS

• The study recommends revising leadership
evaluation tools to include a wider range of attributes beyond traditional leadership charac-
teristics.

PERFORMANCE METRICS

• Clear performance metrics relevant to the organization and directly attributable to leader
influence should be used for evaluation. Examples include productivity, market share,
commissions, or external ratings of team performance. Tracking these metrics over time for
individual leaders, given the low representation
of Black leaders in many organizations, can
provide insights into potential stereotyping.

2. **Perception-Based Reform:** The study suggests implementing perception-based reforms alongside or
as an alternative to traditional diversity initiatives.

INDIVIDUALIZED INFORMATION: Providing specific information about Black leaders (and I
would add all leaders for transparency's sake),
such as educational background, accomplishments, and personal stories, is recommended.

• This can help by personalizing the leader and
busting stereotypes about the experience and
skill of leaders of color.

ADDRESSING PREVAILING INFORMATION: Efforts should be made to ensure that information circulating within the organization doesn't

reinforce negative stereotypes about Black leaders.

- This could involve showcasing successful Black leaders and their achievements throughout the organization.
- Education could also be included as part of continuous improvement to help disrupt stereotyping.[49]

Those are all good ideas, but they will take effort and work. Those responsible for evaluating and assessing competency for leadership should receive support. We often talk about the role that coaching, mentorship, and additional learning can play for Black leaders and other leaders of color. I suggest that those same tools be extended to those white leaders and leaders of color responsible for hiring, promotion, and general evaluations. People with managerial power should not be left to their own devices without frameworks and guidance. This is not an "equity lens." Instead, it is a framework of continuous learning and improvement designed to help spot and disrupt stereotyping and competency checking. Coaching can help managers move the conversation from "I" am not doing "this or that" to "This is something that happens," and we need to be aware of and disrupt it.

When it comes to how people of color can support leaders of color, it's not about accepting bad or poor behavior under the guise of solidarity, but about checking and managing your own expectations. We must turn away from the "scarcity mindset" that posits there can only be "one," and stop requiring Black and other leaders of color to work twice as hard to be rated half as good as their white peers.

How do we do this? By helping employees across the board realize that Black and other leaders of color are frequently underresourced, lack full authority, and struggle to hold their position while dealing with the same stressors as their employees of color. No one is superhuman or unbreakable. This is unacceptable and must change and it's something I think even people of color miss when they see Black and other leaders of color in positions of authority. I know I did.

When I was younger, I would reach out to Black people in positions of authority—such as reaching out by email to a TV news director or by phone to the hiring manager for a major retailer—and be surprised by their limited and, at times, evasive responses. Some of them may have been maintaining their "only" status, but as I've gotten older and moved through these processes myself, on top of my work as a coach, I have seen firsthand how many people do not have—or perhaps more accurately, have not been given—the authority that should have come with their position because of competency checking and white supremacy. White leaders can hire an all-white team, and no one bats an eye, but if Black or other leaders of color hire even two or three nonwhite people, it becomes a problem.

One of the people Dr. Staples interviewed for her research on Black women in senior administrative positions in higher education made this point. "I hired three associate deans, two of whom were Black. But I know that . . . people would not pay any attention to the fact that the dean's office had a bunch of white men in it if it was a white man [doing the hiring]. I knew that with all the Black people in the dean's office, people would pay attention to it."[50] And pay attention to it they did, with the source of the complaint coming from a surprising place: "Word got back to me that one of my Black women colleagues was saying that I was preferencing Black people."[51] Something no one, regardless of color, says when a slate of hires is all white; this is the way it's always been, but it's not how it's supposed to *be*. As people of color, we must give each other grace, hold each other to realistic standards, and rip down the scarcity mindset screen that distorts our relationships.

This is where employee resource groups (ERGs) can be very helpful in creating solidarity and advancing understanding and education. Mentors of color can also break down that fear-based reaction to seeing other people of color in predominately white spaces. White people can stop making "unicorns" out of Black people and holding up one single Black experience as the standard, positively or negatively. When companies stop promoting the scarcity mindset and the myth of the empty or broken pipeline and treating anyone they do hire as the vaunted exception, and when Black and other people of color reject the idea that only a few of us can exist in the same professional space at the same time, well, just imagine the possibilities.

Embarking on the journey of transformation within our organizations after decades—in some cases, centuries—of standard practice is not just a box to check or a shallow embrace of DEI. It is a deep dedication to fairness and justice that must be reflected in our daily actions and choices. Wonderland can be in our rearview—if we leave behind our outdated preconceptions and biases, we stand to step into a reality where everyone's potential can be recognized, nurtured, and cultivated. The path forward requires continuous effort, commitment, and a collective will to change. We create an environment where everyone can thrive, first by recognizing that we do not live in a color-blind meritocracy, and never have. White supremacy and its many vines are all around and within us. But that doesn't make us bad; it makes us human, and we can thrive together as humans by empowering all leaders with the tools to dismantle stereotypes and biases. This isn't just about supporting Black leaders and leaders of color; it's about strengthening our organizations. And our organizations must engage directly in this fight because despite the legal challenges, pushback, and the work of the hidden hand, there are still some tools left and a few creative ways to help us achieve these goals, but it will be imperative that we all understand when, why, and how to wield them.

CHAPTER 9

The Tools

Power concedes nothing without a demand. It never did, and it never will.

—Frederick Douglass

WHILE THE US Supreme Court threw a wrench into efforts to address racism in higher education, delivering a blow to one of the critical tools for advancement, affirmative action in college admissions, as I write this affirmative action in the workplace **remains** legal. Still, there is much concern and fear that this tool will also be removed from the already limited toolbox available to us, one we use to keep open even the smallest cracks in the doors of opportunity. My intention in this chapter is to provide information that can help readers push back on some of the common myths about affirmative action, the Equal Employment Opportunity Commission (EEOC), and DEI and provide a framework for these remedies arguing for their usefulness and using the tools directly. Whether you're a seasoned HR professional, a C-suite leader, a team manager, a frontline worker, or an employee navigating the impact of competency checking, knowing these tools goes beyond mere usage. You must understand why they exist in the first place. From my perspective, many diversity initiatives, particularly those seeking to increase Black inclusion, falter because:

1. Solution designers often lack a deep understanding of the true problem.
2. A "paint-by-numbers" approach falls short for complex and nuanced issues.

Such responses can be a by-product of people in power refusing to change course and remove exclusivity from their hiring practices and within their ranks or because of a lack of knowledge. Therefore, before diving into the "how-to," we must delve into the "why" and the "what."

Affirmative Action

Attacks on Affirmative Action, EEOC protections, and DEI are driven mainly by mis- and dis-information. Affirmative action was never designed through law or policy to promote or hire "unqualified" Black people; this is a myth.[1] That narrative is simply another iteration of the same rhetoric that has dogged all efforts, from Reconstruction to today, to uncover and account for the hidden hand of systemic inequity and, specifically, anti-Black bias. The issue was and still is that it is often harder for qualified Black people to obtain employment or advancement *because* they are Black.[2] The obverse of this is the myth that all white people are inherently qualified for whatever positions they seek or hold, which is ridiculous; meanwhile, Black people must meet every qualification (and sometimes more) to hold whatever position they seek. That itself is a symptom of anti-Blackness, which expresses itself in the workplace as persistent and consistent competency checking.

During my interview with Deena Pierott, the founder of iUrban Teen, a STEM (science, technology, engineering, mathematics) and arts nonprofit, we talked about how constant competency checking was one of the reasons she left a local government job and started her own business. "No matter what I did, you know, and what mountains I moved—and I moved a lot—no matter what programs I created, that they still use, they still didn't feel that I was competent to do them. I had employees comment that I was an affirmative action hire. I saw the resume of the white gentleman competing against me; if you looked at our resumes side by side, night and day, it was clear that I was overqualified for that role, and he didn't even have the experience."[3]

The people who accused Deena of being an affirmative action hire believed the myths. But just like everything else in the workplace, we can't track what we don't measure. Affirmative action can involve setting *goals* for increasing the representation of women and people of color in the workplace if their representation in that workplace is less than their availability in the current workforce. This approach encourages organizations to identify and address barriers that might limit the inclusion of these groups. Some in Deena's workplace may have believed the myth that affirmative action is "reverse discrimination" as opposed to company policies designed to seek and recruit women and minorities for employment opportunities, including opportunities in positions to which they may have been historically (including recent history) denied access. Affirmative action requires that all candidates be assessed equitably and without bias based on job-relevant criteria. The "reverse discrimination" myth seems to imply that simply ensuring underrepresented people are included in a candidate pool is so offensive—so outside the norms, we've been taught through centuries of racist precedent—as to be discriminatory against white people. Even some people of color where Deena worked may have believed the myth that affirmative action harms the self-esteem of women and people of color, a narrative pushed by some conservatives who say these programs hurt Black people by giving them "unearned" advantages. These same people blame the existence of these programs, not the existence of systemic racism, for negative stereotypes about Black people in the workplace.

Why?

If you believe that the "why" of affirmative action is to help supposedly intellectually inferior people access opportunities they don't deserve, you are going to think that the "pipeline" is broken or that no one is even in there. And if you think you are "giving" people an opportunity, through your benevolence and largesse, from the perch of "ownership" of that opportunity, you will have a different approach than if you understand your goal is to remove artificial blockages. Suppose you understand deeply that these blockages have and continue to prevent ordinary everyday people, some good, some bad, some average, and some who are brilliant, from the opportunities that they and everyone else should have access to. In that case, it will change how you design your solutions.

While Black men, women, and children have worked from the moment they were forced onto American soil, they were, by design, never meant to be equal participants in the American workforce. Their labor was only meant to enrich the lives of those who owned them. It could be argued, then, that the Civil War was about the disruption of that right: "In the 11 states that eventually formed the Confederacy, four out of ten people were slaves in 1860, and these people accounted for more than half the agricultural labor in those states. In the cotton regions, the importance of slave labor was even greater."[4]

When Black people were legally freed, the idea of them securing employment in competition—and on equal footing with—white people toward their own financial enrichment was a heresy that was met with extreme violence and anger.[5] Today, people who seek to minimize the myriad negative impacts of slavery will mention that there were free Black people in the South and the North who worked for wages. That is true. However, it is also true that the percentage of free Black people in the United States at the start of the Civil War was a scant 10 percent.[6] Over half of them lived in the North, where they held jobs commensurate with their status: women were cooks, maids, laundresses, and for men, other types of manual labor, restaurants, rail yards, and generally service-industry positions. Free Black people were either paid less than their white counterparts or given housing and land (sharecropping) to work that ultimately only yielded a minuscule stipend in exchange for their labor.[7] White restaurant owners were so opposed to paying free Black employees a wage that tipping was introduced to the American workforce right after slavery's end. Roberto Ferdman writes, "The restaurant industry, which was hiring newly freed slaves as tipped workers, really wanted the right to hire these workers but pay them next to nothing. So they put forth this idea that they were valueless and really shouldn't have to be paid by their employers. They essentially made the argument that newly freed slaves should get a zero-dollar wage."[8] Of course, tipping is still a tactic that is used today by many service-industry employers looking to keep hourly pay at below-livable rates. [9]

From the end of slavery until well into the 1970s, most Black workers were employed in low-wage and so-called low-skilled jobs. And while data on the state of the Black workforce, specifically related to "white-collar" employment before 1970, is limited, we do know that Black people were also employed as educators, nurses, social workers, postal workers, and in some clerical positions, but almost always exclusively within Black communities.[10] Not because they were unqualified for higher-paying jobs in white communities, or incompetent, but because, to paraphrase Lincoln, someone must be the "inferior" race.[11]

That fallacy of assumed inferiority has led to high hurdles and outright barriers to employment and advancement today. It is those barriers and blockages that have and continue to divert access and inclusion for Black Americans. It's never been a matter of laziness, intelligence (or lack thereof), or incompetence. So, affirmative action exists to enforce fairness, *not* provide special treatment. My own mother once applied for a job at a local hospital in the early 1960s, well before affirmative action existed; after the interview, she watched the hiring manager crumple up her application and throw it in the garbage. Like my mother, that hiring manager was a woman, but she was white, and therefore felt the need to protect the system of inequality that had put her in a position of power she felt she deserved, and my mother didn't. As I said, affirmative action didn't exist yet, but this hiring manager knew my mother was unqualified and incompetent because of her skin color. This was the situation before affirmative action.

The marginal assistance that affirmative action has provided Black people has given them a shot at employment. However, its introduction to American working life didn't fundamentally change long-held workplace cultures and corporate practices. As a teenager looking for work in the 1980s, I applied for a job at a national clothing store and noticed that everyone working on the sales floor were young white women. Regardless, I applied, but I never heard back. I was not terribly surprised when, in 2003, a group of young Black, Hispanic, and Asian people filed a class-action lawsuit against Abercrombie & Fitch, alleging racial discrimination in their hiring practices.[12] In 2004, the company settled with the rejected applicants and those current employees who were essentially "hidden" from the sales floor because of the color of their skin. In 2016, an investigative report uncovered how some temporary placement agencies were caught using code words like *chocolate cupcakes* and *kitties* with employers to weed out Black workers, women, LGBTQIA+, and other people of color.[13] That's what's behind the fierce desire to hide the impact of systemic inequity—when you hide the truth, you can promote the lie "we don't have diversity because they are unqualified," as opposed to, "we don't have a diverse workforce because we purposely block it from happening." This is why affirmative action was needed then and is still needed now.

Affirmative action was first introduced to the American conversation by President John F. Kennedy in 1961. He sought to use the financial power of federal government contracts to create "affirmative action" to break down existing racial hiring barriers.[14] After JFK was assassinated, President Lyndon B. Johnson expanded and defined it further. In 1965, in a speech at Howard University, he succinctly described the need for the program: "You do not take a man who for years has been hobbled by chains, liberate him, bring him to the starting line of a race, saying, 'You are free to compete with all the others,' and still justly believe you have been completely fair."[15] But almost immediately that message was flipped on its head and branded "unfair" to white people.

Like the opposition to the Freedman's Bureau, which supported the formerly enslaved after the Civil War, the pushback against affirmative action was almost instantaneous. In his book *Protesting Affirmative Action*, author Dennis Deslippe quotes a 1965 *Wall Street Journal* article covering claims of "reverse discrimination" logged by orchestra players at CBS: "For as long as men are hired and fired based on color alone, America's racial tensions will not subside. Anything that preserves such tensions we call negative action."[16] This argument—which dismisses structural anti-Black racism and countless other discriminations—is a deeply misinformed act of magical realism. It's an intellectual illusion where opponents overlook or deny the reality that such initiatives aim to correct historical and ongoing injustices. These efforts address the harsh truth that individuals have been, and still are, excluded from hiring, promotions, and fair competition due to skin color and persisting negative stereotypes. Deslippe claims that early pushback against affirmative action came from "three sources: . . . labor unionism, colorblind liberalism, and colorblind conservatism."[17]

Affirmative Action: Gender

It is also incredibly telling—and therefore worth expanding on—that the myths around qualifications and affirmative action tend to focus exclusively on Blackness as opposed to the other groups covered and impacted by affirmative action policies. Gender was added as a category in affirmative action in 1967, two years after the passage of the original affirmative action legislation, or Executive Order 11375, which was signed into law by President Johnson. Highlighting the complex interplay of white supremacy and gender, the only reason gender was included in the law was that in 1964, "Congressman Howard Smith (D-VA), Chairman of the Rules Committee and a staunch opponent of civil rights . . . offered an amendment that added sex to Title VII (equal employment opportunity)." While historians say that Smith supported the idea of an Equal Rights Amendment for women, "his amendment to the civil rights bill was likely intended to kill the measure."[18] The inclusion of gender in Title VII of the 1964 Civil Rights Act opened the door for advocacy groups like the National Organization for Women (NOW) to lobby for women to be included in affirmative action.[19] I think a legitimate question to ask today is, Was Congressman Howard W. Smith's goal to kill the Civil Rights Act of 1964 or dilute its impact on Black people? Whatever the answer, the impact speaks for itself. Affirmative action has had a profound impact on the lives of white women in education and the workforce.

Data from the Bureau of Labor Statistics corroborates this profound impact, revealing a fourfold increase in college degree attainment among women since 1970 and showing that over 50 percent of those in management and professional roles now are women.[20] And while women are still overrepresented in jobs historically associated with gender, such as teachers and nurses, white women in particular have made significant strides. White women are more likely than any other group of women to work in high-paying "professional" fields, such as management, medicine, technology, and law.[21] Yet it seems, based on their voting patterns and their opposition, including taking legal action, that most white women do not see the impact or connection between their success and affirmative action. I attribute this to both the desire by some to maintain white supremacy and the stunning effectiveness of messaging by those who wield the "hidden hand."[22] While white women can be competency-checked in the workplace, there appears to be no widespread campaign to frame their very presence as the result of unqualified, incompetent people being gifted employment above others in the same way that those who oppose affirmative action frame the conversation when discussing Black people in the workplace. The clear difference between the fate of Black people under affirmative action and white women under the same is that white women are white. Proof enough that affirmative action can and has worked, but that there is a persistence in anti-Black bias that requires us to lean into race-based affirmative action and other race-conscious efforts to reduce the unique blockages—both internal and external— against Black and other people of color as they seek to secure and retain employment and advance in the workplace.

We can learn something else from the relative success of white women in the workplace under affirmative action: maintaining that success requires enforcement and is not guaranteed. For example, they, as well as other women, still endure a disproportionate amount of workplace harassment, specifically sexual harassment, as the explosion of the #MeToo movement, originated by Black social activist Tarana Burke and popularized by the actress Alyssa Milano, proved.[23] Data from the US Equal Employment Opportunity Commission (EEOC) between 2018 and 2021 shows that women filed the vast majority of the sexual harassment charges received by the EEOC.[24] To see this in action, we must look no further than the events at Activision.

In 2021, the California Department of Fair Employment and Housing sued Activision Blizzard, one of the world's largest and most successful videogame companies, for gender-based discrimination and harassment, including unwanted groping and advances, pay disparity, and blocked promotions for female employees. By December 2023, the company settled a lawsuit for $50 million with the California Civil Rights Department to resolve allegations of discrimination against women in pay and promotions.[25]

EEOC: Administering the Medicine

As I mentioned before, I see systems deploying competency checking and outright discrimination to reject diversity in the workplace in much the same way the body rejects an organ after a transplant. And it's that danger of rejection that necessitates the need for antirejection medication that a person will take for the rest of their life. This is because the body perceives the new organ as a foreign object, a threat. Women, Black people, LGBTQIA+, and other minoritized folks are all human beings, and there is, on the surface, no reason this level of rejection should happen in the workplace. But the "body" of systemic inequity and white supremacy rejects the presence of what it has defined as "foreign." Consequently, there must be a consistent effort to monitor, address, and account for how institutions will try to "reject" the perceived threat. If we say, "Hey, the transplant has happened, and everything is fine, no need for monitoring or medication," then we doom both the patient and the organ to failure. In medicine, that failure is death, and in the workplace, this failure can lead to a type of death: the death of opportunity, new ideas, and hope.

While companies often see the EEOC as an adversary because of its enforcement role, given the current climate they should lean into the preventive and curative factors that the EEOC can provide for their own health. Correctly utilizing the EEOC could prevent problems, open opportunities, and be otherwise utilized to stop the rejection of Black people, women, the disabled, other people of color, LGBTQIA+ people, and everyone covered by it, but it must be used. If the idea of the EEOC bringing its investigative and legal power into the workplace is intimidating to you, I would encourage you to sit with that feeling and interrogate it further. How and why are you threatened by the better treatment of others? And why do you fear *that* more than the legal action that arises when these requirements are not followed? Employers should treat the EEOC like a pharmacy, an entity that provides patients—regardless of race or gender—with what they need for their long-term health and longevity as employees.

Employers can use the EEOC as a valuable resource and legal tool by reframing it. However, the EEOC should be the baseline, not the ceiling; it has done plenty of good, and it has the potential to help ward off internal and external legal challenges against creating an inclusive and diverse workforce that meets the needs of an increasingly diverse consumer base. For example, employers can use it to communicate with their employees why they are taking specific actions based on EEOC requirements. The EEOC can also help strengthen the monitoring of racism and/or discrimination in the workplace and, if necessary, enforcement actions.

On this, we can look to Title VII of the Civil Rights Act of 1964, which the EEOC enforces, to help us with those "hidden blockages," including color-blind policies and competency checking that advantage white people. "Title VII prohibits not only intentional discrimination, but also **practices that appear to be neutral**, but that limit employment opportunities for some racial groups and are not based on business needs. Intentional discrimination occurs when an employment decision is affected by the person's race. It includes not only racial animosity but also conscious or **unconscious stereotypes about the abilities, traits, or performance of individuals of certain racial groups**."[26] This can be a strong justification for examining anti-Black bias, which, through competency checking, is creating artificial blockages that are derailing your hiring, promotions, and retention efforts for Black employees and addressing the specific needs of other employees covered under Title VII.

DEI

Many people think DEI is new. It's not. Most folks only recently heard of it after the 2020 murder of George Floyd and the so-called "racial reckoning" that followed.[27] And as quickly as that recognition came, so too did the "backlash." Now we have people speaking negatively about this initiative and see them actively seeking to "outlaw" diversity, equity, and inclusion, but what does that mean exactly? It's not illegal to be diverse. It's not morally or legally wrong to be inclusive—in fact, it's the exact opposite. Recognizing and accounting for the fact that some people have different experiences from others (equity) is a necessary element of running any business.

The first expression of a workplace DEI initiative was in 1965, when the country's first minority employee resource group (ERG) was formed at Xerox, "spurred by an uprising amongst Black employees who demanded pay equality with their white peers."[28] The recent prominence of DEI is distinguished by the fact that it, for the first time, sought to address anti-Black bias in the workplace head-on. While there have been amazing wins for Black folks in civil rights legislation, there has, in fact, never been a race-specific solution to anti-Black bias that has prioritized the specific needs of Black people in the workplace. The GI Bill didn't do it; affirmative action didn't either; and the Freedman's Bureau, established to help the formerly enslaved, was stopped from doing it by using the same mis- and dis-information we see being thrown around today.[29]

So, when we get to this historical moment like the one in 2020, where the true cost of anti-Black bias floods the airwaves and causes mass self-reflection and even some catharsis for those who have been experiencing America's underbelly for generations, there is inevitably a not-insignificant amount of pent-up frustration, anger, and deferred dreams that have come pouring out of Black people. For the first time, there is a conversation about specific solutions to address anti-Black bias and the impact of white supremacy, in the workplace, directly. That DEI has not accomplished in four years what it took us four hundred years to create mirrors the unrealistically high expectations Black Americans themselves face in the workplace. It is simply too much pressure to put on any one modality, and the idea that this would be a fait accompli is, quite frankly, ludicrous. Yet this is the standard by which people for and against DEI judge its efforts.

Many a think piece has bemoaned the "performative efforts" and lack of real progress from this brief interlude of focus on anti-Black bias.[30] I understand the frustration because I share it: while there has been some incremental progress over the years, it hasn't been nearly enough, with far too many obstacles still in place determined to stymie it. Ironically, I think Black people's disappointment with DEI as a workplace initiative springs from the same source that motivates the white people who push back against it—a misperception about where we are on the racial progress timeline. Part of the problem is that we think the racial progress timeline is linear, going only ever in one direction: toward racial justice.[31] The fact that we continue to hold the misapprehension that there is a straight line from chattel slavery to the first Black president is undermining our efforts to confront and deal with what is actually happening.[32]

The truth is that racial progress is a winding and circuitous route that doubles back constantly and is never guaranteed.[33] In my practice, I hear Black people say, "We're still dealing with this in 2024?" And I hear white people say, "We're still dealing with this in 2024?" Yes. But does that mean modern DEI efforts have been a total failure? No. No one fights this hard against something that isn't, at least on some level, having some impact. The forces—of government, of capitalism, of society itself—that are determined to hold back these efforts and their inarguably positive results would not be so vocal and strategic in trying to cause confusion and create distractions if these efforts didn't matter. Have some companies been "performative" in hiring Black folks for window dressing? I am sure some have, and recent data on retention and diversity seems to signal that many weren't prepared for or serious about maintaining that diversity.[34] But have we also had one of the first direct conversations about the impact of anti-Blackness in the workplace?[35] Yes.

Given the backdrop of history, this obviously is not enough, and we are now faced with the potential to see a "doubling back" of that progress as real questions arise about the staying power of that change. But as tenuous as these advancements are, the rate of change is still too much for some. Older Black folks might call it a "trick bag," a way of getting you into a situation where you are supporting your own demise. This is why I must say to anyone disillusioned by DEI as a strategy, so much so that they want to abandon it, "It's a trap!" Don't give in to nihilism; keep pushing for more change, more inclusion, and more diversity, and demand specifics and tangible action. I worry that a potentially catastrophic convergence of (understandable, albeit regrettable) Black cynicism about DEI and white supremacist antipathy, could together, though for very different reasons, rewrite the narrative, much like the delegitimization of carpetbaggers and scalawags before us, and overwrite our still-nascent efforts before they can lead to lasting change.

It may seem like there will always be an us-versus-them mentality, one that uses divisive language to portray those advocating for change as outsiders or threats to the established order through dehumanization and labeling, but nothing is forever if we choose—actively and repeatedly—to change it. Those techniques were used to justify the enslavement of Black people and continue to be used to justify their ongoing oppression today. Terms like *carpetbagger* and *scalawag* aimed to dehumanize white people who sought to move society forward by reducing them to stereotypes and, most importantly, delegitimizing their work. Likewise, some critics of DEI efforts seek to do the same using delegitimizing labels like *social justice warrior* or mocking terms like *woke*—a term that actually has been used by Black people as far back as the earliest part of the twentieth century to alert each other to be careful. Stay woke. Keep your eyes open literally, figuratively, and spiritually.[36] And, of course, fear-mongering Reconstruction opponents warned of carpet-baggers exploiting the South, while some today paint DEI as undermining established norms or threatening cultural identities.

All of these are tactics used to resist change. DEI initiatives, in particular, seek to alter established power structures and address historical inequalities. This shift can generate anxiety and resistance from those who perceive themselves as benefiting from the current system. I use the term *perceive* intentionally because so many fight to maintain a system that does not benefit them.[37] Through rhetoric, those who oppose this advancement have misrepresented the efforts to address systemic inequity's hidden hand as divisive, exclusionary, or promoting reverse discrimination rather than as efforts to create more inclusive and equitable environments. And because systemic inequity is so deeply baked into our society, it is difficult for the average person to see or, like doctors versus the interstitium of the human body, believe it exists. That disbelief is what allows those who oppose progress to reframe the narrative to promote hostility toward diversity, fear of inclusion, and hatred of equity.

Because I am a consultant working in this space, people often ask me, "Is it hard working with white people who don't understand race? Is it frustrating?" For me, not so much; I know what we weren't taught, so I see how we get here. What tears me apart, what breaks my heart and haunts my soul, are the frustrations and hurts experienced by Black people, specifically young Black people, who are today facing the fact that we have not advanced as far as they were led to believe we had. Not because they don't deserve it or haven't earned it, and not because DEI has failed, but because, as a country, we have failed to fully address and dismantle anti-Black bias in our society and, therefore, in the workplace.

Applying the Tools

Understand that as of today, we stand on a precipice that could easily see over fifty years of nascent workplace advancement undone. It is going to take more than empty platitudes, "DEI lenses," or good intentions to thwart a "color-blind" version of Jim Crow that has the potential to destroy progress and hinder both economic and business growth. This means we must use every law and policy at our disposal. We must also be able to articulate why it behooves us to put the old paradigms to rest once and for all.

"Change Your Thinking, Change Your Life."[38] This is more than just a platitude; it is a critical tool that allows us to, remixing the Carl Jung quote here, make the unconscious conscious so we can stop calling it fate. While it may seem odd that the first tool against systemic inequity I'm presenting is a "new age" axiom, especially after just saying that platitudes will not be enough, as the saying goes, *think* about it: If you look around your workplace, from leadership to frontline workers, and see few to no Black people, a scant few other people of color, and women bunched up in "traditional" roles such as administrative support and human resources, it is a clear sign that something is wrong in that workplace. How can there be no Black people in the entire country "qualified" for positions within your company? In what world are Black women less ambitious than white women or white men? What is more likely is that there are seen and unseen blockages preventing them from either accessing, succeeding in, or staying at a given company or workplace.

Writing in the *Atlantic*, Gillian B. White cites a National Bureau of Economic Research (NBER) paper, authored by Costas Cavounidis of the University of Warwick and Kevin Lang of Boston University, that "attempts to demonstrate how discrimination factors into company decisions, and creates a feedback loop, resulting in racial gaps in the labor force." Cavounidis and Lang found that "[t]o keep a job, Black workers also must meet a higher bar. Only when Black workers are monitored and displayed a significantly higher skill level than their white counterparts would they stand a significant chance of keeping their jobs. . . . But even in instances where the productivity of Black workers far exceeded their white counterparts, there was still evidence that discrimination persisted, which could lead to lower wages or slower promotions."[39]

So, how can you find those blockages and remove them? If you are a C-suite executive, a nonprofit organization, an HR professional, or a construction site manager, and you believe what Charles Scharf, the Wells Fargo CEO, said about there being no pipeline of Black talent, then you must first confront and change your underlying assumptions. *Change your thinking.* If you are looking for "unicorns," aka holding Black candidates and workers to higher standards, then you will indeed have a hard time finding a pipeline full of them. To identify the internal or external blockages that are preventing women, other people of color, LGBTQIA+ people, and disabled folks from accessing opportunities while not losing sight of the unique impact of anti-Blackness, you are going to want to ask yourself practical questions.

1. **WHO SUCCEEDS HERE, AND WHO DOESN'T?** A client of mine, a Black person, found out the answer

to that question when a position of advancement came up, and though they were highly qualified for the position, they were not even considered. The position required specialized knowledge and industry experience, with higher education preferred. Arguably, my client met all three requirements for this new position but had only been in the industry for three years. Much to my client's surprise, the new position was given to a white candidate who was promoted and allowed to complete their education and acquire the specialized knowledge that is required for the job *after* the fact. There's nothing wrong with allowing people to learn and grow into a position; we should do it more. However, Black employees find this rarely happens to them. Instead, they must meet and exceed all the requirements to even be considered, and that is competency checking in action.

2. **ARE YOU LOOKING FOR A REAL PERSON, OR ARE YOU LOOKING FOR A "SUPER TOKEN?"** Dr. Elizabeth "Dori" Tunstall, the first Black dean of the Faculty of Design at OCAD University, defines the term thus: "I define [a super token] as an individual from a marginalized group or groups whose talents are so desired by institutions that the [institutions] can overcome their innate aversion to the individual's identities to have access to those talents."[40] This person often has a top-tier degree, exceptional experience and skill, but frequently has yet to ascend to a leadership position. When they do, they are often the "first" in their field. There's nothing wrong with someone being the first, but if your company is a midtier business in a small to midsize city that does

not routinely recruit white people of that caliber, ask yourself why a Black person would need to be of that caliber to work there. Is it competency checking? Is it the unspoken blockage that doesn't allow you to see the Black community college graduate the same way you see the white community college graduate who already works there?

3. **HOW HEAVILY ARE YOU USING THE SHADOW HIRING PIPELINE?** The "shadow hiring pipeline" is, by its nature, a racially closed hiring loop that seems neutral on its face, but isn't. When a company says they are paying referral bonuses or when they prioritize or make easier entry for referrals from friends, family members, and business connections they are perpetuating a racially exclusionary process that seems race-neutral but, much like the GI Bill, ends up overwhelmingly benefiting white people.

In addition to the questions above, you can simply ask people for their input. Conduct focus groups with outside consultants and use anonymous surveys with employees to gain insights into their experiences with the hiring and promotion processes. Ask questions like "What blockages have you encountered that have impacted your experience in hiring, promotion, or retention at this company?" Ask if there have been incidents of competency checking, as defined in this book, that they have encountered. Use that information to make changes, including process, training, and management.

Finally, you must monitor. As discussed in this chapter, we must all be on the lookout for the ways in which the system will continue to try to reject the perceived "foreign" presence of nonwhite employees. For this, look to retention and advancement data. Consistently reinforce your commitment to an equitable workforce through training, modeling, and action. That includes being prepared to enforce your stated standards and norms and being willing to remove employees who refuse to learn and grow in an inclusive environment.

Of course, all of this relies on acknowledging that there is a problem. Certain people are missing from your workplace, not because they are unqualified, not because they don't exist, but because of current and historical fictions around intelligence, access, and opportunity. Everyone must agree that diverse employees or candidates are *not* the problem. They are not hard to find. The system built to hire, promote, and retain them, however, *is* a problem, and the artificial blockages the system creates, like competency checking, must be accounted for and removed.

Removing those blockages externally is just the first step. Internally, workplaces must foster a corporate culture where employees feel valued and respected regardless of their background. And like any other corporate culture initiative, this means you may need to take affirmative steps to educate, train, and, if necessary, separate from those who are blocking the advancement and inclusion of women, Black people, people of color, and other minoritized groups in the workplace. As a CEO or HR professional, you must ask your company *and* yourselves why you fear drawing lawsuits from inclusion rather than exclusion. One consultant I know was recently dealing with a company that was hesitant to address the issue of an employee beginning each morning's meeting on a work site by saying "88." According to the Anti-Defamation League, "88" (or, more accurately, 8–8, representing the eighth letter of the alphabet, *H*, twice in a row) is a white supremacist numeric symbol and shorthand for "Heil Hitler."[41] Or in the case of allegations, lawsuits, and a class action that was brought against Tesla where "240 Black factory workers in California described rampant racism and discrimination at the electric automaker's San Francisco Bay Area plant, including frequent use of racial slurs."[42] Or again what happened to the women of Activision Blizzard. How does it get this bad?

Adam Levitt, whom I referenced earlier in this book, is a founding partner of DiCello Levitt and my former classmate at Northwestern University, Pritzker School of Law. His firm does complex litigation, including class actions, and he provided me with an assessment of what his firm is seeing that proves the examples above are not exaggerated. "The legal actions we're pursuing reveal a disturbing trend of implicit biases deeply embedded within corporate cultures, making it exceptionally challenging for Black individuals to achieve equitable treatment."[43]

Nowhere is this seen more than in the trades and on construction sites where there seems to be a "wink and a nod" culture combined with, from what I have observed, what can only be described as a fear by employers of their own employees. In her groundbreaking piece in the *Philadelphia Inquirer*, "How Black Workers Got Locked Out of Construction's Best Jobs," Juliana Feliciano Reyes covers Black people's history and present status in the trades in that city. She sheds considerable light on the profound racial and gender imbalances within the construction industry and in Philadelphia in particular. While the national landscape also reveals a predominance of white workers within the building trade unions at odds with the population, Philadelphia's scenario is even more striking. As of 2012, the local construction union's workforce was predominantly male and predominantly white, not reflecting the city's diverse demographic, which is nearly 50 percent Black.[44] Other research has shown that while Hispanic workers make up more of the construction workforce, depending upon the state, they find themselves locked out of management or supervisory roles and relegated instead to roles that carry higher risks and offer lower wages. These workers also face a greater incidence of work-related injuries and subsequent health issues than their white, non-Hispanic peers.[45] Reyes's investigation underscores the entrenched barriers perpetuating these disparities, calling for introspection and action within the industry to dismantle these blockages.

The tools still at our disposal include "changing our thinking," EEOC protections, and, at this moment, affirmative action in the workplace. But whatever happens, legally, there is still a business and moral case for the expansion, not the retraction, of diversity, inclusion, and opportunity as a stabilizing force for the betterment in our society.

Getting Creative

Personally, I see clear similarities between advancing DEI and the concept of "new market expansion." Expanding DEI efforts mirror the entering of new foreign markets because of systemic racism and sexism. Black consumers, Hispanic consumers, and women are still developing markets that for years were either excluded, artificially depressed, mocked as "racial mascots," or treated as secondarily necessary.[46] Just as businesses wouldn't shy away from a promising foreign market due to initial challenges, they shouldn't retreat from diversifying their workforce and consumer base out of fear of pushback. The long-term rewards (like a new consumer base, new product ideas and creation, and more profitability) outweigh the short-term hurdles. The idea that someone would say that you cannot and should not try to understand and recruit from a diverse workforce or that you should not understand how to market to and sell to a diverse consumer base is the path of obsoletion. This means that those companies that can afford it may need to take the lead in pressing court matters regarding their rights as institutions, the restriction of free speech, and anticompetitive interference.

And here's how they might do that—by taking a page from the playbook of those who, often using fake plaintiffs,[47] manipulate the intent of civil rights legislation to promote a supposedly "color-blind" society that favors white people, use the existing law in a new way. One avenue might be Citizens United. The Supreme Court decision in *Citizens United v. Federal Election Commission* (2010)[48] fundamentally changed the landscape of campaign finance law by ruling that corporate funding of independent political broadcasts in candidate elections cannot be limited under the First Amendment. This decision has broad implications for corporate speech and could potentially be used by companies to push back against anti-DEI efforts. Here's how companies might leverage this decision and the First Amendment to support DEI initiatives:

- **Corporate Free Speech Rights:**
  Citizens United recognized that corporations have a right to free speech under the First Amendment. Companies can argue that DEI initiatives are a form of corporate speech that reflects their values and business interests. Any government action or legislation that seeks to limit or ban DEI efforts could be challenged as an infringement on the company's free speech rights.

- **Expressing Corporate Values:**
  DEI efforts can be framed as part of the company's expression of its values and identity. Just as Citizens United allowed corporations to express political opinions through funding, companies can argue that promoting DEI is an expression of their organizational philosophy and commitment to social issues.

- **Opposition to Government Overreach:**

  Companies might argue that anti-DEI regulations represent an overreach of government authority, attempting to control or restrict the messages that companies can support or promote. This aligns with the broader Citizens United argument against governmental restrictions on speech.

- **Economic Interests as Speech:**

  In Citizens United, the court acknowledged that speech is not less protected because it is "corporate speech." Companies can argue that DEI initiatives are economically beneficial by fostering a more inclusive workplace, which can enhance innovation, employee satisfaction, and customer relations. Therefore, restrictions on DEI efforts could be seen as a restriction on economic interest.

- **Political Advocacy and Contributions:**

  Under Citizens United, companies have the right to engage in political advocacy. Companies could argue that supporting DEI initiatives, including lobbying against anti-DEI legislation, is a form of political speech. They could also financially support candidates or policies that favor DEI under the same principles upheld in Citizens United.

What the future holds for affirmative action in the workplace is unclear. However, until the US Supreme Court invalidates this legislation, employers should see it as a powerful tool for making life fairer for employees and for the sake of growth and profit as a company. Should the court reverse course, employers must be ready to fight back and establish their rights as corporations in a free market to "win the future" by leaning into, not retreating from, securing a creative and diverse workforce and providing goods and services to a majority diverse consumer base. Corporations must see a diverse, equitable, and inclusive workforce as a moral *and* strategic imperative. They must treat this as a Key Performance Indicator (KPI) for the business's success.[49] In a free-market capitalist system, corporations can make the argument that the historical and current exclusion of women, people of color, and LGBTQIA+ workers is bad for their bottom lines to the tune of $16 trillion, the economic toll of racism on Black Americans.[50] This means less money to spend, fewer new businesses, fewer new job creators, and, as birth rates decline, fewer future workers.

To access a more inclusive and equitable future, we must work intentionally to account for and move past these fictions around race, intelligence, and inclusion, including the fiction of linear progress and advancement. We can do this with intentional efforts, those rooted in deep understanding, compassion, and the collective desire to do better, so, let's get to work.

CHAPTER 10

Let's Get to Work

The world as we have created it is a process of our thinking. It cannot be changed without changing our thinking.[1]

Author Unknown

AS I ARRIVE at the final chapter in this book, I come back once again to the role our "thinking" must play in bringing about change. The only way to truly deal with the impact of competency checking in the workplace is to acknowledge that it is happening. Once we do that, we can begin to shift our thinking from "diversity is an almost impossible problem to solve" to "diversity is something that *should* be happening *but for* intentional and unintentional blockages that are preventing its natural flow." If we shift our thinking, we can begin to do the real work of removing those blockages, using the legal tools we just reviewed, our workplace policies and procedures, and a reexamination of how we do business rooted in a changed mindset.

Here's an example: Black entrepreneurs overwhelmingly report being "over-mentored and underfunded."[2] Alcide Honoré, the CEO and cofounder of e-billing company Billseye, says Black founders have a harder time getting the trust of investors. Investors seem stuck in the first principle of competency checking, namely the *assumption* of Black intellectual inferiority or lack of qualifications. This manifests as hypervigilance, a degree of oversight that does not allow Black founders to do what white founders say you must do to succeed—fail. Honoré says, "If you don't get the opportunity to fail, it's very hard to develop a successful product in the long run."[3] This peculiar dynamic sees Black founders subjected to extreme and excessive supervision disguised as mentorship because of assumed incompetence. It is further expressed as investors hesitating to invest significant amounts of money into Black business ideas. A 2020 McKinsey report revealed that white entrepreneurs start businesses with approximately three times more capital than Black business owners: $107,000 versus $35,000.[4]

The assumption of white competence combined with regular allowances for failure can have extreme, even life-and-death consequences. Elizabeth Holmes infamously raised $945 million from venture capitalists and powerful tech and media moguls such as Larry Ellison and Rupert Murdoch for a product that didn't—couldn't—work. Had Holmes been a Black woman, her company Theranos's underlying weaknesses would have been discovered well before she was able to receive any funding. Conversely, if, as a Black woman, she had a product that worked, current history and statistics tell us she would have been unlikely to reach the level of funding Holmes did.[5]

Of course, Holmes isn't the only one, there's this headline from an August 2022 article in *Forbes*: "Adam Neumann Gets a $350 Million Do-Over and Diverse Entrepreneurs Barely Get a Start."[6] Neumann cofounded WeWork, which was valued at $47 billion before a swift, colossal plunge left it valued at around $4 billion. Much of the coworking-office-space company's troubles have been attributed to Neumann's alleged bad decisions and reckless leadership style, though it didn't stop other venture capital firms from considering new investments worth hundreds of millions of dollars in Neumann's ideas.[7] But it's a different story for Black entrepreneurs. According to Shaun Harper, a tenured professor in the Marshall School of Business at the University of Southern California, "Even if their ideas are good (and perhaps substantively better and financially more promising than Neumann's), diverse innovators are often deemed too risky or not sufficiently proven. Ironically, Neumann's failure has been proven."[8]

Mentorship isn't a bad thing. In fact, Neumann and Holmes could both have benefited from longer-term mentorship, more oversight, and less initial funding until they could, as Black founders must, prove that the fundamentals of success were truly present in their ideas and plans. And just like mentorship in the venture capital investing space, mentorship in the workplace can be rooted in the first principle of competency checking: the assumption of Black intellectual inferiority. Mentorship that is based on the idea that all Black people need remedial help to succeed in the workplace is almost destined to fail as a method to bring in or retain more Black people in the workplace. This is because the second principle of competency checking is activated whenever these already competent Black adults and other people of color are revealed to be either equal to or exceeding their mentors and/or peers. This manifests as surprise and unease that can lead to the Black employee being seen as "arrogant" when they assert their knowledge and skill, or dissolve into a "pet-to-threat" scenario. Even in the best-case scenario, it can lead to the Black or other employee of color being seen as so "unexpectedly different" that they become tokenized.

There are clear solutions to issues like overmentoring and underfunding, especially in the entrepreneurial space. First, and most simply: treat Black founders and other people of color the same way you treat white founders. This means that if most white founders do not have to endure "remedial classes" to get a pittance of investment, then neither should anyone else. If you believe these kinds of actions are necessary because you believe white founders are inherently more qualified, then you need to check your assumptions. Some white founders may have more education from elite universities, but as the Holmes case proves, that doesn't mean they don't need oversight; in some cases, they shouldn't be considered qualified at all. Some white founders didn't even finish or go to graduate school, such as Neumann, who dropped out of graduate school to start his entrepreneurial journey. WeWork was what is called a "unicorn" in entrepreneurial speak, a company that has reached a value of $1 billion—rarefied air for a start-up.[9] But it is important to know that even among this elite group, according to Ilya Strebulaev, a finance professor at Stanford Graduate School of Business, "Fewer than a third of unicorns based in the United States have a founder who went to a B-school."[10] And it's not just the unicorns where we see diversity in education. "Clearly, you don't need an MBA to be an entrepreneur. After all, most entrepreneurs don't have MBAs, and more than half don't even have bachelor's degrees."[11]

If the reason you believe that Black entrepreneurs and other entrepreneurs of color need this remedial help is that they don't have MBAs, then why aren't the white entrepreneurs without MBAs held to the same standard? Black Americans hold 10 percent of all MBA's granted, 17 percent if you include for-profit business schools, which means that, once again, this isn't a pipeline issue.[12] These entrepreneurs exist. But Black entrepreneurs shouldn't have to meet a standard—namely, having an MBA—that a majority of white entrepreneurs aren't held to in order to receive funding. When it comes to Black founders and their ideas, I'm told, "People don't want to take a risk with their money; they want to invest in something they are going to get a return on." But if that's the case, how do they account for what the statistics say about venture capital–backed start-ups? According to research cited by the Harvard Online Forum on Corporate Governance, "Approximately 75% of venture-backed startups fail—the number is difficult to measure, however, and by some estimates, it is far greater."[13] If investors feel more "risk-averse" when it comes to Black and other founders of color, competency checking is occurring, because what makes the failure of Black and other founders of color so different from the 75 percent or more white people who already fail in this space? Only the color of the skin that "risk" comes in.

The key here is removing the blockages that are higher expectations of education and assumptions of inferiority. We also have to remove the blockage that is seeing Black failure as endemic of Blackness and white failure as an inevitable hurdle on the path to guaranteed success. Removing these blockages looks like acknowledging that race-based assumptions are behind the low funding for Black founders and other founders of color, not their ability, education, or risk profile. It looks like redesigning mentorship programs to target the specific needs of all entrepreneurs, even white ones with elite education. It looks like creating mentorship programs for venture capitalists to help coach *them* through competency checking and broaden their understanding of how to assess all investments without relying on faulty, even racist, assumptions. It will take recognizing that intentionality was required to get us here, and it will take intentionality to address the issue at the heart of Black entrepreneurship: a lack of access to funds. That would look like earmarking funds for those who have been systematically denied access. But even as I write this, efforts such as the Fearless Fund—which was devised to invest in female entrepreneurs of color—have been stopped by the courts. Again, it's no coincidence that the legal challenge against the Fearless Fund was brought by the same group that led the fight to take down affirmative action in higher education. While those groups claim to be promoting fairness and equity and "colorblindness," they are, in fact, seeking to continue race-based competency checking and stop us from using the "antirejection" medications necessary to address white supremacy's mission to exclude Black people specifically from full participation in American life.

I began this chapter focusing on entrepreneurs for good reason. Very often, Black and other people of color have said, in response to hostility in the workplace, "We should start our own businesses." And many have, me included. But the truth of the matter is that not everyone wants or is designed for the life of an entrepreneur, and as we saw, there is a big blockage in the entrepreneurial space around equitable access to funding for those who do. Most working-class people in the United States work hourly or salary-earning jobs. Some people love the certainty of the workplace and like being a part of a team as opposed to the sole owner and operator. Some people need the retirement benefits or health insurance that wage-based employment provides. This means we cannot cede the workplace—corporate, nonprofit, governmental, the trades, or otherwise—to the issue of white supremacy. As my friend Carolyn told me when we discussed the need for this book, "Just like Black lives, Black livelihoods matter too."

Removing Blockages

So much about the way race operates in our society is hidden, but a lot of it hides in plain sight. Two legal concepts illuminate this: in Latin, *de jure*, which means in accordance with the law or because of the law; and *de facto*, which means in reality or actuality. An example of this is de jure housing segregation, which was at one time mandated by law. In a 2017 interview with NPR, Richard Rothstein discussed how local, state, and federal housing policies mandated segregation by "redlining areas where African-Americans lived as too risky for mortgage guarantees and subsidizing builders who produced subdivisions for whites only, under the condition that homes not be sold to African-Americans."[14] Rothstein, speaking about his 2017 book *The Color of Law*, pointed out the FHA's influence: "It was in something called the Underwriting Manual of the Federal Housing Administration, which said that 'incompatible racial groups should not be permitted to live in the same communities.' Meaning that loans to African-Americans could not be insured."[15]

But over time, and even though the law no longer mandated segregated housing, it became de facto housing segregation, which is basically how we live today. But the thing about de facto is that it often sits on top of de jure. In other words, the de facto way things are done today results from the impact of historical de jure: this is how things have always been, so this is how we'll continue to do them.

When considering workplace discrimination, there are explicitly illegal acts, such as discrimination based on skin color, age, gender, and other factors stated in antidiscrimination laws. This is because, at one time, discrimination based on those factors was either tolerated by or mandated by the law—*de jure*. However, there is also *de facto* discrimination, which is not often discussed when it comes to the workplace. When it comes to de facto race-based discrimination in the workplace, the real elephant in the room is one we've already met: referral-based hiring.

Referral-based hiring, which we touched on in chapter 9, is a practice where current employees refer potential candidates for job openings. On the surface, referral-based hiring may appear neutral, as it is based on personal connections and recommendations, but in practice, the result is de facto discrimination. There are several reasons for this, made up of a mix of the long-term results of historical de jure discrimination, such as housing discrimination, and de facto discrimination, such as the homogeneity of a company's workforce. This means that if the existing makeup of the workforce and the social and business networks that have developed as a result are homogeneous, then the results of referral-based hiring will be a "de facto" reflection of that.

This isn't by accident. Research and common sense tell us that there's a strong correlation between residential and workplace segregation. This segregation leads to a lack of interracial interaction, which hinders the formation of friendships between Black and white people.[16] According to a 2022 report from the Public Religion Research Institute, "White Americans' friendship networks are on average 90% white, unchanged from 91% in 2013."[17] Conversely, according to PRRI, Black American friend groups have diversified, going from 83 percent Black to 78 percent Black.

This type of de facto segregation because of de jure segregation is also why we have what is called "occupational segregation." Racial occupational segregation describes the uneven distribution of racial and ethnic minorities across various industries and job categories. Like how gender segregation operates, this form of segregation manifests both horizontally and vertically. Horizontally, it influences the specific industries that racial minorities are more likely to occupy. Vertically, it impacts their upward mobility and career advancement.[18] This segregation shapes not only the job opportunities available to Black and other people of color, but also their potential for progression in the workplace.[19]

Both of these factors clearly illustrate why referral-based hiring overwhelmingly benefits white people. Most white people are not villainously keeping Black people out of this backdoor pipeline. However, the fact that almost everyone ignores the de facto discriminatory nature of the referral-based pipeline starts to feel a lot like the maintenance of white supremacy, consciously or unconsciously. Data from Glassdoor shows that referral candidates receive offers at a higher rate than candidates who secured job interviews through online applications, colleges, universities, staffing agencies, or recruiters.[20] Basically, all the ways the vast majority of Black and other people of color find employment.

Instead of addressing the clear inequity in this system, the blame and the burden of it all are placed on Black and other people of color. They are often coached on "how to network better" and admonished to "lean in more," which leads to even more remedial remedies that assume Black incompetence and not the real culprit, white ignorance of the factors at play. In the research on race and networks in the job search process from the *American Sociological Review*, they identify one of the factors as "network access." "Black and white job seekers utilize their networks at similar rates, but network-based methods are less likely to lead to job offers for African Americans."[21] In other words, Black job seekers receive fewer job leads because these networks are segregated.

The same research also highlights another factor, what is called "network returns." This means that even when Black job seekers utilize their networks as much as white job seekers, the benefits are often reduced due to the lesser influence of their connections within organizations and racial biases that devalue referrals from nonwhite people. A friend of mine who works at a large tech company once vented to me about their frustrations with referral base hiring, saying, "When I refer people, it seems they are rarely interviewed and never hired, but when my white colleagues refer people, they at least seem to get an interview, and some get hired."

No amount of networking or sponsorship or so-called color-blind faith can overcome a system that isn't designed for you. "When you know better, do better,"[22] as the saying goes. We must do better here. We cannot look at a system we know is de facto segregated, providing significant benefits for those with access to it, and pretend it's fair. Zippia, the online career services website, gives us the bottom line: "Referrals are four times more likely to be offered a job than website applicants [and] . . . employee referrals account for 30–50% of all hires."[23]

My honest recommendation is that we end referral-based hiring. But because I also live in the real world, I would see employers limit referral-based hiring and bring that 30–50 percent down to 15 percent or 10 percent of all hires. Even as you begin to bring down the number of referral hires, audit your process and results. Which referrals get "real" consideration? Is there a pattern of referrals from Black and other people of color not getting to either the interview or hiring stage? If so, you must retool your process or consider scrapping it. Because while many employers worry about legal action related to promoting diversity, equity, and inclusion, they must also factor in legal action related to these "unnatural" blockages. In 2022, the newsletter of the New Jersey Business and Industry Association reported on a bakery in New York that paid "$850,000 to resolve allegations it discriminated against female, Black, and Asian applicants in the recruitment process by relying exclusively on referrals from existing employees to hire cashiers, packers, and bakers."[24] One of the key reasons the threat of a lawsuit worked to change the practice at this bakery is that it had a federal contract to provide baked goods to the U.S. Military Academy at West Point. As a result, it was found to be in violation of "an executive order which prohibits federal contractors from discriminating in employment based on race, color, religion, gender, sexual orientation, or national origin."[25] This again speaks to the need for legal, often federal, oversight that can act as the proper "medicine," which in this case is the executive order used to address the rejection of qualified Black and other people of color from the workplace. Ultimately, it is the responsibility of workplaces to do the work of removing these unnatural blockages that are limiting access for Black and other people of color in hiring, advancement, and retention.

Lest you think this kind of hegemony only impacts racial diversity, it also impacts intellectual diversity. When a company hires people based on who-knows-who, they bottleneck the hiring pool, limiting the many ways diversity would otherwise occur naturally. In his book *The Diversity Bonus*, Scott E. Page details how multiple diversity factors can help a company's hiring practices, saying that thinking of multifactor diversity as a bonus can "enable us to see how our differences can make us more innovative, resilient, and prosperous. It points to how we might enlarge the pie instead of negotiating over the size of our current slice."[26]

Nobel Prize–winning economist Gary Becker is credited with the finding that *more profitable* companies are *less biased*, ultimately proving that discrimination, be it de jure or de facto, is bad for business. Teasing apart why that might be I came upon this line from the *New York Times* article, about the race-based resume name audit, that we discussed earlier, and it stopped me in my tracks: "Economists said that could be because the more profitable companies benefit from a more diverse set of employees. It could also be an indication that they had more *efficient business processes* in H.R. and elsewhere."[27] As someone who has consulted with large and small for-profit businesses, nonprofits, and governmental agencies,

I can confidently say they all suffer from a lack of efficient business processes, "in H.R. and elsewhere." That lack of efficacy is causing multiple problems, from communication to the execution of work to the ability to expand or maintain market share and size. So, curing for the de facto discrimination that is built into referral-based hiring may have significant benefits for other business functions. This is because it will force the company to slow down and use *intentionality* not just in hiring but in *everything* they do.

While there is a solid argument to be made that referral-based hiring broadly harms workplaces, I must ground us in the fact that eliminating or reducing its impact is just the start. As research across industries has shown, "race remains a fundamental determinant"[28] in hiring, advancement, and retention.

Hiring

When we talk about hiring, we frequently talk about the "pipelines" of talent. There is the aforementioned backdoor pipeline of referral-based hiring we just discussed. And for those coming in the more formal and complex "front door," there's the new-talent pipeline, and then there's the pipeline that gives us managers. There's also the lateral-hiring pipeline, frequently populated by those seeking to advance their careers in a new workplace, and the leadership pipeline. Each one of these "pipelines" has specific blockages that prevent the flow of racial diversity in the workplace.

So, let's take an even deeper dive into the study that used names as racial markers. What that study found was that discriminatory practices are baked into some corporate cultures and those practices *are* the blockages—the vines of race-based stereotyping and assumptions (when we see a "Black" name) that were seeded at the founding of this country and have wound through time and continue to gum up our current systems. In the case of the audit, the blockages in question were assumptions about Black intellectual inferiority, competency, and qualifications, all of which were based on stereotypes triggered by a name and not on the actual, individual employee. We know how this happens; consciously or subconsciously, we "shift standards" once we know a person's race, leading us to see the exact same resume or memo as inferior. Even in the face of competency, we deploy goal-based stereotyping, and we use competency checking to validate or disprove a person's qualifications, which either blocks or sets a higher bar for hiring, retention, and advancement. It's not a mystery. So, while the audit did find that "the results demonstrate how entrenched employment discrimination is in parts of the U.S. labor market—and the extent to which Black workers start behind in certain industries,"[29] it also found something else.

When it came to the companies that discriminated the least at the entry level, researchers found that "access to a centralized HR department in the selection of applications has an important effect on the level of discrimination."[30] This is because when the calls came from a centralized HR department, they seemed to have more of a process and showed less urgency to get the position filled. However, the researchers found that "[w]hen [the calls] came from individual hiring managers at local stores or warehouses . . . [t]hese messages often sounded frantic and informal."[31] The *New York Times* quotes one of the researchers, Professor Patrick Klines, as saying, "That's when implicit biases kick in . . . [but slowing down and] thinking about things, which steps to take, having to run something by someone for approval, can be quite important in mitigating bias."[32]

My own experiences confirm this for me. A more formal hiring process is indeed one of the tools that can help mitigate this kind of race-based blockage. In practice, it looks like clear, deliberate, consistent, and consistently applied processes and procedures. That might sound easy, but it's not. Many companies, even large, well-established ones, are not deliberate in their hiring process. They are either hurrying to meet a need, restructuring after downsizing, or rolling out a new product, and this leads to them making decisions in a rush, relying on referrals, and deploying what Daniel Kahneman called "System 1" thinking. In his book *Thinking, Fast and Slow*, Kahneman explains that humans deploy two types of thinking: System 1 and System 2. System 1 is fast, intuitive, and emotional; it operates automatically and quickly, with little effort and no sense of voluntary control. System 2, on the other hand, allocates attention to the effortful mental activities that demand it, including complex computations. It is slower, more deliberate, and more logical.[33] When we engage in System 1 thinking, it is easier for our conscious and unconscious biases to guide our decision-making, and this is something all humans do. Maybe if we can lean into the fact that humans do this, we can depersonalize it and move away from the "I am not doing this, I am not part of the problem" place of internal resistance to "this is what it means to be human, so I need to check myself."

The best way to check yourself—or in this case, your business—is to do regular hiring audits. Look at who got hired and who didn't, then cross-check by looking at the names. Do you notice any patterns? Of course, this is easier for large companies, and the research did indicate that the amount of name bias present in entry-level hiring might have been underestimated. While this audit didn't look at Asian and Hispanic/Latinx surnames, other research suggests they are also contacted less than white people but more than Black people, which again speaks to the *unique* impact of anti-Black bias in the workplace.[34]

The audit also found that diverse recruiters tend to help mitigate or outright remove race-based competency-checking blockages in entry-level hiring. Companies that discriminated the least in the audit had a diverse team of recruiters; about 40 percent of their recruiters were people of color.[35] On top of that, these companies also actively deepened their candidate pools by reaching out to diverse populations and expanding their definition of a "qualified" candidate. This means that the most successful companies relied on skills-based versus degree-requirement hiring. As we've already discussed, there is no doubt that skills-based hiring can open opportunities and does not mean hiring "less qualified" people; however, because "race remains a fundamental determinant,"[36] we must still audit and closely examine skills-based hiring. We must audit this hiring to see who gets the benefit of the doubt, whose skills are deemed sufficient, and who is still being arbitrarily competency-checked to have either more skills or additional education.

The report also found that there was "less bias in hiring [when there was] more regulatory scrutiny—like at federal contractors, or companies with more Labor Department citations."[37] Once again, the facts speak to the overwhelming need for the presence and use of "antirejection" medication, regulatory scrutiny, and federal requirements, all of which have cracked open the doors of opportunities for Black and other people of color.

Interestingly, according to the *Times* article, the research found that having "a chief diversity officer, offering diversity training or having a diverse board—were not correlated with decreased discrimination in entry-level hiring."[38] I would be interested to know what type of training wasn't correlated. Was it a generic "plug-and-play" type of DEI training, or was it DEI training designed for that particular company (and those engaged in hiring at that company)? This matters because, in my experience, training designed to help a specific company uncover how racism blocks hiring at *that* company or in that industry can have a much greater impact. Specifically, customized training can help operationalize DEI. For example, training on how competency checking has and continues to impact the hiring of medical professionals is going to be different than training on how it has impacted construction workers. Getting that specific information is going to help make the changes to hiring in those fields "operational," meaning these changes become a part of, not an addition to, how the process functions. Without this knowledge, knowing what types of training were offered that the study found "not helpful," I find the statement that training wasn't a factor impacting entry-level hiring—specious.

What we do know is that it is critical that we remove blockages in our hiring practices and the early stages of employment. It is not just a matter of fairness and true corrective equality, but of economic necessity. "Black and Hispanic students are substantially more likely than students of other races and ethnicities to wind up underemployed," according to a 2024 article by Business Insider, "The Permanent Detour," which discussed the findings of a 2024 report that headlined its conclusion thusly: "Most US Graduates Who Start Their First Job Underemployed Can't Find College-level Jobs 10 Years Later."[39] The article, citing the research, went on to illuminate the devastating consequences of early-in-life underemployment: "Most who start out underemployed stay underemployed . . . 74 percent of those underemployed at the five-year mark are still underemployed 10 years after their first job."[40]

Advancement

Because of the domino effect of underemployment on Black people at every stage of their careers, it is imperative that companies learn to see this as one of the key blockages in the leadership pipeline. Workplaces must make it their business to acknowledge the existence of—and expand the search for—leaders of color. Training will be required to do this effectively. We're talking about navigating internal resistances in the form of subjective bias and potential external scrutiny, as well. We must do this because, as we have seen, waiting for people to learn to do this on their own is futile, and intervention is necessary.

How does this kind of intervention happen? The first step is to put the ever-shifting performance goalposts *down*. According to Skipp Spriggs, a former senior executive vice president and chief HR officer at TIAA, leading human resources strategies for a global workforce, "[W]hen it comes to Black talent, there is an expectation that they have to have all the pieces in order to be considered."[41] Spriggs, who in his thirty-five-year career has served in senior roles at Fortune 500 companies like Boston Scientific, Home Depot, Levi Strauss, and Cigna, was speaking about the findings of a 2019 report by the consulting firm Korn Ferry on the state of Black chief financial officers, aka P&L leaders, in corporate America. Spriggs went on to say, "Organizations . . . need to consider whether Black leaders are asked to prove themselves in ways that their peers are not. If Black leaders are typically more experienced, more credentialed, or more agile than other employees before being promoted, then organizations must examine their established practices and address the challenge head-on."[42] Interestingly, this research confirms what the EPI and others have found regarding the economic impacts of underemployment, indicating that "Black professionals often get stuck in middle management, typically in functional roles,"[43] which means not only are qualified professionals getting stuck in the pipeline, but so are their wages.

While the Korn Ferry report clearly articulates some of the

blockages faced by Black professionals, I think it could have gone further. The report zeroes in on the function of sponsorship as well as other techniques to clear the way for Black professionals. While I believe those tactics should be deployed and can help, there are even more direct ways to address this issue: by focusing on promotions internally, and externally, by doing what I call "laterally hiring up."

In the event of racial imbalance—an overrepresentation of one group, usually white people, and an underrepresentation of another group, frequently Black and other people of color—in a given workplace, internal hiring can promote bias rather than mitigate it. But again, the word *intentionality* comes to mind because if you slow down and think about how bias is showing up in promotions in the workplace, that can help remove a very real blockage in what otherwise appears to be an empty hiring pipeline.

"Too often, organizations miss opportunities to unleash diverse talent at lower levels and from different functional backgrounds and experiences."[44] This insight from a report by the Global Leadership Series confirms the frustrations of current Black employees in the workplace. Many report seeing white colleagues with equal to or even, at times, lesser skills, knowledge, or education than them advance within the company while they are passed over.[45] While sponsorship is a key part of successfully navigating the workplace for everyone, Black and other people of color should also be able to advocate for and earn promotions for themselves. But this is complicated by the fact that Black people, in particular, regularly face backlash from white managers when they attempt to self-advocate. They are pegged as entitled or egotistical for the same self-advocacy seen as a positive coming from other groups.[46]

My issue with sponsorship when it comes to Black people in the workplace is that it promotes competency checking and white supremacy by tacitly acknowledging that Black people cannot advocate for themselves without risking that backlash. This then places the sponsor, usually a white person, in a paternalistic role of vouching for the competency of the Black employee and promoting the Black employee in ways the employee cannot. Dr. Jiaqing (Kathy) Sun, an assistant professor at the London School of Economics and Political Science and coauthor of a study on Black self-advocacy in the workplace, says, "When managers perceive the violation of their stereotypical 'norm' of Black employees, they feel uneasy and thus react negatively."[47]

This is where training, a chief diversity officer, and board involvement can all have an impact. HR professionals need to be trained to "issue spot" when it comes to advancing Black and other people of color in the workplace. If a manager or HR professional conducts a promotion audit and discovers that there are Black and other people of color with excellent reviews and skills but who are not actually being promoted, the HR professional must be able to identify potential causes. To follow this example further, let's say that the HR rep speaks with the employee's manager and finds out that their self-advocacy hurt them. The HR manager, through training, knows this is a race-based blockage. HR professionals must be empowered to work with managers to show them how self-advocacy should not be a promotional blockage for Black employees. HR should be able to provide opportunities for training on this specific issue and other hiring-related blockages.

This is where a chief diversity officer could back up the HR professional, by being responsible for showing the relevant data to the hiring manager and communicating with senior leadership. The goal would be to help the manager break the pattern by rooting the conversation in data and the concept. Company-wide training will similarly be important, because that conversation between manager and HR should not be the first time the manager has heard about competency checking, or about the impact of these race-based blockages. These are internal solutions to a preexisting internal problem. But what if you don't have enough Black people and other people of color in your companies to promote internally? You can use that method I mentioned earlier, what I call "laterally hiring up."

Millions of underemployed Black people are ready, willing, and able to take on more responsibility and work. If an employer is looking for directors, associate vice presidents (AVPs), and vice presidents (VPs), they must expand their sights to include managers, directors, or AVPs from competitors or closely aligned industries. By providing these lateral-up promotions, an employer can open an entirely new pipeline of diverse employees.[48]

"What about qualifications?" I've heard this question too many times to count. To answer it, I would refer you back to chapter 4 and the myth of qualifications. I would also ask you to consider this question once posed by Lauren Rollins, founding president and CEO of the Western Massachusetts Policy Center, whose personal journey to professional leadership was long and arduous because of systemic racism and relentless competency checking: "Have you considered asking yourself WHY your jobs/roles are structured the way they are? Why are the qualifications and credentials what they are? To whom are those credentials really important? Is it because it works? Or is it because that's the way it's always been?"[49]

Communication

When it comes to race-based blockages and competency checking in the workplace, there are countless things I could point out, and I have covered many of them in this book. But my goal has always been to point you to the source of these systemic ills, and to highlight its most recognizable manifestations in your working life, regardless of your job or industry. But of those many issues, one stands out to me: the profound impact of race-based miscommunication and misunderstanding. Because, like everything else related to removing race-based blockages in the workplace, addressing this particular challenge thoughtfully and deliberately can be transformative for all.

As I've said in previous chapters, despite the prevalence of personality tests and communication-style assessments in modern corporate environments, these tools often fall short. This is because they fail to consider how deeply race and other perceptual filters—gender, class, ethnicity, and linguistic background—shape interpersonal interactions. This leads to us ignoring how those things impact how messages are sent and received in society and in the workplace. As a friend of mine once said to me, "I went through all the testing to tell me I was a 'blue communicator,' and I felt frustrated, because the problems I was having with communication in the workplace came down to me being Black."

All of us would do well to explicitly call out the importance of communicating across race, gender, class, ethnicity, and language. To me, addressing these issues is where the rubber really meets the road. From what I have seen, race-based miscommunication and misunderstanding are key factors in poor performance reviews, disciplinary actions, and hostile work culture complaints. Without understanding how identities inform our interpersonal interactions, you are inevitably setting people who are not a part of the dominant culture and its communication style up for failure.

Let's say a company hosts a "team building" event for its entire staff. Participants are encouraged to share an anecdote from their childhood. While this seems like a simple request, this type of activity can be extremely stressful for Black and other people of color who may be concerned about revealing information that would inadvertently confirm a negative stereotype. According to an article in the *Harvard Business Review* on diversity and authenticity in the workplace, researchers interviewed over three hundred young African American, Hispanic, and other racial-minority professionals seeking admittance to an elite MBA program, they found that those surveyed were uncomfortable opening up to white coworkers.[50] The reason, in short, was fear: "fear that personal information highlighting their race (termed *status-confirming disclosure*) might reinforce the stereotypes that can undermine performance reviews and prevent progress toward leadership roles."[51] As one Black executive in the study said, "I don't feel safe sharing information that might later be used against me."

Black and other people of color know that almost everything they say is constantly being seen and heard through perceptual filters such as race-based stereotyping and competency checking. If I say, "I was such a bad speller as a child, but then I won a spelling bee in the eighth grade," my concern would be that all the other person heard was "She can't spell." Any spelling or other mistakes made after that would confirm that I am incompetent, and because of perceptual filters, this confirmation would be attributed to my race. Of course, there are others for whom these types of "shares" are uncomfortable, such as people who endured childhood trauma or people who struggled financially or with their sexuality or their gender identity. All these people would be forced to either lie or appear standoffish and be perceived as "not team players." This then leads to situations like one described in the article, in which a Black man, Marcus, who worked in international banking, found his career stalling despite high performance. As Marcus's manager told him, "You are really good at your job, but the problem is that the partners feel they don't really know you."

While I think the researchers hit the nail on the head when it comes to the concerns Black and other people of color have with self-disclosure in the workplace, I was troubled and saddened by where they placed the blame. "Many other minority members fail to understand that their career mobility can be affected by their colleagues' feelings of familiarity or closeness with them. And even for those who do understand this, building workplace relationships across racial boundaries can be difficult."[52] First of all, everyone understands this, but it is not safe or reasonable to expect everyone to *do* it. Second, whiteness is given a pass, and the burden and the onus is placed on Black and other people of color to "overcome" their inability to share, not on the concept of whiteness and how it's seen as a flattened culture with no distinct style of communication, just a "normal" one.

The thing is, whiteness *does* have distinct styles of communication, differences that can be as perplexing as a foreign language for nonnative speakers of whiteness. Kusum Crimmel, head of the Dissecting Whiteness project, explains, "The different voice tones used for various situations, the expression and understanding of body language, the word choice and sentence structure in oral communication, and the references . . . All of this is culture-specific, but because white people don't see ourselves as having a distinct culture, white 'space' is seen as a common territory in which everyone feels comfortable and safe."[53] Compare that to the *Harvard Business Review* article, which put the onus of miscommunication on Black and other people of color in the workplace, there was no real discussion about how white people communicate and their feelings and assumptions around sharing personal information.

What white people fail to understand is that they have a

culturally specific way of communicating, and they are impacted by race-based perceptual filters because of that culture. It is widely acknowledged that cross-cultural communication as a field of study began in the 1940s to help foreign service officers, white and male, understand "foreign" cultures.[54] In the last twenty-plus years, scholars have started to unravel how whiteness has shaped communication practices and assumptions and how it acts as a key driver in the reproduction of racial power structures. For employers who invest millions in personality typing and communication style identification, I argue it would be far better to spend some money on what really matters in your workplace: understanding and identifying the ways employees are miscommunicating across real and existing differences and leading by example so they can learn how they too can do better.

As a consultant, I have the privilege of getting to poke my head into multiple organizations on a short-term basis. In this role, I have seen firsthand the many ways miscommunication is truly "the man behind the curtain," a terrible workplace Oz that we must acknowledge and dispel. The issue is so widespread that I decided to develop two e-learning modules: Communicating Across Difference, part one and part two. In part one, I focus on the difference between stereotyping and cultural competency, and I also go through the six patterns of cultural difference, cross-generational and racial communication, and how authority, confidence, and gender collide. In part two, I address the complexities of today's diverse workforce. I created these modules to fill a need: We currently have the most diverse professional workforce at any time in our national history. That diversity includes age, race, gender, sexual orientation, language diversity, and more. But we seem to forget that for most of our history, we were segregated in the workplace by class, income, gender, and race. This means we must invest in learning to understand what it means to communicate across *these* differences.

I want to pause here to acknowledge that when I talk about communicating across difference as it relates to race, people are rightfully concerned about stereotyping. I believe the goal is to learn from general understandings that provide context and build cultural competency, but that doesn't mean we use those general understandings to stereotype, "write off," or otherwise oversimplify our ideas about another person. The difference can be explained as that between reading one book and saying you know everything about a topic and having a library of information that you have cultivated over time.

Here's an example: I once worked with a manager who was having difficulty training an employee. The manager said that every time they went over certain steps with the trainee, the trainee would respond, "I know," "I know," "I know." Curious, I asked the manager a few simple questions about their interaction with the trainee—Are they following the steps? Are they focused on you? Are they looking in another direction? What is their body language saying? Soon it became clear that the trainee was indeed listening and focusing, but the manager felt disrespected hearing "I know" in response to everything they said. The manager mentioned to me that the trainee was Hispanic/Latinx. I asked the manager if they knew if English was the trainee's first language. The answer was that it was not—it was Spanish. In American English, when somebody says, "I know," we assume they're giving us sass, right? We hear, "Uh, I *know*, so stop talking to me," or "**I know**, and I don't need you to tell me." That's the subtext we hear, but not what's being said. As someone who has taken courses in Spanish and lived in Mexico for a period, I know that when speaking in another language, you sometimes use words incorrectly, or, in other cases, you use them correctly, but they don't land in the same way they do in your native tongue.

What I didn't say to the manager was, "Oh, this person is a Spanish speaker; all people who speak Spanish mean *this* when they say *that*." Because *that* would have been stereotyping. What I did tell them was how I know that when speaking another language, we sometimes misuse words. I told the manager that everything else contextually seemed to indicate the person was engaged in learning, so I suggested that they ask a few questions when going through the steps with the trainee. "I notice after each step you say, 'I know.' Have you already learned this, or are you simply acknowledging each step as I am explaining it?" This miscommunication could have cost the trainee their job, all because the manager was so frustrated and felt that they weren't being heard, simply because of the phrase "I know." Everything else about the interaction was being filtered through those two words. Now, it could be that the trainee wasn't interested or wasn't good at their job, but the only way we can get to the truth of the matter is by removing perceptual filters and the blockage that miscommunication, especially language-based, presents.

What can we do to identify and change this? Well, like with any major issue, we must first acknowledge that it is happening. I use this wonderful video on miscommunication during my training sessions, a TED-Ed YouTube channel presentation by Katherine Hampsten, PhD, who focuses on the power of intentional listening and understanding. There are several key takeaways from her talk that I am always eager to share with others. The first is "Seek to understand as you seek to be understood."[55] This principle calls for a more deliberate and thoughtful approach to communication, emphasizing the necessity of listening over merely waiting for an opportunity to respond. I often tell clients that if they start speaking the second the last syllable has left the previous speaker's mouth, they likely weren't listening at all and especially not to the last bit of information, which is often the most important. This means you are responding to what you believe was said, not what was actually said.

In her talk, Dr. Hampsten explains how we can think of communication between people as a game of catch with a lump of clay. "As each person touches it, they shape it to fit their own unique perceptions based on any number of variables, like knowledge or past experience, age, race, gender, ethnicity, religion, or family background. Simultaneously, every person interprets the message they receive based on their relationship with the other person and their unique understanding of the semantics and connotations of the exact words being used."[56] This means that when we are passing the proverbial clay of communication back and forth with another person, we must remember that we are interpreting their message, and as Dr. Hampsten says, "Our perceptual filters continually shift meanings and interpretations."[57]

One of those perceptual filters impacting Black people at work has to do with their perceived "tone." In her book, *So You Want to Talk About Race*, Ijeoma Oluo defines tone policing as "someone (usually a privileged person) in a conversation about oppression [shifting] the conversation from the oppression being discussed to the way it is being discussed. Tone policing prioritizes the comfort of the privileged person in the situation over the oppression of the disadvantaged person."[58] I would expand on this to say that Black people, no matter what we are discussing, are tone-policed by a white society that feels entitled to police how we communicate. So, it doesn't have to be a conversation about oppression; it could be a conversation about sales data, but perceptual filters around the historical trope of being uppity can lead to a Black person being seen as egotistical or entitled when they try to promote their successful numbers. Consequently, a Black person has to find a way to speak up for themselves and their accomplishments while simultaneously devaluing their work with self-deprecating humor or understatement so as not to trigger this particular type of tone policing and competency checking. A Black man who is a manager or supervisor must think very carefully about being agitated, as all normal human beings can become, lest the agitation in his tone be interpreted as threatening or frightening. This kind of miscommunication isn't a result of what Black people are doing; it's a result of the perceptual filters that kick in the moment Black people speak. As I've said in other chapters, Black women deal with this ad nauseam. When we speak, we are perceived as being too direct and too decisive, which then is interpreted as angry, rude, or threatening. Speaking from experience, it is emotionally, physically, and psychologically exhausting work to have to do on top of a nine-to-five. The existence of tone policing as a perceptual filter needs to be acknowledged by and corrected by white people in the workplace if it is to be changed going forward. These perceptual filters are rooted in race-based miscommunication and create a particularly stubborn blockage in the career-mobility pipeline, often leading to alienation, unnecessary discipline, and poor performance reviews.

The solution for these issues around communication is fairly simple, comprising regular and consistent training on communicating across differences, active listening, leaning into "System Two" or slowed-down thinking, and being aware of and correcting for perceptual filters. Here's a brief breakdown of each solution:

ACTIVE LISTENING: By intentionally focusing on the speaker's verbal and nonverbal cues, employees can bridge communication gaps that often arise in diverse settings.

EMPATHY: Seeing things from another person's perspective and acknowledging their experiences is crucial. This approach helps understand diverse viewpoints and reduces biases hindering collaboration and trust among team members.

SLOWING DOWN: In fast-paced work environments, it's easy to miss the nuances of communication that are essential for mutual understanding. Taking the time to clarify messages, ask questions, and then ask more questions can bring understanding and prevent many workplace conflicts. Dr. Hampsten, in her TED-Ed talk, says a way to get at this is to say, "This is how I see the problem; how do you see it?"[59]

AWARENESS OF PERCEPTUAL FILTERS: Recognizing how one's own background, culture, and life experiences shape one's communication style is vital. For white people, this will mean recognizing that there are cultural and normative ways in which they communicate that dominate and actively police the workplace around them. This awareness helps individuals identify potential biases and adjust their interactions accordingly, which is key to fostering respectful and productive workplace relationships.

Evan Apfelbaum, an associate professor of management and organizations at Boston University, says that diversity in the workplace "makes us work harder." Apfelbaum states that while communicating in a diverse environment has its challenges, "Diverse groups tend to engage in more rigorous decision-making, more consideration of different perspectives, which lead them to more objective decisions; they're less likely to make certain mistakes."[60] Mistakes like one Dr. Hampsten references in her talk that saw a multimillion-dollar probe crash into the surface of Mars because of miscommunication.[61] Rather, with better communication, a team can, like the consumer products company I worked with, come up with a better tool that serves multiple types of users across ethnicities and expands your product's potential market share. That is the power we can unleash if we commit ourselves to removing race-based blockages in the workplace.

The Road Ahead

After reading about the challenges related to cross-cultural communication—indeed, after reading this book, some may say, "This is too complicated a problem to try to solve." But the truth of the matter is that diversity isn't hard. The blockages of race-based assumptions, competency checking, and perceptual filters—those are hard. They are jammed into every nook and cranny of American life, society, culture, and work, preventing what should be a natural and robust flow of diverse people who all want the same shot at bringing their skills, talent, leadership, and boundless creativity to the American Experiment.

Companies that excel in solving these problems see significant benefits, such as employees feeling more connected, productive, and engaged while seeing opportunities for professional growth. This can lead to lower turnover and a more effective workforce. Many companies already know this because they're deploying these skills at home and abroad. As I mentioned earlier in this book, workplace DEI in the United States mirrors the dynamics of international corporate business management, particularly in fostering inclusive environments. Both functions demand a sophisticated grasp of cultural differences and the development of strategies that accommodate diverse perspectives and practices. In both DEI and international business management, the key to success is the creation of policies and practices that not only acknowledge but embrace cultural differences. This includes promoting open communication that respects all voices, whether addressing identities across race, gender, and sexual orientation in DEI or navigating various cultural norms in global business dealings. Tailoring strategies to specific groups or markets ensures that practices are relevant and effective, fostering an atmosphere where all participants feel valued and part of the organization's mission. If companies can see the domestic workplace as a microcosm of the global market, then we can understand that the skills developed from managing a multicultural workforce are invaluable for global operations. This becomes more necessary as our world becomes more connected virtually and in real life.

I know that some who work in this field are insulted by the pure business case for diversity, equity, and inclusion, and I know some are flummoxed by the purely moral case for it in the workplace. I stand at the intersection. As a society, we have a moral duty to cut away the historical vestiges of anti-Black bias and the myriad ways it limits the full participation of Black Americans in society and the workplace, full stop. I am a human being first and a consultant second. I know people rarely do things just because it's the right thing. As human nature has it, people frequently want to know what's in it for them. This includes things we consider moral, such as having children or donating to a charity (tax write-offs, anyone?). But I can acknowledge the vast spectrum of human nature while also stating unequivocally that the United States cannot continue to be a vibrant leading economy if we insist on devaluing the participation of entire groups in the workplace and withholding widespread generational wealth, that could help this country thrive long into the future.

I'll let you in on a secret: I love this country. My love is driven by a desire to see it progress, improve, and eventually become the best version of itself. The saying goes, "Love means never having to say you're sorry," but in fact, love means just the opposite. I think love really means embracing imperfections, recognizing flaws, and striving for improvement. Not perfection, but balance. This kind of love is truer, deeper, and more enduring. That being said, I can't deny how challenging it is to work in my field and not concede to those who claim to love this country more because they literally wrap themselves and their products in the American flag. Some have said that if you criticize the country in any way they don't agree with, that means you hate it and should leave it.[62] First, I do not hate this country. Second, this is my home, the home of my parents, grandparents, great-grandparents, and great-great-grandparents. They fought for, bled for, and died for my right to be here. If I didn't love this country, I wouldn't continue working so hard toward its transformation—tearing down its ugliness and rebuilding it into something greater, meaningful, beautiful, and true. I wrote this book because I love this country and its people deeply, and I felt compelled to address the pain and frustration that Black Americans, in particular, are experiencing in the workplace, often in silence. Yes, "the arc of the moral universe is long, but it bends toward justice," but it cannot bend on its own; it is the duty of each and every one of us to pull on that arc as hard as we can together to hasten its arrival at justice—for all. I know we can do it!

EPILOGUE

TRADITIONAL BOOK PUBLISHING, as I've learned, is a slow business. Which means I'm writing this in my present; you're reading it in yours. As this book enters its final edits in the waning days of September 2024, President Joe Biden has withdrawn from the presidential race, and Vice President Kamala Harris has become the Democratic nominee. These changes are as historic as they are head-spinning. When it became clear that Harris would be the first mixed-race woman ever nominated for the presidency (her father is Jamaican; her mother was South Asian), the competency checking began immediately. Allegations of her being a "DEI hire," "unintelligent," and, tellingly, "unqualified" ricocheted across the media landscape.[1]

When GOP congressman Tim Burchett questioned the qualifications of Vice President Harris, stating, "Biden said he's gonna hire a Black female for vice president . . . When you go down that route, you take mediocrity . . ."[2] he wasn't just making a political statement. He was perpetuating a deeply entrenched narrative: that Blackness itself is disqualifying.

We know this because when we consider Burchett's own credentials—he holds a bachelor of science degree and tenure as a small-town mayor—and compare them to Vice President Harris's, a woman with a juris doctor who has served as a district attorney, California attorney general, US senator, and vice president, we are left scratching our heads at how he could make such a misinformed statement. By any objective measure,

Harris's qualifications dwarf Burchett's. Yet, his comments reflect exactly what this book is about: the white need to competency-check Black people and other people of color to remind them of their place in America's racial hierarchy.

Harris's presidential run also surfaced the long shadow of the "one-drop rule," which has seen both white, Black, and other people of color questioning her Black identity. Harris was born into a Jim Crow America where white supremacy, not Black people, set the rules for racial identity. Her mother's understanding of this reality led her to ensure that both her daughters were consciously raised within the Black community, fostering their identities as the Black women the world would see them as. The fact that this was the only pragmatic choice is lost on many.

Much like how President Barack Obama's eight years in office could not and did not rectify hundreds of years of anti-Black racism in the United States, Harris's win would not fundamentally change the circumstances that Black and other people of color encounter in the workplace. In fact, many would say that the ongoing backlash to President Obama intensified the resistance to racial inclusion and diversity efforts. Conversely, his election also created a false perception of racial advancement, complicating diversity initiatives in the workplace.

Critics who claim that DEI implies a lack of qualifications for Harris are perpetuating this narrative in their own workplaces, forcing Black and other people of color to navigate a gauntlet of skepticism and continually prove their qualifications in an endless marathon. Former first lady Michelle Obama spoke of this marathon during her speech at the Democratic National Convention: "[Harris] understands that most of us will never be afforded the grace of failing forward . . . [W]e will never benefit from the affirmative action of generational wealth."[3] This backlash isn't new. It is the persistent echo of every effort through-out American history to maintain white supremacy at the cost of nonwhite progress.

About fifteen years ago, I had the profound honor of inter-viewing civil rights icon Harry Belafonte, who shared reflections from his conversations with Dr. Martin Luther King Jr. During a pivotal moment in the civil rights movement, Dr. King ex-pressed a disturbing revelation to his friend: "I've come upon something that disturbs me deeply. . . . We have fought hard and long for integration, as I believe we should have, and I know we will win. But I've come to believe we're integrating into a burning house."

That house still burns today—flames fanned by an "Age of Anger."[4] This era of emotional and psychological tumult is fer-tile ground for populist and identity politics, where frustrations and loneliness not only thrive but can quickly become weapon-ized.[5] Allowing this to continue risks perpetuating divides that undermine the very fabric of our nation.

As we look forward, we must draw on our collective ca-pacity for empathy and understanding to challenge the narra-tives that have long divided us. We must commit to a vision of the workplace and our society where diversity is not seen as a problem to be solved but as a boundless resource waiting to be harnessed. Embracing this vision requires acknowledging the entrenched barriers that people of color face, not only in em-ployment but in all areas of economic and social engagement. Only through collective action can we dismantle these barriers and create a more equitable society.

Here is where I leave you. I hope this book is received as it was intended: as an invitation. A call to action, not just to ac-knowledge the profound challenges we all face, but to actively and even enthusiastically engage in the hard work of dismantling them. It is a plea to embrace our shared humanity's complexity and recommit ourselves and our government to equity, liberty, and justice for all. Our task is to ensure that our workplaces reflect the 350 million people who make up our society and, in doing so, move closer to fulfilling the promise of democracy, our greatest challenge and our most enduring hope.

ACKNOWLEDGMENTS

A Tapestry of Gratitude

This book wouldn't exist without the threads woven by the remarkable people in my life. Let me take you on a journey through time, introducing you to those who shaped me.

Rooted in the Past: A Foundation of Love and Knowledge

My story begins with my mother, Leola Staples Dunn. Her unwavering love and steadfast thirst for knowledge were the bedrock of my upbringing. She instilled in me a curiosity for the world and the courage to question authority. My father, Harry Dunn Jr., also played a pivotal role. He showed me the power of fighting injustice, a fire that burns brightly within me even today.

My family, like many others, was far from perfect. Yet my parents, a united front, instilled in me a sense of self-worth and belonging, and though they are no longer here in their earthly forms, they have left with me the knowledge that I belong in any room that I am in. My sister, Jeanette Dunn, and her children, my niece and nephews, taught me the meaning of "the village." Anthony, Aaron, Andrew, Austin, and Avonda—you are loved. Through shared experiences of sorrow, pain, and laughter, you have gifted me the immeasurable joy of family.

My grandparents, Lester and Velma Staples, showered me with unconditional love. Their home was a haven for exploring the world and Black experiences beyond textbooks. They supported my love of learning, which continues to this day. In fact, it was in their small home that I heard my aunts and uncles debate the day's topics. I soaked in their relentless teasing, disagreements, laughter, and deep knowledge of our Black American history. Without these conversations, I would not be who I am today, so thank you to my uncles, Daniel, Lester Jr., DeBoris, Eddie, Edward, Joseph, and Rasheed. My aunts, Catherine, Vernice, Celestine, Thelma, and Velma. I have too many cousins to list by name, but I must acknowledge Candice—my grandparents would be over the moon if they were alive to see me writing a book and citing their beloved "candy baby" in it. As my grandfather would have said, "Great DAY!"

The Staples family, my root system, is a source of immense strength. Their pride in their heritage and the resilience passed down through generations is a constant source of inspiration. I pay homage to my ancestors, my great-great-grandparents William and Abby Staples, who not only survived the brutal institution of slavery but thrived with an unyielding spirit that continues to propel me forward. My grandmother's family, the Downeys, my paternal grandparents, the Dunns, and the Easons, our story reveals the rich tapestry of American identity. Their Irish, Scottish, Nigerian, and Scandinavian and many other roots contribute to the beautiful tapestry of who I am.

Family and Friends: The Present Support System

Fast-forward to the present, in which I am surrounded by a phenomenal support system. Alicia, my longest friend and sister-in-arms has been a constant source of encouragement, standing by my side in our shared fight for justice. David, my second-oldest friend, has listened to and supported me through all of life's ups and downs.

When it comes to my friends, I have been blessed. To quote Proverbs 27:17: "As Iron sharpens iron, so one person sharpens another." This is true of Traci and Nina, who believed in my potential to be an entrepreneur long before I did. Their faith in me paved the path that led to this book. Carolyn, Adrienne, and Pleschette round out the sisterhood I am blessed to be a part of. Each one of you is a pillar upon which I stand and a soft place to land when I fall.

The Team Behind the Book

Really, none of this would have happened without David Ellis, a bestselling crime fiction author and my law school classmate. David shared his access and connected me with my agent, Susanna Einstein. Susanna, I am deeply grateful for your belief in my book proposal and for guiding me through this journey. My incredible team at HarperCollins: Hollis Heimbouch, publisher; Rachel Kambury, editor; Olivia McGiff, cover designer; Jocelyn Larnick, production supervisor; Alicia Gencarelli, production editor; Jessica Gilo, marketing; and Thomas Pitoniak, copyeditor. Rachel and Hollis deserve a standing ovation. Your editorial expertise, unwavering support, and belief in my story have helped me grow as a writer. To the entire HarperCollins team that worked on this book, I can't thank you enough. I also must thank all the folks at Fortier Public Relations for believing in me and my work.

Shout-out to Brea Baker, who describes herself as "a freedom fighter and writer (in that order)." Brea helped me early on; I called her my training wheels because she helped me figure out what my idea even was and what a book proposal should look like! Durga, a big thank-you for helping me through a bit of writer's block and reminding me to "write how I write, not how others write." Last but certainly not least is Michele G. Michele, you have been more than an administrative professional; you have been the foundation of my business, and your professionalism and skill allow me to fly, so I thank you from the bottom of my heart for your heart work and for sticking with ITBOM LLC all these years.

Looking to the Future: A Legacy of Hope

This book is also dedicated to my niece, Sloane. As I write this, I dream of a future where she can express herself fully and pursue her dreams without limitations.

To all those yet unknown, I acknowledge the unseen shoulders that I stand upon, and I ask you to do the same and stand on the foundation I have laid.

A Heartfelt Thank-You

To Marquette University and the Jesuits who taught me and whom I challenged. To Northwestern University Pritzker School of Law and all my classmates. I want to thank Milwaukee, Wisconsin, the place that gave me my work ethic and common-sense approach, and Portland, Oregon, for being exactly what I needed. To anyone unintentionally omitted, please accept my sincerest apologies.

Finally, thank you to all who have poured into my life, both directly and indirectly. Your contributions, big and small, are deeply appreciated.

NOTES

Introduction

1. "The State of Black Women in Corporate America," n.d., Lean In, https://leanin.org/research/state-of-black-women-in-corporate -america.

2. "Author Minda Harts: How Women of Color Can Get a Seat at the Table," MSNBC, 2020, https://www.msnbc.com/know-your -value/why-50-multicultural-women-are-thinking-about-leaving -their-jobs-n1234734.

3. Lisa Kailai Han, "Unemployment Rate Among Black Americans Jumped in March, Contrasting Overall Trends," CNBC, April 5, 2024, https://www-cnbc-com.cdn.ampproject.org/c/s/www.cnbc .com/amp/2024/04/05/unemployment-rate-among-black -americans-jumps-in-march.html.

4. Chimamanda Ngozi Adichie, "The Danger of a Single Story," n.d., https://www.ted.com/talks/chimamanda_ngozi_adichie_the _danger_of_a_single_story/transcript.

5. Kayla Yup, "Black Women Excluded from Critical Studies Due to 'Weathering,'" Yale School of Medicine, December 1, 2022, https://medicine.yale.edu/news-article/black-women-excluded -from-critical-studies-due-to-weathering/.

6. Jp Julien, Duwain Pinder, Shelley Stewart III, Dominic Williams, and Nina Yancy, "The State of Black Residents: The Relevance of Place to Racial Equity and Outcomes," McKinsey & Company, 2024, https://www.mckinsey.com/bem/our-insights/the-state -of-black-residents-the-relevance-of-place-to-racial-equity-and -outcomes.

7. Nakeia Daniels, interviewed by Shari Dunn, 2023.

8. "Labor Day 2019: Black Workers Endure Persistent Racial Disparities in Employment Outcomes," n.d., Economic Policy Institute, https:// www.epi.org/publication/labor-day-2019-racial-disparities-in -employment/.

9. Claire Cain Miller and Josh Katz, "What Researchers Discovered

When They Sent 80,000 Fake Résumés to U.S. Jobs," *New York Times*, April 8, 2024, https://www.nytimes.com/2024/04/08/upshot/employment-discrimination-fake-resumes.html.

10. Miller and Katz.

11. Miller and Katz.

12. "FedEx Express Race Discrimination," Lieff Cabraser, n.d., https://www.lieffcabraser.com/employment/fedex-express/; Jonathan Stempel, "Appeals Court Overturns $366 Mln FedEx Race Bias Verdict," Reuters, February 2, 2024, https://www.reuters.com/legal/fedex-wins-overturning-366-mln-race-bias-verdict-2024-02-01/.

13. Jhacova Williams and Valerie Wilson. n.d. "Labor Day 2019 | Black Workers Endure Persistent Racial Disparities in Employment Outcomes," Economic Policy Institute, https://www.epi.org/publication/labor-day-2019-racial-disparities-in-employment/.

14. Adam Levitt, interviewed by Shari Dunn, July 20, 2023.

15. Jessica DiNapoli, Imani Moise, and Ross Kerber, "Exclusive: Wells Fargo CEO Ruffles Feathers with Comments About Diverse Talent," Reuters, September 22, 2020, https://www.reuters.com/article/idUSKCN26D2IT/.

16. "Finance & Insurance," n.d., Data USA, https://datausa.io/profile/naics/finance-insurance; "Finance Professional Demographics and Statistics [2024]: Number of Finance Professionals in the US," Zippia, April 5, 2024, https://www.zippia.com/finance-professional-jobs/demographics/.

17. Dana Wilkie, "White Men Disproportionately Win Job Referrals, Get Higher Pay Out of Them," SHRM, December 21, 2023, https://www.shrm.org/topics-tools/news/employee-relations/white-men-disproportionately-win-job-referrals-get-higher-pay.

18. Bill Streeter, "7 Things You Don't Know About Wells Fargo CEO Charlie Scharf," The Financial Brand, May 18, 2022, https://thefinancialbrand.com/news/bank-culture/wells-fargo-ceo-scharf-visa-dimon-89076/.

19. R. Frankham, J. D. Ballou, and D. A. Briscoe, *Introduction to Conservation Genetics* (Cambridge: Cambridge University Press, 2002), https://www.scirp.org/reference/referencespapers?referenceid=1139650.

20. José C. Clemente, Luke K. Ursell, Laura Wegener Parfrey, and Rob Knight, "The Impact of the Gut Microbiota on Human Health: An Integrative View," *Cell* 148 (6): 1258–70, https://doi.org/10.1016/j.cell.2012.01.035.

21. "Biodiversity and Health," World Health Organization, June 3, 2015,

https://www.who.int/news-room/fact-sheets/detail/biodiversity
-and-health.

Chapter 1: Competency Checking Defined

1. John Daves, interviewed by Shari Dunn, June 20, 2023.
2. Daves interview.
3. Sadie Bell, "T-Pain Says He's Written Country Songs for Other Artists but 'Stopped Taking Credit' After Facing 'Racism,'" *People*, February 7, 2024, https://people.com/tpain-written-country -songs-stopped-taking-credit-racism-8567869.
4. Lou Blouin, "Confronting Special Education's Race Problem," University of Michigan–Dearborn News, February 7, 2022, umdearborn.edu/news/confronting-special-educations-race -problem.
5. Blouin.
6. Claude M. Steele and Joshua Aronson, "Stereotype Threat and the Intellectual Test Performance of African Americans," *Journal of Personality and Social Psychology* 69, no. 5 (1995): 797–811, https://doi.org/10.1037/0022-3514.69.5.797.
7. "Stereotype Threat," Rutgers School of Arts and Sciences, accessed November 1, 2023, https://philosophy.rutgers.edu/climate-v2 /climate-issues-in-academic-philosophy/stereotype-threat.
8. Leon F. Litwack, "The White Man's Fear of the Educated Negro: How the Negro Was Fitted for His Natural and Logical Calling," *Journal of Blacks in Higher Education*, no. 20 (1998): 100–108, https://doi.org/10.2307/2999249.
9. Wikipedia, "List of Jim Crow Law Examples by State," last updated February 29, 2024, 15:31, https://en.wikipedia.org/wiki /List_of_Jim_Crow_law_examples_by_state.
10. Stetson Kennedy, *Jim Crow Guide to the U.S.A.: The Laws, Customs, and Etiquette Governing the Conduct of Nonwhites and Other Minorities as Second-Class Citizens* (Tuscaloosa: University of Alabama Press, 1990).
11. Ronald L. F. Davis, "Racial Etiquette: The Racial Customs and Rules of Racial Behavior in Jim Crow America," California State University, Northridge, https://www.oregonsd.org /site/handlers/filedownload.ashx?moduleinstanceid=305 &dataid=1457&FileName=racial%20etiquette%20handout.pdf, accessed February 17, 2024.
12. Law Journal Editorial Board, "Question on Ketanji Brown Jackson's LSAT Score Speaks for Itself," *New Jersey Law Journal*, April 1, 2022, https://www.law.com/njlawjournal/2022/04/01 /question-on-ketanji-brown-jacksons-lsat-score-speaks-for-itself/.

13. Law Journal Editorial Board.

14. Nicole E. Price, Carolyn D. Richmond, and Glenn S. Grindlinger, "Equinox Jury Verdict Serves as Cautionary Tale for Employers," Fox Rothschild, June 9, 2023, https://shorturl.at/fkvxG.

15. Adedayo Akala, "Cost of Racism: U.S. Economy Lost $16 Trillion Because of Discrimination, Bank Says," NPR, September 23, 2020, www.npr.org/sections/live-updates-protests-for-racial-justice /2020/09/23/916022472/cost-of-racism-u-s-economy-lost-16 -trillion-because-of-discrimination-bank-says.

16. Alicia Moore, interviewed by Shari Dunn, October 15, 2023.

17. Tiffany Trotter, "Recruiters Play a Key Role in Diversity and Inclusion in the Workplace," *Black Enterprise*, July 8, 2020, www .blackenterprise.com/how-recruiters-play-a-key-role-in-diversity -and-inclusion-in-the-workplace/#:~:text=%E2%80%9CWhile%20 ultimately%20the%20final%20hiring,diverse%2C%E2%80%9D%20 said%20Kimberly%20B.

18. Meredith Metsker, "The Top Alternative Careers for Journalists," Lightcast.io, January 28, 2019, https://lightcast.io/resources /blog/the-top-alternative-careers-for-journalists.

19. Matthew Weeks, Kelly P. Weeks, and Emily C. Watkins, "Using the Shifting Standards Model of Stereotype-based Judgments to Examine the Impact of Race on Compensation Decisions," *Journal of Applied Social Psychology* 51, no. 3, https://doi.org/10.1111 /jasp.12724.

20. Trevor Bates, interviewed by Shari Dunn, July 31, 2023.

21. Debra Cassens Weiss, "Partners in Study Gave Legal Memo a Lower Rating When Told Author Wasn't White," *ABA Journal*, April 21, 2014, https://www.abajournal.com/news/article /hypothetical_legal_memo_demonstrates_unconscious_biases.

22. Weiss.

23. Calvin Schermerhorn, "Why the Racial Wealth Gap Persists, More than 150 Years After Emancipation," *Washington Post*, June 19, 2019, https://www.washingtonpost.com/outlook/2019/06/19 /why-racial-wealth-gap-persists-more-than-years-after -emancipation/.

24. Schermerhorn.

25. Justin Elliott et al., "A 'Delicate Matter': Clarence Thomas' Private Complaints About Money Sparked Fears He Would Resign," ProPublica, December 18, 2023, https://www.propublica.org/article /clarence-thomas-money-complaints-sparked-resignation-fears -scotus; Alena Botros, "Clarence Thomas' Billionaire Benefactor Inherited a Commercial Real Estate Empire—His Father Was Once the Largest Landlord in the US," *Fortune*, April 14, 2023,

https://fortune.com/2023/04/14/who-is-harlan-crow
-commercial-real-estate-billionaire-clarence-thomas/.

26. Henry Louis Gates Jr., "Who Really Invented the 'Talented Tenth'?" PBS, accessed Oct. 24, 2023, www.pbs.org/wnet /african-americans-many-rivers-to-cross/history/who-really -invented-the-talented-tenth/.

27. Nicholas Kristof, "Pull Yourself Up by Bootstraps? Go Ahead, Try It," *New York Times*, February 19, 2020, https://www.nytimes .com/2020/02/19/opinion/economic-mobility.html.

28. Christopher D. DeSante, "Working Twice as Hard to Get Half as Far: Race, Work Ethic, and America's Deserving Poor," *American Journal of Political Science* 57, no. 2 (April 2013): 342–56.

29. *Black-ish*, season 7, episode 9, "First Trap," directed by Chris Robinson, written by Melanie Boysaw, aired February 9, 2021, on ABC.

30. Kellie Hwang, "'Are You Really a Doctor?': Physician on Indianapolis Flight Says She Was Racially Profiled," *Indianapolis Star*, November 2, 2018, https://www.indystar.com/story /news/2018/11/02/dr-fatima-cody-stanford-tamika-cross -delta-airlines-racial-profiling/1856290002/.

31. Joanne Finnegan, "Dear Delta: This Is What 'Actual Physicians' Look Like," Fierce Healthcare, October 17, 2016, https://www .fiercehealthcare.com/practices/young-black-doctor-says -flight-attendant-assumed-she-was-not-actual-physician.

Chapter 2: The Roots of Competency Checking

1. Samuel A. Cartwright, "Diseases and Peculiarities of the Negro Race," *DeBow's Review* 11, no. 1 (1851).

2. Linda Villarosa, "How False Beliefs in Physical Racial Difference Still Live in Medicine Today," *New York Times*, August 14, 2019, www.nytimes.com/interactive/2019/08/14/magazine/racial -differences-doctors.html.

3. Kelly M. Hoffman et al., "Racial Bias in Pain Assessment and Treatment Recommendations, and False Beliefs About Biological Differences Between Blacks and Whites," *Proceedings of the National Academy of Sciences of the United States of America* 113, no. 16 (April 19, 2016): 4296–4301, doi: 10.1073 /pnas.1516047113.

4. Ta-Nehisi Coates, *Between the World and Me* (New York: Spiegel & Grau, 2015).

5. Robert P. Baird, "The Invention of Whiteness: The Long History of a Dangerous Idea," *Guardian*, April 20, 2021.

6. Facing History and Ourselves, "Inventing Black and White,"

accessed October 30, 2023, www.facinghistory.org/resource
-library/inventing-black-white.

7. Facing History and Ourselves.

8. Theodore W. Allen, *The Invention of the White Race: The Origin
    of Racial Oppression*, vol. 1 (London: Verso, 1994); Michelle Al-
    exander, *The New Jim Crow: Mass Incarceration in the Age of
    Colorblindness* (New York: New Press, 2013), 24.

9. Taunya Lovell Banks, "Dangerous Woman: Elizabeth Key's Free-
    dom Suit—Subjecthood and Racialized Identity in Seventeenth
    Century Colonial Virginia," *Akron Law Review* 41, no. 3, article
    5 (2008).

10. Facing History and Ourselves, *Race and Membership in American
    History: The Eugenics Movement* (Brookline, MA: Facing History
    and Ourselves, 2002).

11. Frances Frank Marcus, "Louisiana Repeals Black Blood Law,"
    New York Times, July 6, 1983.

12. Ira Berlin, interview, *Race: The Power of an Illusion*, PBS, ac-
    cessed February 27, 2024, https://www.pbs.org/race/000
    _About/002_04-background-02-08.htm.

13. "A Quote by George Carlin," n.d., https://www.goodreads.com
    /quotes/17908-that-s-why-they-call-it-the-american-dream
    -because-you.

14. Robin D. G. Kelley, interview, *Race: The Power of an Illusion*, PBS,
    https://www.pbs.org/race/000_About/002_04-background-02-05
    .htm.

15. Howard Zinn, *A People's History of the United States* (New York:
    Harper Perennial, 1995), 1319.

16. Edmund Morgan, *American Slavery, American Freedom* (New
    York: Norton, 1975), 328.

17. John Blake, "Did Black Lives Matter to Abraham Lincoln? It's
    Complicated," CNN, March 14, 2021.

18. Erin Blakemore, "Jim Crow Laws Created 'Slavery by Another
    Name,'" *National Geographic*, February 5, 2020, https://www
    .nationalgeographic.com/history/article/jim-crow-laws-created
    -slavery-another-name; Douglas A. Blackmon, *Slavery by Another
    Name: The Re-Enslavement of Black Americans from the Civil War
    to World War II* (New York: Doubleday, 2008).

19. Olivia B. Waxman, "The Legacy of the Reconstruction Era's Black
    Political Leaders," *Time*, February 7, 2022.

20. "Carpetbaggers & Scalawags," History, June 24, 2010, https://
    www.history.com/topics/american-civil-war/carpetbaggers
    -and-scalawags; Ted Tunnell, "Creating 'The Propaganda of His-

tory': Southern Editors and the Origins of 'Carpetbagger and Scalawag,'" *Journal of Southern History* 72, no. 4 (2006): 789–822, https://doi.org/10.2307/27649233.

21. History.com, "Carpetbaggers,"

22. Tunnell, "Creating 'The Propaganda of History.'"

23. Tunnell.

24. Tunnell.

25. Jonathan Swift, *The Examiner*, September 11, 1710.

26. Library of Congress, "The African American Odyssey: A Quest for Full Citizenship," accessed October 30, 2023, https://www.loc .gov/exhibits/african-american-odyssey/reconstruction.

27. Ira Katznelson, "What America Taught the Nazis," *Atlantic*, November 2017; Becky Little, "How the Nazis Were Inspired by Jim Crow," History, August 4, 2023; James Q. Whitman, *Hitler's American Model: The United States and the Making of Nazi Race Law* (Princeton, NJ: Princeton University Press, 2018).

28. Emerging Civil War, "Echoes of Reconstruction: Who the Hell Was William Dunning & Did He Distort Reconstruction History?" January 28, 2023, https://emergingcivilwar.com/2023/01/28 /echoes-of-reconstruction-who-the-hell-was-william-dunning -did-he-distort-reconstruction-history/.

29. Emerging Civil War.

30. Loving v. Virginia, 388 U.S. 1 (1967).

31. Scott L. Miller, "The Origins of the Presumption of Black Stupidity," *Journal of Blacks in Higher Education*, no. 9 (Autumn, 1995): 78–82.

32. Henry Louis Gates Jr., "How Reconstruction Still Shapes Racism in America," *Time*, April 2, 2019, time.com/5562869/reconstruction -history/.

33. Julian Mark, "A Law That Helped End Slavery Is Now a Weapon to End Affirmative Action," *Washington Post*, November 7, 2023, https://www.washingtonpost.com/business/2023/11/06 /civil-rights-act-1866-dei-affirmative-action/.

34. Mark.

35. Thomas Nast, Alfred R. Waud, Henry L. Stephens, James E. Taylor, J. Hoover, George F. Crane, and Elizabeth White. n.d, "Reconstruction and Its Aftermath—the African American Odyssey: A Quest for Full Citizenship | Exhibitions (Library of Congress)," https://www .loc.gov/exhibits/african-american-odyssey/reconstruction.html.

36. "Cornerstone Speech," American Battlefield Trust, accessed October 31, 2023, www.battlefields.org/learn/primary-sources /cornerstone-speech.

37. Deneen L. Brown, "Remembering 'Red Summer,' When White Mobs Massacred Blacks from Tulsa to D.C.," *National Geographic*, June 19, 2020.

38. Brown, "Red Summer,"

39. Alexis Clark, "Tulsa's 'Black Wall Street' Flourished as a Self-Contained Hub in the Early 1900s," History, March 29, 2023, https://www.history.com/news/black-wall-street-tulsa-race-massacre.

40. Adam Harris, "How Reconstruction Created American Public Education," *Atlantic*, November 13, 2023, https://www.theatlantic.com/magazine/archive/2023/12/reconstruction-education-black-students-public-schools/675816/.

41. "Schools and Education During Reconstruction," PBS, accessed October 31, 2023, https://www.pbs.org/wgbh/americanexperience/features/reconstruction-schools-and-education-during-reconstruction/#:~:text=The%20Freedmen%E2%80%99s%20Bureau%20puts%20money,building%20%2D%2D%20to%20create%20schools.

42. Kumari Devarajan, "Ready for a Linguistic Controversy? Say 'Mmhmm,'" NPR, August 17, 2018, accessed October 31, 2023, www.npr.org/sections/codeswitch/2018/08/17/606002607/ready-for-a-linguistic-controversy-say-mhmm#:~:text=He%20says%20plantation%20owners%20worried,%2C%22%20as%20Rickford%20puts%20it.

43. David Shenk, "The Truth About IQ," *Atlantic*, July 28, 2009, www.theatlantic.com/national/archive/2009/07/the-truth-about-iq/22260/.

44. "Building the Myth of Black Inferiority," *Encyclopaedia Britannica*, accessed October 31, 2023, www.britannica.com/topic/race-human/Building-the-myth-of-Black-inferiority.

Chapter 3: Color Blinded

1. Matthew F. Delmont, *Half American: The Heroic Story of African Americans Fighting World War II at Home and Abroad* (New York: Viking, 2022), 271.

2. Olivia B. Waxman, "The Story Behind the Blinding of Isaac Woodard," *Time*, March 30, 2021, https://time.com/5950641/blinding-isaac-woodard/.

3. DeNeen L. Brown, "A Black WWII Veteran Was Beaten and Blinded, Fueling the Civil Rights Movement," *Washington Post*, March 31, 2021, https://www.washingtonpost.com/history/2021/03/31/isaac-woodard-truman-integration-military/.

4. Michael J. Bennett, *When Dreams Came True: The GI Bill and the Making of the Modern America* (McLean, VA; Brassey's, 1996), 26.

5. Charles Hurd, "Democracy Challenged," *Opportunity*, no. 23 (Spring 1945): 63, quoted in Ira Katznelson, *When Affirmative Action Was White: An Untold History of Racial Inequality in Twentieth-Century America* (New York: Norton, 2006), 118.

6. Suzanne Mettler, "How the GI Bill Built the Middle Class and Enhanced Democracy," Scholars Strategy Network, January 1, 2012, https://scholars.org/contribution/how-gi-bill-built-middle-class-and-enhanced.

7. OpenStax College, "A New Social Order: Class Divisions," May 7, 2014, https://pressbooks-dev.oer.hawaii.edu/ushistory/chapter/a-new-social-order-class-divisions/.

8. Mark Ledesma, "WWII Veteran Reflects on G.I. Bill Benefits, Offers Advice to Today's Veterans," *VA News*, January 20, 2017, https://news.va.gov/34599/wwii-veteran-reflects-on-g-i-bill-benefits-provides-sage-advice-to-recent-veterans/.

9. Mettler, "GI Bill."

10. U.S. Department of Defense, "75 Years of the GI Bill: How Transformative It's Been," accessed December 17, 2023, https://www.defense.gov/News/Feature-Stories/story/Article/1727086/75-years-of-the-gi-bill-how-transformative-its-been/.

11. Liam Bailey, "How Will Millennials Spend US$90 Trillion?" Knight Frank, February 28, 2024, https://www.knightfrank.com/research/article/2024-02-28-how-will-millennials-spend-us90-trillion.

12. "Why American School Segregation Didn't End with Brown v. Board of Education," Reading Partners, March 16, 2023, https://readingpartners.org/blog/why-american-school-segregation-didnt-end-with-brown-v-board-of-education/#:~:text=In%201964%2C%2010%20years%20after,were%20attending%20predominantly%20white%20schools.

13. Tom Porter, "A Land Fit for (Some) Heroes: How the GI Bill Helped White Vets More Than Black Ones," History Department, Bowdoin College, July 27, 2023, https://www.bowdoin.edu/history/news-and-events/a-land-fit-for-some-heroes-how-the-gi-bill-helped-white-vets-more-than-black-ones.html; Richard Rothstein, *Segregated by Design*, https://www.segregatedbydesign.com/.

14. Robert Levinson, "Many Black World War II Veterans Were Denied Their GI Bill Benefits. Time to Fix That," War on the Rocks, September 11, 2020, https://warontherocks.com/2020/09/many-black-world-war-ii-veterans-were-denied-their-gi-bill-benefits-time-to-fix-that/.

15. Charles G. Bolte and Louis Harris, *Our Negro Veterans* (Public Affairs Committee, 1947), 20, https://archive.org/details /ournegroveterans00bolt/mode/2up.

16. Students for Fair Admissions v. Harvard, 600 U.S. 181 (2023).

17. *Harvard*, 600 U.S. at 188.

18. Plessy v. Ferguson, 163 U.S. 537, 551 (1896).

19. Cedric Merlin Powell, *Post-Racial Constitutionalism and the Roberts Court* (Cambridge: Cambridge University Press, 2023).

20. Dayna Bowen Matthew, Edward Rodrigue, and Richard V. Reeves, "Time for Justice: Tackling Race Inequalities in Health and Housing," Brookings Institution, October 19, 2016, https:// www.brookings.edu/articles/time-for-justice-tackling-race -inequalities-in-health-and-housing/.

21. *Harvard*, 600 U.S. at 385.

22. Cedric Merlin Powell, "Reconstruction, Retrogression, Retrenchment, and the Roberts Court," Fifteen Eighty-Four, November 10, 2022, https://www.cambridgeblog.org/2022/11 /reconstruction-retrogression-retrenchment-and-the-roberts -court/.

23. Transcript of Oral Argument at 68, *Harvard*, 600 U.S. 181.

24. Kevin M. Levin, "Chief Justice John Roberts Explains Why the Civil War Was Fought and Gets It Wrong," *Civil War Memory* (blog), Substack, June 30, 2023, https://kevinmlevin.substack .com/p/chief-justice-john-roberts-explains.

25. Debate at Charleston, Illinois, September 18, 1858, Abrahamlincoln.org, accessed December 5, 2023, https:// abrahamlincoln.org/features/speeches-writings/abraham -lincoln-quotes/#:~:text=%E2%80%9CI%20will%20say%20 then%20that,white%20people%3B%20and%20I%20will.

26. Debate at Charleston, Illinois.

27. Marcus A. Banks, "Cancer Cells Could Travel Through the Interstitium: Study," *Scientist*, April 19, 2021, https://www .the-scientist.com/cancer-cells-could-travel-through-the -interstitium-study-68680.

28. Petros C. Benias et al., "Structure and Distribution of an Unrecognized Interstitium in Human Tissues," *Scientific Reports* 8 (March 27, 2018), https://www.nature.com/articles/s41598 -018-23062-6.

29. Michelle Alexander, "Tipping Is a Legacy of Slavery," *New York Times*, February 5, 2021, https://www.nytimes.com/2021/02/05 /opinion/minimum-wage-racism.html.

30. Jeneen Interlandi, "Why Doesn't America Have Universal Health Care? The Answer Has Everything to Do with Race," *New York*

Times, August 14, 2019, https://www.nytimes.com/interactive /2019/08/14/magazine/universal-health-care-racism.html.

31. Nicholas Confessore, "'America Is Under Attack': Inside the Anti-D.E.I. Crusade," *New York Times*, February 8, 2024, https:// www.nytimes.com/interactive/2024/01/20/us/dei-woke -claremont-institute.html.

32. Beth Reinhard and Josh Dawsey, "How a Trump-Allied Group Fighting 'Anti-White Bigotry' Beats Biden in Court," *Washington Post*, December 12, 2022, https://www.washingtonpost.com /politics/2022/12/12/stephen-miller-america-first-legal -biden-race-policies/.

33. Patrick Young, "Andy Johnson Said That Equality for Blacks Is Discrimination Against Whites: Veto of Civil Rights Act of 1866," *The Reconstruction Era* (blog), June 29, 2019, https:// thereconstructionera.com/andy-johnson-said-that-equality -for-blacks-is-discrimination-against-whites-veto-of-civil-rights -act-of-1866/.

34. Eric Foner, *Reconstruction: America's Unfinished Revolution, 1863–1877* (New York: Harper & Row, 1988).

35. "A Working Definition of Racism: Revised 7/88 by Ricky Sherover-Marcuse," n.d., https://docplayer.net/41346059-A-working -definition-of-racism-revised-7-88-by-ricky-sherover-marcuse.html.

36. Jason Wilson, "Activist Who Led Ouster of Harvard President Linked to 'Scientific Racism' Journal," *Guardian*, January 31, 2024, https://www.theguardian.com/world/2024/jan/31/rightwing -activist-christopher-rufo-ties-scientific-racism-journal.

37. Gavin Evans, "The Unwelcome Revival of 'Race Science,'" *Guardian*, March 2, https://www.theguardian.com/news/2018/mar/02/the -unwelcome-revival-of-race-science; Joel Z. Garrod, "A Brave Old World: An Analysis of Scientific Racism and BiDil," *McGill Journal of Medicine*, December 1, 2020, https://doi.org/10.26443/mjm .v9i1.499/.

38. Wyatte Grantham-Philips, Geoff Mulvihill, and the Associated Press, "Fortune 100 Companies Are Getting Swarmed by Republican AGs Using the Supreme Court Affirmative Action as a Lever into the Workplace," *Fortune*, July 15, 2023, https://fortune .com/2023/07/15/affirmative-action-13-republican-attorney -general-letter-corporate-ceos-fortune-100/.

39. Mike Freeman, "Claim of NASCAR Bias Against White Men Isn't Just Buffoonery. It's Downright Dangerous," *USA Today*, November 4, 2023, https://www.usatoday.com/story/sports/columnist /mike-freeman/2023/11/04/nascar-discrimination-eeoc-white -men-diversity/71428107007/.

40. Todd A. Price and Mackensy Lunsford, "The Receipts: Documented Discrimination Against Black Farmers," *Tennessean*, November 17, 2022, https://www.tennessean.com/in-depth/news/american-south/2022/11/16/the-receipts-documented-discrimination-against-black-farmers/69609225007/.

41. Reinhard and Dawsey, "How a Trump-Allied Group."

42. Kaanita Iyer and Chris Boyette, "Texas Governor Signs Bill to Ban DEI Offices at State Public Colleges," CNN, June 15, 2023, https://www.cnn.com/2023/06/15/politics/greg-abbott-texas-dei-office-ban-colleges/index.html.

43. "Gov. Greg Abbott Tells State Agencies to Stop Considering Diversity in Hiring," CBS News, February 9, 2023, https://www.cbsnews.com/texas/news/greg-abbott-diversity-hiring/.

44. "Gov. Greg Abbott Tells State Agencies."

45. Brent Staples, "How Italians Became 'White,'" *New York Times*, October 12, 2019, https://www.nytimes.com/interactive/2019/10/12/opinion/columbus-day-italian-american-racism.html.

Chapter 4: The Myth of Qualifications

1. Michael Weishan, "The Real Gentleman's C," Franklin Delano Roosevelt Foundation, https://fdrfoundation.org/the-real-gentlemans-c/.

2. Fareed Zakaria, "Why University Presidents Are Under Fire," CNN, December 10, 2023, https://www.cnn.com/2023/12/08/opinions/israel-palestine-antisemitism-american-universities-zakaria/index.html.

3. "The First Harvard Graduate," *Harvard Crimson*, September 27, 2009, https://www.thecrimson.com/article/1890/12/9/the-first-harvard-graduate-the-following/.

4. "A History of Privilege in Higher Education," Best Colleges, July 17, 2020, https://www.bestcolleges.com/news/analysis/2020/07/17/history-privilege-higher-education/.

5. Jérôme Karabel, *The Chosen: The Hidden History of Admission and Exclusion at Harvard, Yale, and Princeton*, 2025, 20 https://dash.harvard.edu/bitstream/handle/1/12701500/2007_asq_karabel.pdf?sequence=1.

6. Christopher P. Wilson, "'Unleavened Bread': The Representation of Robert Grant," *American Literary Realism, 1870–1910* 22, no. 3 (1990): 17–35, http://www.jstor.org/stable/27746414.

7. Weishan, "The Real Gentleman's C."

8. Karabel, *The Chosen*, 20; Harold S. Wechsler, "The Rationale for Restriction: Ethnicity and College Admission in America,

1910–1980," *American Quarterly* 36, no. 5 (1984): 643–67, 644, https://doi.org/10.2307/2712865.

9. Karabel, *The Chosen*, 86.

10. Wechsler, "The Rationale for Restriction," 648, citing *The Qualified Student: A History of Selective College Admission in America* (New York: Wiley-Interscience, 1977), ch. 7

11. Tirupathi Reddy, "The Eugenic Origins of IQ Testing: Implications for Post-Atkins Litigation," *Depaul Law Review*, Spring 2008, https://via.library.depaul.edu/cgi/viewcontent.cgi?article=1270&context=law-review.

12. "Crossing the Bar—Not the Primrose Path: Educating Lawyers at the Turn of the Last Century," State Bar of Michigan, https://www.michbar.org/journal/Details/Crossing-the-Bar--Not-the-Primrose-Path-Educating-Lawyers-at-the-Turn-of-the-Last-Century?ArticleID=99.

13. Wechsler, "The Rationale for Restriction."

14. "History of Bar Exam—Formation and Evolution of UBE," UWorld Legal, February 11, 2023, https://legal.uworld.com/bar-exam/history-and-changes/.

15. "Crossing the Bar—Not the Primrose Path," citing Jerold S. Auerbach, *Unequal Justice: Lawyers and Social Change in Modern America* (Oxford: Oxford University Press, 1997), 95.

16. "Crossing the Bar—Not the Primrose Path," citing Auerbach, *Unequal Justice*, 95

17. Carl C. Brigham, *A Study of American Intelligence* (Princeton, NJ: Princeton University Press, 1923), 180, accessed through Cornell University Library Digital Collections Bookreader, https://reader.library.cornell.edu/docviewer/digital?id=hearth4221299#page/208/mode/1up.

18. Brigham, 157–81.

19. Brigham, 194.

20. "A Brief History of the SAT," Best Colleges, https://www.bestcolleges.com/blog/history-of-sat/.

21. Michael Milov-Cordoba, "Beyond 'Valid and Reliable': The LSAT, ABA Standard 503, and the Future of Law School Admissions," *NYU Law Review*, December 22, 2020, https://www.nyulawreview.org/issues/volume-95-number-6/beyond-valid-and-reliable-the-lsat-aba-standard-503-and-the-future-of-law-school-admissions/.

22. "African Americans and the American Labor Movement," National Archives, October 6, 2022, https://www.archives.gov/publications/prologue/1997/summer/american-labor-movement.html.

23. David E. Bernstein, "Licensing Laws: A Historical Example of the Use of Government Regulatory Power Against African Americans," 31 *San Diego L. Rev.* 89 (1994), available at https://digital .sandiego.edu/sdlr/vol31/iss1/5.

24. Bernstein, 90.

25. Bernstein, 103.

26. Bernstein.

27. Travis Watson, "Union Construction's Racial Equity and Inclusion Charade," *Stanford Social Innovation Review*, June 14, 2021, https://ssir.org/articles/entry/union_constructions_racial _equity_and_inclusion_charade#bio-footer.

28. "Union Construction."

29. Brigham, A Study of American Intelligence, 194.

30. "Union Construction."

31. Zakaria, "Why University Presidents Are Under Fire."

32. National Center for Education Statistics, "Fast Facts: Race/ Ethnicity of College Faculty (61)," https://nces.ed.gov/fastfacts /display.asp?id=61.

33. "History Professor Demographics and Statistics [2024]: Number of History Professors in the US," Zippia, July 21, 2023, https:// www.zippia.com/history-professor-jobs/demographics/.

34. National Center for Education Statistics, "Fast Facts."

35. "Quickfacts," U.S. Census Bureau, https://www.census.gov /quickfacts/fact/table/US/RHI825222.

36. "The Unequal Race for Good Jobs: How Whites Made Outsized Gains in Education and Good Jobs Compared to Blacks and Latinos," CEW Georgetown, April 6, 2020, https://cew.georgetown .edu/cew-reports/raceandgoodjobs/.

37. "The Unequal Race for Good Jobs."

38. "Why Are Employment Rates So Low Among Black Men?," Brookings Institution, May 16, 2023, https://www.brookings .edu/articles/why-are-employment-rates-so-low-among-black -men/.

39. "Why Are Employment Rates So Low?"

40. Rasha Kardosh, Asael Y. Sklar, Ariel Goldstein, Yoni Pertzov, and Ran R. Hassin, "Minority Salience and the Overestimation of Individuals from Minority Groups in Perception and Memory," *Proceedings of the National Academy of Sciences of the United States of America* 119, no. 12 (2022), https://doi.org/10.1073 /pnas.2116884119.

41. Kardosh et al.

42. Kardosh et al.

43. Matthew Weeks, Kelly P. Weeks, and Emily C. Watkins, "Using

the Shifting Standards Model of Stereotype-Based Judgments to Examine the Impact of Race on Compensation Decisions," *Journal of Applied Social Psychology* 51, no. 3 (2020), https://doi.org/10.1111/jasp.12724.

44.　Gillian B. White, "Black Workers Really Do Need to Be Twice as Good," *Atlantic*, June 27, 2018, https://www.theatlantic.com/business/archive/2015/10/why-black-workers-really-do-need-to-be-twice-as-good/409276/.

45.　Margaret Barthel, "Black Men Need More Education than White Men to Get Jobs," *Atlantic*, August 11, 2014, https://www.theatlantic.com/education/archive/2014/08/black-men-need-more-education-to-get-the-same-jobs/375770/, citing Rory O'Sullivan, Konrad Mugglestone, and Tom Allison, "Closing the Race Gap: Alleviating Young African American Unemployment Through Education," Young Invincibles, accessed January 14, 2024, https://younginvincibles.org/the-atlantic-black-men-need-more-education-than-white-men-to-get-jobs/.

46.　Barthel, citing O'Sullivan et al.

47.　Leniece F. Brissett, "I Help Organizations Hire People—and Watch White Candidates Get Favored Again and Again," Vox, August 31, 2016, https://www.vox.com/2016/8/31/12694276/unconscious-bias-hiring.

48.　Brissett.

49.　Brissett.

50.　Jhacova Williams and Valerie Wilson, "Labor Day 2019 Black Workers Endure Persistent Racial Disparities in Employment Outcomes," Economic Policy Institute, August 27, 2019, www.epi.org/publication/labor-day-2019-racial-disparities-in-employment/.

51.　"Tokenism," Wikipedia, May 3, 2024, https://en.wikipedia.org/wiki/Tokenism.

52.　"Say Goodbye to MBTI, the Fad That Won't Die," LinkedIn, September 17, 2013, https://www.linkedin.com/pulse/20130917155206-69244073-say-goodbye-to-mbti-the-fad-that-won-t-die/.

53.　Lisa Wong Macabasco, "'They Become Dangerous Tools': The Dark Side of Personality Tests," *Guardian*, April 6, 2021, https://www.theguardian.com/tv-and-radio/2021/mar/03/they-become-dangerous-tools-the-dark-side-of-personality-tests.

54.　Macabasco.

55.　Benjamin Hardy, "Most Personality Tests (like Myers-Briggs) Are Junk Science and Can Make You Cling to a Label—Instead, Focus on Making Meaningful Change," Business Insider, July 2, 2020, https://www.businessinsider.com/most-personality-tests-junk-science-make-you-cling-to-label-2020-7.

56. Now, let me briefly explain why I use *Hispanic/Latinx*. While working with clients, most people at those companies who identify as Hispanic have stated that they prefer *Hispanic* to *Latinx*. A 2020 report on Hispanic identity from the Pew Research Center seems to bear this out, with the majority of those who have a preference preferring to be called Hispanic, so I seek to honor what people have told me directly that they prefer to be called and balance that with the knowledge that they do not speak for all people from their group. Mark Hugo Lopez, "Hispanic Identity," Pew Research Center, Hispanic Trends Project, May 30, 2020, https://www.pewresearch.org/hispanic/2013/10/22/3-hispanic-identity/.

57. "I Don't Do 360 Degree Performance Reviews—This Is Why," LinkedIn, May 31, 2021, https://www.linkedin.com/pulse/i-dont-do-360-degree-performance-reviewsthis-why-katica-roy/.

58. A. T. Wynn and S. J. Correll, "Combating Gender Bias in Modern Workplaces," in B. Risman, C. Froyum, and W. Scarborough, eds., *Handbook of the Sociology of Gender* (Cham: Springer, 2018), 511, https://doi.org/10.1007/978-3-319-76333-0_37.

59. "Who Really Said These 5 Famous Phrases?," Google Arts and Culture, https://artsandculture.google.com/story/who-really-said-these-5-famous-phrases/JAXh1xsiCEHOqw?hl=en. Though Albert Einstein is credited as saying this famous quote it was in fact Rita May Brown.

60. G. F. Dreher, J.-Y. Lee, and T. A. Clerkin, "Mobility and Cash Compensation: The Moderating Effects of Gender, Race, and Executive Search Firms," *Journal of Management* 37, no. 3 (2011): 651–81, https://doi.org/10.1177/0149206310365728.

61. Jessica Guynn, "What Is Code-Switching? Why Black Americans Say They Can't Be Themselves at Work," *USA Today*, February 9, 2024, https://www.usatoday.com/story/money/careers/2024/02/01/code-switching-meaning-black-americans-at-work/72370895007/.

62. "Executive Order Emphasizes Skills over Degrees for Federal Jobs," SHRM, https://www.shrm.org/topics-tools/news/talent-acquisition/executive-order-emphasizes-skills-degrees-federal-jobs.

63. Caroline Colvin, "Why Skills-Based Hiring May Be the Future of DEI," HR Dive, June 7, 2023, https://www.hrdive.com/news/why-skills-based-hiring-may-be-future-of-dei/652341/; "Our History," Opportunity@Work, March 3, 2021, https://opportunityatwork.org/our-history/.

64. "Researchers Examine Effects of a Criminal Record on Prospects for Employment," CSG Justice Center, March 10, 2020, https://csgjusticecenter.org/2014/09/23/researchers-examine-effects-of-a-criminal-record-on-prospects-for-employment/.

65. "Researchers Examine Effects."

Chapter 5: Unmasking Imposter Syndrome

1. "Author Minda Harts: How Women of Color Can Get a Seat at the Table," MSNBC, 2020, https://www.msnbc.com/know-your-value/why-50-multicultural-women-are-thinking-about-leaving-their-jobs-n1234734.

2. Ruchika Tulshyan and Jodi-Ann Burey, "Stop Telling Women They Have Imposter Syndrome," *Harvard Business Review*, August 4, 2022, https://hbr.org/2021/02/stop-telling-women-they-have-imposter-syndrome.

3. Tulshyan and Burey.

4. Tulshyan and Burey.

5. Pauline Rose Clance and Suzanne Imes, "The Imposter Phenomenon in High Achieving Women: Dynamics and Therapeutic Intervention," *Psychotherapy* 15, no. 3 (1978): 241–47, https://doi.org/10.1037/h0086006.

6. Clance and Imes.

7. Clance and Imes.

8. Tulshyan and Burey, "Stop Telling Women They Have Imposter Syndrome."

9. "Second Wave Feminism Primary Sources & History," Gale, https://www.gale.com/primary-sources/womens-studies/collections/second-wave-feminism.

10. Clance and Imes, "The Imposter Phenomenon."

11. Hunter Vermeer, "Belles and Bondswomen: Historical Treatment of Southern Antebellum Women," Texas Woman's University, https://twu.edu/history/ibid/previous-ibid-issues/ibid-a-student-history-journal-volume-15-spring-2022/belles-and-bondswomen-historical-treatment-of-southern-antebellum-women/.

12. Saira Rao and Regina Jackson, "White Women Must Do More to Confront Racism," *Time*, December 3, 2022, https://time.com/6227993/white-women-perfection-anti-racism/.

13. "The Infantilization of Women in Mainstream Media and Society," *Verdict* (blog), April 23, 2021, https://www.theverdictonline.org/post/the-infantilization-of-women-in-mainstream-media-and-society.

14. Corinne Moss-Racusin et al., "Science Faculty's Subtle Gender Biases Favor Male Students," *Proceedings of the National*

Academy of Sciences of the United States of America 109, no. 41 (2012): 16474–79, https://doi.org/10.1073/pnas.1211286109.

15. Moss-Racusin et al.

16. Tulshyan and Burey, "Stop Telling Women They Have Imposter Syndrome."

17. "Human Resources Manager Demographics and Statistics: Number of Human Resources Managers in the US," July 21, 2023, https://www.zippia.com/human-resources-manager-jobs/demographics/.

Chapter 6: For Black Girls Who've Considered Quitting When Sisterhood Would've Been Enough

1. Ekaette Kern, interviewed by Shari Dunn, June 15, 2023.

2. Deborah Tannen, *You Just Don't Understand: Women and Men in Conversation* (New York: HarperCollins, 1990), 3.

3. Tannen.

4. "Missing White Woman Syndrome: The Media Bias Against Missing People of Color," NPR, June 8, 2023, https://www.npr.org/2023/06/06/1180499403/missing-white-woman-syndrome-the-media-bias-towards-missing-people-of-color.

5. Awesomely Luvvie, "About the Weary Weaponizing of White Women Tears," Awesomely Luvvie, May 28, 2020, https://awesomelyluvvie.com/2018/04/weaponizing-white-women-tears.html.

6. "Research Confirms That Black Girls Feel the Sting of Adultification Bias Identified in Earlier Georgetown Law Study," Georgetown Law School, n.d., https://www.law.georgetown.edu/news/research-confirms-that-black-girls-feel-the-sting-of-adultification-bias-identified-in-earlier-georgetown-law-study/.

7. A. G. Halberstadt et al., "Racialized Emotion Recognition Accuracy and Anger Bias of Children's Faces," *Emotion* 22, no. 3 (2022): 403–17, https://doi.org/10.1037/emo0000756, citing Hugenberg and Bodenhausen 2003; Halberstadt et al., 2018.

8. Halberstadt et al.

9. Halberstadt et al.

10. Pierott Deena, executive director, iUrban Teen, interviewed by Shari Dunn, June 27, 2023.

11. Kevin Donahue, Tina Gilbert, Melinda Halpert, and Portia Robertson Migas, "The Infuriating Journey from Pet to Threat: How Bias Undermines Black Women at Work," *Forbes*, June 29, 2021, https://www.forbes.com/sites/forbeseq/2021/06/29/the-infuriating-journey-from-pet-to-threat-how-bias-undermines-black-women-at-work/?sh=434d30a76490.

12. "Voices in the Workplace," Management Leadership for Tomorrow,

https://info.mlt.org/voices-from-the-workplace-minority-employees
-experience-with-racism-thank-you?submissionGuid=df6ea7d5
-7b17-4622-bb3a-a6ea87af88f2.

13. D. G. White, *Ar'n't I a Woman? Female Slaves in the Plantation South* (New York: Norton, 1985), 29.

14. Ekaette Kern, interviewed by Shari Dunn, June 15, 2023.

15. Dr. Tina Opie, interviewed by Shari Dunn, July 12, 2023.

16. Juatise Gathings, interviewed by Shari Dunn June 30, 2023.

17. Gathings interview.

18. Gathings interview.

19. R. W. Livingston, A. S. Rosette, and E. F. Washington, "Can an Agentic Black Woman Get Ahead? The Impact of Race and Interpersonal Dominance on Perceptions of Female Leaders," *Psychological Science* 23, no. 4 (2012): 354–58, https://doi .org/10.1177/0956797611428079.

20. Calvin John Smiley and David O. Fakunle, "From 'Brute' to 'Thug': The Demonization and Criminalization of Unarmed Black Male Victims in America," *Journal of Human Behavior in the Social Environment* 26, nos. 3–4 (2016): 350–66, https://doi.org /10.1080/10911359.2015.1129256.

21. Livingston, Rosette, and Washington, "Can an Agentic Black Woman Get Ahead?"

22. Morgan Murrell, "Ava DuVernay on Beyoncé Renaissance Film: Made Me So Emotional," BuzzFeed, November 26, 2023, https:// www.buzzfeed.com/morganmurrell/ava-duvernay-renaissance -film-beyonce-emotional-reaction.

23. Kayla Yup, "Black Women Excluded from Critical Studies Due to 'Weathering,'" Yale School of Medicine, December 1, 2022, https:// medicine.yale.edu/news-article/black-women-excluded-from -critical-studies-due-to-weathering/.

24. Arline T. Geronimus, "The Weathering Hypothesis and the Health of African-American Women and Infants: Evidence and Speculations. Ethnicity and Disease 2, no. 3 (1992): 207–21.

25. Arline T. Geronimus, Margaret T. Hicken, Danya E. Keene, and John Bound, "'Weathering' and Age Patterns of Allostatic Load Scores Among Blacks and Whites in the United States," *American Journal of Public Health* 96, no. 5 (2006): 826–33, https:// doi.org/10.2105/ajph.2004.060749.

26. Daryn O'Neal, "Lincoln University Administrator's Suicide Sparks Conversation About Mental Health," *Hilltop* (blog), January 30, 2024, https://thehilltoponline.com/2024/01/29/lincoln -university-administrators-suicide-sparks-conversation-about -mental-health/; "'Misogynoir': American Contempt for Black

Women and How to Change It," Center for the Study of Race, Ethnicity and Equity, Washington University, https://cre2.wustl.edu/i2/innovation-space/misogynoir-american-contempt-for-black-women-and-how-to-change-it/.

27. Christine E. Stanik, Susan M. McHale, and Ann C. Crouter, "Gender Dynamics Predict Changes in Marital Love Among African American Couples," *Journal of Marriage and Family* 75, no. 4 (2013): 795–807, https://doi.org/10.1111/jomf.12037; Bria Overs, "Black Women Are More Likely to Be Breadwinners. That's Not a Bad Thing," Word in Black, April 29, 2023, https://wordinblack.com/2023/04/black-women-are-more-likely-to-be-breadwinners/.

28. Kara Kyles, interview by Shari Dunn, November 21, 2023.

29. "Black Women Helping Close the Gender Gap as the Fastest Growing Group of Entrepreneurs," press release, GoDaddy, https://aboutus.godaddy.net/newsroom/news-releases/press-release-details/2023/Black-women-helping-close-the-gender-gap-as-the-fastest-growing-group-of-entrepreneurs/default.aspx.

30. "VCs: This Is Why You're Not Investing in Black Women, and Here's How to Change That," Crunchbase News, March 21, 2022, https://news.crunchbase.com/diversity/black-women-vc-diversity-ty-heath-linkedin/.

31. Ruth Umoh, "Uncle Nearest, the Black and Woman-Owned Whiskey Brand, Approaches Unicorn Status After Latest Raise," *Fortune*, February 14, 2024, https://fortune.com/2024/02/14/uncle-nearest-black-owned-whiskey-liquor-bhm-founder/.

32. Dominic-Madori Davis, "Fearless Fund's Arian Simone on Why a Downturn Is Business as Usual for Minority Founders," TechCrunch, June 16, 2022, https://techcrunch.com/2022/06/15/fearless-funds-arian-simone-on-why-a-downturn-is-business-as-usual-for-minority-founders/.

33. "Venture Capital Fund for Black Women in Epic Legal Battle Against Conservatives with an Agenda," BET, November 21, 2023, https://www.bet.com/article/qzg2vm/fearless-fund-lawsuit-arian-simone-interview.

34. Associated Press, "Grant Program for Black Women Business Owners Is Discriminatory, Appeals Court Rules," NPR, June 4, 2024, https://www.npr.org/2024/06/03/g-s1-2649/fearless-fund-grant-program-appeal-ruling.

35. Aj Hess, "The Real Reason Latina and Black Women Founders Don't Receive VC Funding," *Fast Company*, March 31, 2023, https://www.fastcompany.com/90870053/why-latina-and-black-women-founders-dont-receive-vc-funding.

36. Agatha Agbanobi, "Creating Psychological Safety for Black Women at Your Company," *Harvard Business Review*, May 22, 2023, https://hbr.org/2023/05/creating-psychological-safety-for-black-women-at-your-company.

37. "The State of Black Women in Corporate America," Lean In, https://leanin.org/research/state-of-black-women-in-corporate-america.

38. "'Gendered Ageism': Discrimination Against Older Women in the Workplace," Halunen Law, September 21, 2023, https://www.halunenlaw.com/gendered-ageism-discrimination-against-older-women-in-the-workplace/; Jessica Bennett, "Stop Telling Women Their Most Valuable Asset Is Their Youth," *Time*, August 7, 2014, https://time.com/3087527/stop-telling-women-our-most-valuable-asset-is-our-youth/.

Chapter 7: It's Not Just Black and White (or American)

1. H. G. Biswas, "Colonialism, Imperialism, and White Supremacy," *International Journal of Policy Sciences and Law* 1, no. 1 (2020): 414, http://ijpsl.in/wp-content/uploads/2021/09/Colonialism-Imperialism-White-Supremacy_Hema-Georgina-Biswas.pdf.

2. Gerald Goodwin, "'You and Me-Same Same' and 'They Called Me "Monkey"'": Conflicting African American Views of Vietnamese Civilians," World History Connected, https://worldhistoryconnected.press.uillinois.edu/14.2/goodwin.html.

3. Harmeet Kaur, "The Term 'Asian American' Has a Radical History," CNN, May 4, 2022, https://www.cnn.com/2022/05/04/us/history-of-term-asian-american-cec/index.html.

4. Kaur.

5. Kaur.

6. "Success Story, Japanese-American Style," *New York Times*, January 9, 1966, https://www.nytimes.com/1966/01/09/archives/success-story-japaneseamerican-style-success-story-japaneseamerican.html.

7. Cathy Park Hong, *Minor Feelings: An Asian American Reckoning* (New York: One World, 2020), 190.

8. Hong, 9.

9. Scarlett Wang, "The 'Tiger Mom': Stereotypes of Chinese Parenting in the United States," Applied Psychology OPUS (Online Publication of Undergraduate Studies), New York University, n.d., https://wp.nyu.edu/steinhardt-appsych_opus/the-tiger-mom-stereotypes-of-chinese-parenting-in-the-united-states/.

10. Bic Ngo and Stacey J. Lee, "Complicating the Image of Model

Minority Success: A Review of Southeast Asian American Education," *Review of Educational Research* 77, no. 4 (2007): 415–53, https://doi.org/10.3102/0034654307309918.

11. Shannon Greenwood, "Asian Americans and the 'Forever Foreigner' Stereotype," Pew Research Center, November 30, 2023, https://www.pewresearch.org/race-ethnicity/2023/11/30/asian-americans-and-the-forever-foreigner-stereotype/.

12. Viet Thanh Nguyen, "Asian Americans Are Still Caught in the Trap of the 'Model Minority' Stereotype. And It Creates Inequality for All," *Time*, June 26, 2020, https://time.com/5859206/anti-asian-racism-america/.

13. Jennifer Lee, "'Bamboo Ceiling' Asian Americans Face in Workplace Is Holding Sturdy," *San Francisco Chronicle*, October 12, 2023, https://www.sfchronicle.com/opinion/openforum/article/bamboo-ceiling-mighty-sturdy-workplace-18397939.php.

14. Lee.

15. "Defining Diaspora: Asian, Pacific Islander, and Desi Identities," Cross-Cultural Center, California State University, San Marcos, n.d., https://www.csusm.edu/ccc/programs/diaspora.html.

16. Jackson G. Lu, Richard E. Nisbett, and Michael W. Morris, "Why East Asians but Not South Asians Are Underrepresented in Leadership Positions in the United States," *Proceedings of the National Academy of Sciences of the United States of America* 117, no. 9 (2020): 4590–4600, https://doi.org/10.1073/pnas.1918896117.

17. Lu, Nisbett, and Morris.

18. Lu, Nisbett, and Morris.

19. Kimmy Yam, "Asian American Women Fall Off by 80% at Corporate Leadership Levels, a New Report Says," NBC News, September 14, 2022, https://www.nbcnews.com/news/asian-america/asian-american-women-fall-80-corporate-leadership-levels-new-report-sa-rcna46546.

20. Hong, *Minor Feelings*.

21. Hong.

22. Vivek Ramaswamy, "Ann Coulter on the N Word," video, 2024, https://www.youtube.com/watch?v=nUa1KkxyOmA.

23. Joseph Konig, "After Racist Jacksonville Shooting, Ramaswamy Defends Denying Existence of White Supremacy," Spectrum News NY1, August 27, 2023, https://ny1.com/nyc/all-boroughs/news/2023/08/27/after-racist-jacksonville-shooting--ramaswamy-defends-denying-existence-of-white-supremacy.

24. Hong, *Minor Feelings*.

25. Kurek, *Eyes Wide Cut*.

26. Amy Qin, "California Could Become the First State to Ban Caste Bias as Prejudices Linger," *New York Times*, September 8, 2023, https://www.nytimes.com/2023/09/08/us/california-caste -discrimination.html#:~:text=lawsuit%20last.

27. Vina M. Goghari and Mavis Kusi, "An Introduction to the Basic Elements of the Caste System of India," in *Frontiers in Psychology*, U.S. National Library of Medicine, December 21, 2023, https://www.ncbi.nlm.nih.gov/pmc/articles/P.

28. "Fisher v. University of Texas at Austin," American Civil Liberties Union, June 23, 2016, https://www.aclu.org/cases/fisher-v -university-texas-austin.

29. Kali Holloway, "Inside the Cynical Campaign to Claim That Affirmative Action Hurts Asian Americans," 2023, *Nation*, August 9, 2023, https://www.thenation.com/article/society/affirmative-action -asian-americans/.

30. Kimmy Yam, "Experts Say Framing Affirmative Action as Anti-Asian Bias Is 'Dangerous,'" NBC News, January 26, 2022, https:// www.nbcnews.com/news/asian-america/experts-say-framing -affirmative-action-anti-asian-bias-dangerous-rcna13544.

31. Holloway, "Inside the Cynical Campaign."

32. Yam, "Experts Say."

33. Carlos Aguilar, "Tenoch Huerta Mejía and the Beauty of Representation in 'Wakanda Forever,'" *New York Times*, November 16, 2022, https://www.nytimes.com/2022/11/16/movies/tenoch -huerta-mejia-wakanda-forever.html.

34. Combahee River Collective Statement, 1977, *Black Past* (blog), August 29, 2019, https://www.blackpast.org/african-american -history/combahee-river-collective-statement-1977/; "Loretta Ross on the Phrase 'Women of Color': Sociological Images," The Society Pages, March 26, 2011, https://thesocietypages.org /socimages/2011/03/26/loreta-ross-on-the-phrase-women-of -color/.

35. "Loretta Ross," *The Balm* (podcast), https://xraypod.com/show /the-balm.

36. *The American Heritage Guide to Contemporary Usage and Style* (Boston: Houghton Mifflin Harcourt, 2005), 356.

37. Kee Malesky, "The Journey from 'Colored' to 'Minorities' to 'People of Color,'" NPR, March 31, 2014, https://www.npr.org /sections/codeswitch/2014/03/30/295931070/the-journey -from-colored-to-minorities-to-people-of-color.

38. Luke Pearson, "Who Identifies as a Person of Colour in Australia?" ABC Radio National, December 1, 2017.

39. Sandra E. Garcia, "Where Did BIPOC Come From?" *New York*

Times, June 17, 2020, https://www.nytimes.com/article/what
-is-bipoc.html.

40. Garcia.

41. Garcia.

42. "Damon Young," *GQ*, August 19, 2020, https://www.gq.com
/contributor/damon-young.

43. James Baldwin, *The Cross of Redemption: Uncollected Writings*,
edited by Randall Kenan (New York: Pantheon, 2010), 136.

44. Baldwin, 135.

45. Baldwin.

46. "Audre Lorde Quotes (Author of *Sister Outsider*)," n.d., https://
www.goodreads.com/author/quotes/18486.Audre_Lorde.

47. Brent Staples, "How Italians Became 'White,'" *New York Times*,
October 12, 2019, https://www.nytimes.com/interactive/2019
/10/12/opinion/columbus-day-italian-american-racism.html.
"The newcomers also chose to live together in Italian neighbor-
hoods, where they spoke their native tongue, preserved Italian
customs, and developed successful businesses that catered
to African-Americans, with whom they fraternized and inter-
married. In time, this proximity to blackness would lead white
Southerners to view Sicilians, in particular, as not fully white
and to see them as eligible for persecution—including lynching—
that had customarily been imposed on African-Americans.";
"Irish and Blacks: The Ties That Bind," editorial, *Chicago Tri-
bune*, March 17, 1993, updated August 10, 2021, https://www
.chicagotribune.com/1993/03/17/irish-and-blacks-the-ties
-that-bind/. "Also a part of the Irish-African legacy of the 19th
Century were the true 'black Irish,' Americans who combined in
them the blood of both an island's immigrants and a continent's
captives: Jesuit Patrick Healy, born to a Roscommon who illegally married an enslaved Georgian woman, became known both
as the first black American to earn a Ph.D. and a president of
Georgetown University. His brother James Healy won installa-
tion as America's first black Catholic bishop in 1875. That was
probably not long after the wedding of Muhammad Ali's maternal
great-grandparents, a 'free colored woman' and a County Clare
immigrant, and perhaps during the lifetime of the great-great
Irish grandfather Alice Walker celebrates."

48. Staples, "How Italians Became 'White.'" "Few who march in Columbus Day parades or recount the tale of Columbus's voyage
from Europe to the New World are aware of how the holiday
came about or that President Benjamin Harrison proclaimed it
as a one-time national celebration in 1892—in the wake of a

bloody New Orleans lynching that took the lives of 11 Italian immigrants."

49. Art McDonald, "How the Irish Became White," n.d., https://sites.pitt.edu/~hirtle/uujec/white.html.

50. George Packer, "Banning Words Won't Make the World More Just," *Atlantic*, March 2, 2023, https://www.theatlantic.com/magazine/archive/2023/04/equity-language-guides-sierra-club-banned-words/673085/.

51. Deb Nielsen, Emily Ballantyne, Faatimah Murad, and Melissa Fournier, "4.3 Colonialism in Canada," Pressbooks, September 7, 2022, https://opentextbc.ca/workintegratedlearning/chapter/colonialism-in-canada/.

52. Aimé Césaire, *Discourse on Colonialism*, translated by Joan Pinkham (New York: Monthly Review Press, 1972), 43.

53. "Residential School History," National Centre for Truth and Reconciliation, Canada, October 26, 2021, https://nctr.ca/education/teaching-resources/residential-school-history/.

54. Uday Rana, "8 in 10 Black Canadians Say They Still Face Discrimination at Work: Report," Global News, February 6, 2024, https://globalnews.ca/news/10273423/black-history-month-kpmg-survey-workplace/.

55. Sandramc, "Black Canadians See Workplaces as Epicentres of Racism, While 90 Per Cent See It as a Serious Problem in the Criminal Justice System - News@York," News@York, October 2, 2023, https://www.yorku.ca/news/2023/06/13/black-canadians-see-workplaces-as-epicentres-of-racism-while-90-per-cent-see-it-as-a-serious-problem-in-the-criminal-justice-system/.

56. Sandramc.

57. J. D. Edgerton and L. W. Roberts, "Cultural Capital or Habitus? Bourdieu and Beyond in the Explanation of Enduring Educational Inequality," *Theory and Research in Education* 12, no. 2 (2014): 193–220, https://doi.org/10.1177/1477878514530231.

58. "Discrimination," CNCDH, n.d., https://www.cncdh.fr/presentation/themes-daction/discriminations.

59. Robin Richardot, "9 in 10 Black People in Mainland France Say They Are Victims of Racist Discrimination," *Le Monde*, February 15, 2023, https://www.lemonde.fr/en/france/article/2023/02/15/91-of-black-people-in-metropolitan-france-say-they-are-victims-of-racist-discrimination_6015940_7.html.

60. Mark Brown, "Accent Discrimination Is Alive and Kicking in England, Study Suggests," *Guardian*, June 12, 2022, https://www.theguardian.com/uk-news/2022/jun/12/accent-discrimination-is-alive-and-kicking-in-britain-study-suggests.

61. Laura Smith-Spark, Nima Elbagir, and Barbara Arvaniti-dis, "'The Greatest Trick Racism Ever Pulled Was Convincing England It Doesn't Exist,'" CNN, June 22, 2020, https://www.cnn.com/2020/06/22/europe/black-britain-systemic-racism-cnn-poll-gbr-intl/index.html.

62. "Landmark Report Reveals 75% of Women of Colour Have Experienced Racism at Work," Fawcett Society, May 25, 2022, https://www.fawcettsociety.org.uk/news/landmark-report-reveals-75-of-women-of-colour-have-experienced-racism-at-work.

63. Aayat Ali, "52% of Black Women in the UK Plan to Leave Their Jobs," AllWork, July 14, 2022, https://allwork.space/2022/07/52-of-black-women-in-the-uk-plan-to-leave-their-jobs/.

64. "Author Minda Harts: How Women of Color Can Get a Seat at the Table," MSNBC, 2020, https://www.msnbc.com/know-your-value/why-50-multicultural-women-are-thinking-about-leaving-their-jobs-n1234734.

65. "Global Majority," Wikipedia, February 9, 2024, https://en.wikipedia.org/wiki/Global_majority.

Chapter 8: Leading in Living Color

1. Portland State University, Toni Morrison, Primus St. John, John Callahan, Susan Callahan, and Lloyd Baker, "Black Studies Center Public Dialogue, Part 2," 1975, Special Collections, Oregon Public Speakers, University Library, Portland State University, 90, http://archives.pdx.edu/ds/psu/11309.

2. Jennifer Betts, "Alice in Wonderland Quotes That Are Curiously Inspiring," In Your Dictionary, 2021, https://www.yourdictionary.com/articles/alice-wonderland-trippy-quotes.

3. Kara Kyles, interviewed by Shari Dunn November 21, 2023

4. "A Black Woman's Boss Told Her Being 'Articulate and Sharp' Made Her 'Intimidating' and Ineligible for Promotion, She Says," TheGrio, March 13, 2024, https://thegrio.com/2024/03/12/a-black-womans-boss-told-her-being-articulate-and-sharp-made-her-intimidating-and-ineligible-for-promotion-she-says/.

5. "Trading Glass Ceilings for Glass Cliffs: A Race to Lead Report on Nonprofit Executives of Color," Building Movement, February 9, 2022, https://buildingmovement.org/reports/trading-glass-ceilings-for-glass-cliffs-a-race-to-lead-report-on-nonprofit-executives-of-color/. "Leaders of color" include Black, Latino/Hispanic, Asian, Middle Eastern, and Mixed-Race.

6. "Being Black in Corporate America: An Intersectional Exploration," Coqual, July 17, 2023, https://coqual.org/reports/being-black-in-corporate-america-an-intersectional-exploration/.

7. "Nonprofit Executives and the Racial Leadership Gap: A Race to Lead Brief," Building Movement, February 19, 2021, https://buildingmovement.org/reports/nonprofit-executives-and-the-racial-leadership-gap-a-race-to-lead-brief/.

8. "Nonprofit Executives and the Racial Leadership Gap."

9. Dan Parks, "Deep Disparities Persist in Finances of Nonprofits Led by White People and People of Color," *Chronicle of Philanthropy*, June 8, 2022, https://www.philanthropy.com/article/deep-disparities-persist-in-finances-of-nonprofits-led-by-white-people-and-people-of-color.

10. "Trading Glass Ceilings for Glass Cliffs."

11. "'There Can Only Be One' Syndrome and How People of Color Can Also Uphold White Supremacy and Injustice," Nonprofit AF, August 24, 2020, https://nonprofitaf.com/2020/08/highlander-syndrome-and-how-people-of-color-can-also-uphold-white-supremacy-and-injustice/.

12. "A Quote from Through the Looking-Glass and What Alice Found There," n.d., https://www.goodreads.com/quotes/199404-the-red-queen-shook-her-head-you-may-call-it.

13. Kara Kyles, interviewed by Shari Dunn, November 21, 2023.

14. Kyles interview.

15. "Trading Glass Ceilings for Glass Cliffs."

16. "The Push and Pull: Declining Interest in Nonprofit Leadership," Building Movement, January 25, 2024, https://buildingmovement.org/reports/push-and-pull-report/.

17. "The Push and Pull."

18. "The Push and Pull."

19. "Trading Glass Ceilings for Glass Cliffs."

20. Candice L. Staples, "Hidden Figures: An Examination of the Career Trajectories of Black Women in Senior Administrative Positions" (PhD diss., University of Maryland, College Park, 2020), 214.

21. Staples, 192.

22. Audrey Williams June and Brian O'Leary, "How Many Black Women Have Tenure on Your Campus? Search Here," *Chronicle of Higher Education*, May 27, 2021, https://www.chronicle.com/article/how-many-black-women-have-tenure-on-your-campus-search-here.

23. Teneille Gibson, "Why Are Black Women Only 2% of Tenured Professors?" NBC4 Washington, February 11, 2024, https://www.nbcwashington.com/discover-black-heritage/why-are-black-women-only-2-of-tenured-professors/3537459/.

24. Gibson.

25. Kenneth D. Gibbs, Jacob Basson, Imam M. Xierali, and David A. Broniatowski, "Decoupling of the Minority PhD Talent Pool and Assistant Professor Hiring in Medical School Basic Science Departments in the US," *eLife (Cambridge)* 5 (2016), https://doi .org/10.7554/elife.21393.

26. Gibbs, Basson, Xierali, and Broniatowski, "Decoupling of the Minority PhD Talent Pool."

27. Elizabeth Weise and Jessica Guynn, "Black and Hispanic Computer Scientists Have Degrees from Top Universities, but Don't Get Hired in Tech," *USA Today*, July 20, 2020, https://www.usatoday .com/story/tech/2014/10/12/silicon-valley-diversity-tech -hiring-computer-science-graduates-african-american-hispanic /14684211/. "Using data from the Computing Research Association, which surveyed 179 U.S. and Canadian universities, and the National Center for Education Statistics (NCES)."

28. Weise and Guynn.

29. Weise and Guynn.

30. National Center for Education Statistics, "Bachelor's Degrees Conferred by Postsecondary Institutions, by Race/Ethnicity and Field of Study: Academic Years 2020–21 and 2021–22," https:// nces.ed.gov/programs/digest/d23/tables/dt23_322.30.asp.

31. Weise and Guynn.

32. "Korn Ferry Study Reveals U.S. Black P&L Leaders Are Some of the Highest Performing Executives," Korn Ferry, October 8, 2019, https://www.kornferry.com/about-us/press/korn-ferry-study -reveals-united-states-black-pl-leaders-are-some-of-the-highest -performing-executives-in-the-us-c-suite#:~:text=Despite%20 the%20wealth%20of%20talent,none%20of%20whom%20 are%20women.

33. "Korn Ferry Study."

34. "Korn Ferry Study."

35. "Korn Ferry Study."

36. Ken Belson, "Two Black Coaches Join Brian Flores's Lawsuit Against the N.F.L.," *New York Times*, April 7, 2022, https://www .nytimes.com/2022/02/01/sports/football/brian-flores-giants -discrimination-lawsuit.html.

37. Justin Gomer and Shaun Ossei-Owusu, "Coaching While Black: Race, Leadership, and the National Football League," *Journal of Sport and Social Issues*, December 2022, https://doi .org/10.1177/01937235221144435.

38. Gomer and Ossei-Owusu.

39. Guilherme Gleich, "The Indianapolis Colts Hire Jeff Saturday, a High School Coach, as Interim Head Coach," *New York Times*,

October 24, 2022, https://www.nytimes.com/2022/11/08/sports/football/jeff-saturday-colts-nfl-coach.html.

40. Gleich.
41. Andrew M. Carton and Ashleigh Shelby Rosette, "Explaining Bias Against Black Leaders: Integrating Theory on Information Processing and Goal-Based Stereotyping," *Academy of Management Journal* 54(6) (2011): 1141–58, https://doi.org/10.5465/amj.2009.0745.
42. Carton and Rosette.
43. Carton and Rosette, 1143.
44. Carton and Rosette.
45. Carton and Rosette, 1152.
46. Diandra "Fu" Debrosse, interviewed by Shari Dunn, August 9, 2023.
47. "A Quote from Alice in Wonderland," n.d., https://www.goodreads.com/quotes/458856-my-dear-here-we-must-run-as-fast-as-we.
48. "A Quote from Through the Looking Glass," n.d., https://www.goodreads.com/quotes/12608-when-i-use-a-word-humpty-dumpty-said-in-rather.
49. Carton and Rosette, "Explaining Bias."
50. Staples, "Hidden Figures," 125.
51. Staples, 126.

Chapter 9: The Tools

1. "Affirmative Action: Myth versus Reality," Diversity, Equity, and Inclusion, SUNY Upstate, 2023, accessed December 29, https://www.upstate.edu/diversityinclusion/policies-and-procedures/aa/myth_reality.php.
2. "Hiring Discrimination Against Black Americans Hasn't Declined in 25 Years," *Harvard Business Review*, August 30, 2021, https://hbr.org/2017/10/hiring-discrimination-against-black-americans-hasnt-declined-in-25-years.
3. Pierott Deena, executive director, iUrban Teen, interviewed by Shari Dunn, June 27, 2023.
4. "The Economics of the Civil War," EHnet, accessed November 29, 2023, https://eh.net/encyclopedia/the-economics-of-the-civil-war/.
5. "Southern Violence During Reconstruction," 2023, PBS, https://www.pbs.org/wgbh/americanexperience/features/reconstruction-southern-violence-during-reconstruction/.
6. Aaron O'Neill, "United States: Black and Slave Population 1790–1880," Statista, June 21, 2022, https://www.statista.com/statistics/1010169/black-and-slave-population-us-1790-1880/.
7. Matt Mullen, "Sharecropping: Definition and Dates," History,

March 29, 2023, https://www.history.com/topics/black-history/sharecropping. "It often resulted in sharecroppers owing more to the landowner (for the use of tools and other supplies, for example) than they were able to repay."

8. Roberto A. Ferdman, "I Dare You to Read This and Still Feel Good About Tipping," *Washington Post*, November 24, 2021, https://www.washingtonpost.com/news/wonk/wp/2016/02/18/i-dare-you-to-read-this-and-still-feel-ok-about-tipping-in-the-united-states/. "Tipping became popularized by restaurant owners who didn't want to pay Black workers after the passage of the 15th Amendment."

9. "I Dare You to Read This."

10. E. Ginzberg and D. Hiestand, "Mobility in the Negro Community: Guidelines for Research on Social and Economic Progress, United States Commission on Civil Rights, Clearinghouse Publication No. 11, 1968, retrieved December 29, 2023, from chrome-extension://efaidnbmnnnibpcajpcglclefindmkaj/https://www2.law.umaryland.edu/marshall/usccr/documents/cr11011.pdf; Cindy Long, "A Hidden History of Integration and the Shortage of Teachers of Color," National Education Association, accessed December 29, 2023, https://www.nea.org/nea-today/all-news-articles/hidden-history-integration-and-shortage-teachers-color.

11. Abraham Lincoln," Abrahamlincoln.org, accessed December 5, 2023, https://abrahamlincoln.org/features/speeches-writings/abraham-lincoln-quotes/#:~:text=%E2%80%9CI%20will%20say%20then%20that,white%20people%3B%20and%20I%20will.

12. "Abercrombie & Fitch Employment Discrimination," Legal Defense Fund, April 19, 2022, https://www.naacpldf.org/case-issue/abercrombie-fitch-employment-discrimination/.

13. Julia B. Chan, 2021. "Decoding Discrimination in America's Temp Industry," Reveal, 2021, July 1, https://revealnews.org/podcast/decoding-discrimination-in-americas-temp-industry/.

14. Matthew Green, "Timeline: A Heated History of Affirmative Action in America," KQED, June 30, 2023, https://www.kqed.org/news/11954709/timeline-a-heated-history-of-affirmative-action-in-america.

15. "Commencement Address at Howard University: 'To Fulfill These Rights,'" June 4, 1965, American Presidency Project, https://www.presidency.ucsb.edu/documents/commencement-address-howard-university-fulfill-these-rights#:~:text=You%20do%20not.

16. Dennis Deslippe, *Protesting Affirmative Action: The Struggle over Equality After the Civil Rights Revolution* (Baltimore: Johns Hopkins University Press, 2012), 2, quoting "Negative Action," *Wall Street Journal*, August 23, 1965.

17. "Regents of the University of California v. Bakke (1978)," Legal Information Institute, accessed December 22, 2023, https://www .law.cornell.edu/wex/regents_of_the_university_of_california_v _bakke_(1978)#:~:text=Primary%20tabs,Regents%20of%20the%20 University%20of%20California%20v.,Civil%20Rights%20Act%20 of%201964.

18. "Women's Rights and the Civil Rights Act of 1964," 2022, National Archives, June 17, 2022, https://www.archives.gov /women/1964-civil-rights-act.

19. "Women's Rights and the Civil Rights Act of 1964."

20. "Women in the Labor Force: A Databook: BLS Reports," U.S. Bureau of Labor Statistics, March 1, 2022, https://www.bls.gov /opub/reports/womens-databook/2021/home.htm.

21. "Women in the Labor Force."

22. "Is Sisterhood Conditional? White Women and the Rollback of Affirmative Action," Tim Wise, August 7, 2010, http://www .timwise.org/1998/09/is-sisterhood-conditional-white-women -and-the-rollback-of-affirmative-action/; Nikole Hannah-Jones, "What Abigail Fisher's Affirmative Action Case Was Really About," ProPublica, June 23, 2016, https://www.propublica .org/article/a-colorblind-constitution-what-abigail-fishers -affirmative-action-case-is-r.

23. "Me Too Movement," *Encyclopaedia Britannica*, https://www .britannica.com/topic/Me-Too-movement.

24. "Sexual Harassment in Our Nation's Workplaces," U.S. Equal Employment Opportunity Commission, accessed December 24, 2023, https://www.eeoc.gov/data/sexual-harassment-our-nations -workplaces.

25. "Civil Rights Department Announces Settlement Agreement to Resolve Employment Discrimination and Equal Pay Lawsuit Against Activision Blizzard," press release, California Civil Rights Department, December 15, 2023, https://calcivilrights .ca.gov/2023/12/15/civil-rights-department-announces -settlement-agreement-to-resolve-employment-discrimination -and-equal-pay-lawsuit-against-activision-blizzard/; Andy Chalk, "Activision Blizzard Employees Stage Walkout to Demand Bobby Kotick's Removal," *PCGamer*, November 16, 2021, https://www .pcgamer.com/activision-blizzard-employees-stage-walkout-to -demand-bobby-koticks-removal/; Kris Holt, "Activision Blizzard Continues to Remove Employees Amid Misconduct Allegations," Engadget, January 17, 2022, https://www.engadget.com/activision -blizzard-departures-discipline-bobby-kotick-212356578.html.

26. "Title VII of the Civil Rights Act of 1964," U.S. Equal Employment

Opportunity Commission, https://www.eeoc.gov/statutes/title
-vii-civil-rights-act-1964.

27. Candice Norwood, "Racial Bias Trainings Surged After George
Floyd's Death. A Year Later, Experts Are Still Waiting for 'Bold'
Change," PBS, May 25, 2021, https://www.pbs.org/newshour
/nation/racial-bias-trainings-surged-after-george-floyds-death
-a-year-later-experts-are-still-waiting-for-bold-change.

28. "A Brief History of DEI, Pt. 1," Get Reframe, July 24, 2023,
https://getreframe.com/colon-blog-post/a-brief-history-of
-dei-pt-1/.

29. "The Freedman's Bureau! An Agency to Keep the Negro in Idle-
ness at the Expense of the White Man. Twice Vetoed by the
President and Made a Law by Congress. Support Congress &
You Support the Negro Sustain the President & You Protect the
White Man," n.d., Library of Congress, https://www.loc.gov
/item/2008661698/.

30. Helen Ubiñas, "2020 Called for a Racial Reckoning. 2022 Is Proof of
Its Failure," *Philadelphia Inquirer*, October 14, 2022, https://www
.inquirer.com/opinion/racism-incidents-2022-los-angeles-city
-council-penn-state-20221014.html; Perry Bacon Jr., "The Racial
Reckoning Led to Lots of Talk but Little Real Change," *Washington Post*, January 15, 2023 https://www.washingtonpost.com
/opinions/2023/01/15/black-lives-matter-george-floyd-protests
-policy-change/.

31. E. Bonilla-Silva, *Racism Without Racists: Color-Blind Racism and
the Persistence of Racial Inequality in America* (Lanham, MD:
Rowman & Littlefield, 2017).

32. M. W. Kraus et al., "The Social Psychology of Misperceiving Racial Economic Equality," *Perspectives on Psychological Science*
14, no. 6 (2019): 899–921.

33. I. N. Onyeador et al., "Disrupting Beliefs in Racial Progress:
Reminders of Persistent Racism Alter Perceptions of Past, but
Not Current, Racial Economic Equality," *Personality and Social Psychology Bulletin* 47, no. 5 (2021), 753–65, https://doi
.org/10.1177/0146167220942625. "Given that this discourse
envisions racial progress unfolding in one direction, linearly,
naturally, and perhaps, automatically (Hur & Ruttan, unpub-
lished manuscript), it may serve to undermine, rather than
propel, robust efforts to eradicate racism and its resultant racial disparities."; L. Seamster and V. Ray, "Against Teleology in
the Study of Race: Toward the Abolition of the Progress Para-
digm," *Sociological Theory*, 36(4) (2018): 315–42, https://doi
.org/10.1177/0735275118813614.

34. Michele McGovern, "Diversity Recruitment Is Healthy; Diversity Retention Isn't: 6 Things HR Needs to Do Now," *HRMorning* (blog), June 13, 2023, https://www.hrmorning.com/articles /diversity-retention/.

35. Rachel Minkin, "Diversity, Equity and Inclusion in the Workplace," Pew Research Center, Social and Demographic Trends Project, May 17, 2023, https://www.pewresearch.org/social -trends/2023/05/17/diversity-equity-and-inclusion-in-the -workplace/#dei-measures-and-their-impact.

36. Luiza Dreasher, "A Point of View: The Cultural Appropriation of 'Stay Woke' and the Need for Redefining Contemporary Narratives," Inclusion Solution, July 20, 2023, https://theinclusionsolution .me/a-point-of-view-the-cultural-appropriation-of-stay-woke -and-the-need-for-redefining-contemporary-narratives/.

37. Jonathan M. Metzl, *Dying of Whiteness: How the Politics of Racial Resentment Is Killing America's Heartland* (New York: Basic Books, 2019).

38. Ernest Holmes, *Change Your Thinking, Change Your Life: A Practical Course in Successful Living* (Science of Mind, 1984).

39. Costas Cavounidis and Kevin Lang, "Discrimination and Worker Evaluation," 2015, https://doi.org/10.3386/w21612, as cited by Gillian B. White, "Black Workers Really Do Need to Be Twice as Good," *Atlantic*, June 27, 2018, https://www.theatlantic .com/business/archive/2015/10/why-black-workers-really-do -need-to-be-twice-as-good/409276/.

40. Suzanne LaBarre, "The Rise of 'Supertokenism'—and What Organizations Get Flat Wrong about DEI," *Fast Company*, June 7, 2022, https://www.fastcompany.com/90751644/the-rise-of -supertokenism-and-what-organizations-get-wrong-about-dei.

41. "88," Center on Extremism, August 1, 2023, https://extremismterms .adl.org/resources/hate-symbol/88.

42. Janie Har, "Black Workers at California Tesla Factory Allege Rampant Racism, Seek Class-Action Status," AP News, June 7, 2023, https://apnews.com/article/tesla-racism-black-lawsuit -class-action-21c88bddf60eca702560be58429495de.

43. Adam Levitt, interviewed by Shari Dunn, July 20, 2023.

44. Juliana Feliciano Reyes, "How Black Workers Got Locked Out of Construction's Best Jobs," *Philadelphia Inquirer*, August 30, 2022, https://www.inquirer.com/news/inq2/more-perfect-union -trade-construction-racism-pennsylvania-20220830.html.

45. "Hispanic Workforce in California Face More Dangerous Conditions," n.d., https://www.geklaw.com/news/dangerous.html; Emilie Openchowski, "Latino Workers Are Often Segregated into Bad

Jobs, but a Strong U.S. Labor Movement Can Boost Job Quality and U.S. Economic Growth," Equitable Growth, October 12, 2022, https://equitablegrowth.org/latino-workers-are-often-segregated -into-bad-jobs-but-a-strong-u-s-labor-movement-can-boost-job -quality-and-u-s-economic-growth/.

46. "Desegregating the Dollar: African American Consumerism in the Twentieth Century," 1998, https://www.jstor.org/stable/j .ctt9qfnzd.; Tamar Freundlich, "Marketing to Women: What We Can Learn from the Past Century," Promo, April 29, 2021, https://promo.com/blog/marketing-to-women-what-we-can -learn-from-the-past-century; "Latinos and Advertising," Race & Ethnicity in Advertising, https://raceandethnicity.org/exhibits /show/latinos-and-advertising/latinos-and-advertising; Michael Twitty, "Before the Civil Rights Movement, It Was Common to Call Something 'Racist.' What Happened?" NBC News, June 21, 2020, https://www.nbcnews.com/think/opinion/aunt-jemima-uncle -ben-deserve-retirement-they-re-racist-myths-ncna1231623.

47. David Dayen, "Supreme Court Decides Fake Plaintiffs Are Good Plaintiffs," The American Prospect, June 30, 2023, https:// prospect.org/justice/2023-06-30-supreme-court-decides-fake -plaintiffs-good/.

48. "Citizens United v. FEC, 558 U.S. 310 (2010)." n.d. Justia Law. https://supreme.justia.com/cases/federal/us/558/310/.

49. A six-year study by the consulting firm McKinsey showed that ethnically and culturally diverse companies enjoy a profitability margin up to 36 percent higher than their less diverse counter- parts. The gap grows to 48 percent when comparing the most and least gender-diverse enterprises.

50. Saijel Kishan, "Racism and Inequity Have Cost the U.S. $16 Tril- lion, Wall Street Economist Says," Bloomberg, October 20, 2020, https://www.bloomberg.com/news/articles/2020-10-20/racism -and-inequity-have-cost-the-u-s-16-trillion-wall-street-economist -says.

Chapter 10: Let's Get to Work

1. This quote is often misattributed to Albert Einstein and a letter pub- lished in the *New York Times* in 1946. Einstein said, "A new type of thinking is essential if mankind is to survive and move towards higher levels." "Atomic Education Urged by Einstein; Scientist in Plea for $200,000 to Promote New Type of Essential Thinking," *New York Times*, May 25, 1946, Times Machine, https://timesmachine .nytimes.com/timesmachine/1946/05/25/issue.html.

2. "'Overmentored and Underfunded': Diverse Entrepreneurs Dish on

Legal Tech Startup Experience," Legaltech News, March 9, 2023, https://www.law.com/legaltechnews/2022/03/14/overmentored -and-underfunded-diverse-entrepreneurs-dish-on-legal-tech -startup-experience/?slreturn=20240322225640.

3. "'Overmentored and Underfunded.'"

4. David Baboolall et al., "Building Supportive Ecosystems for Black-Owned US Businesses," McKinsey Institute for Black Economic Mobility, October 29, 2020, https://www.mckinsey.com /industries/public-and-social-sector/our-insights/building -supportive-ecosystems-for-black-owned-us-businesses.

5. Erin Griffith and Erin Woo, "Elizabeth Holmes Found Guilty of Four Charges of Fraud," New York Times, July 8, 2022, https:// www.nytimes.com/live/2022/01/03/technology/elizabeth -holmes-trial-verdict#elizabeth-holmes-guilty.

6. Shaun Harper, "Adam Neumann Gets a $350 Million Do-Over and Diverse Entrepreneurs Barely Get a Start," Forbes, August 17, 2022, https://www.forbes.com/sites/shaunharper/2022/08/16 /entrepreneurial-inequity-is-exacerbated-with-new-investment -into-failed-wework-founder-adam-neumann/?sh=5faa0e4343c5.

7. Harper. "Venture capital firm Andreessen Horowitz is reportedly investing $350 million in Flow, a new real estate company that disgraced WeWork co-founder Adam Neumann is creating. Flow's valuation exceeds $1 billion. Andreessen Horowitz, which is also referred to as a16z, has never invested more in a round of funding for any company, according to the New York Times."

8. Harper.

9. James Chen, "Unicorn: What It Means in Investing, with Examples," Investopedia, April 3, 2024, https://www.investopedia. com/terms/u/unicorn.asp.

10. Marc Ethier, "Do You Need an MBA to Found a Unicorn? History Says . . . Probably Not," Yahoo Finance, July 5, 2023, https://finance.yahoo.com/news/mba-found-unicorn-history-says-120415236.html?guccounter=1&guce_referrer =aHR0cHM6Ly93d3cuZ29vZ2xlLmNvbS8&guce_referrer _sig=AQAAAIsG5bA1FkKatS5PUCSt5Z9Hk6tXIH _Ku16X2D1gOhXJg74Oea7bHHoklUtoGOvziFwULK-HL8J_eGW3 _TNu5uVsvS8sQ-j4DVwUFhKshHKsL0Yib2j7Ho6HnxwM 15dQi9guxAvYaox1krOS4Z9N9akrLXb7mmskvqL3V-yuGZKy.

11. Patrick Mullane, "Do You Need an MBA to Be an Entrepreneur? It Depends," Forbes, January 8, 2024, https://www.forbes.com /sites/patrickmullane/2024/01/08/do-you-need-an-mba-to -be-an-entrepreneur-it-depends-/?sh=a2bb15a7a796.

12. Kristy Bleizeffer, "In GMAC'S First-Ever Global Report on Diversity,

Some Surprising Discoveries," Poets&Quants, October 28, 2021, https://poetsandquants.com/2021/10/26/in-gmacs-first-ever -global-report-on-diversity-some-surprising-discoveries/2/.

13. "Startup Failure," Harvard Law School Forum on Corporate Governance, September 29, 2023, https://corpgov.law.harvard .edu/2023/09/29/startup-failure/.

14. Terry Gross, "A 'Forgotten History' of How the U.S. Government Segregated America," NPR, May 3, 2017, https://www.npr .org/2017/05/03/526655831/a-forgotten-history-of-how-the -u-s-government-segregated-america.

15. Gross; Richard Rothstein, *The Color of Law: A Forgotten History of How Our Government Segregated America* (New York: Liveright, 2018).

16. Ted Mouw and Barbara Entwisle, "Residential Segregation and Interracial Friendship in Schools," *American Journal of Sociology* 112, no. 2 (2006): 394–441, https://doi.org/10.1086/506415.

17. "PRRI Survey: Friendship Networks of White Americans Continue to Be 90% White," PRRI, June 15, 2022, https://www.prri .org/press-release/prri-survey-friendship-networks-of-white -americans-continue-to-be-90-white/.

18. Donald Tomaskovic-Devey, "Gender and Racial Inequality at Work: The Sources and Consequences of Job Segregation," *Economic Geography* 70 (1993).

19. Tomaskovic-Devey.

20. D. S. Pedulla and D. Pager, "Race and Networks in the Job Search Process," *American Sociological Review* 84, no. 6 (2019): 983–1012, https://doi.org/10.1177/0003122419883255.

21. Pedulla and Pager.

22. Quote often attributed to Maya Angelou from Oprah Winfrey. "The Powerful Lesson Maya Angelou Taught Oprah," video, n.d., https://www.oprah.com/oprahs-lifeclass/the-powerful-lesson -maya-angelou-taught-oprah-video.

23. Jack Flynn, "25 Incredible Employee Referral Statistics: Facts About Employee Referrals in the U.S," Zippia, June 28, 2023, https://www.zippia.com/advice/employee-referral-statistics/.

24. Joanne Degnan, "Hiring Based Solely on Staff Referrals Can Violate Anti-Discrimination Laws," New Jersey Business & Industry Association, May 16, 2022, https://njbia.org/hiring-based -solely-on-staff-referrals-can-violate-anti-discrimination-laws/.

25. Degnan.

26. Scott E. Page, *The Diversity Bonus: How Great Teams Pay Off in the Knowledge Economy* (Princeton, NJ: Princeton University Press, 2017), 221.

27. Claire Cain Miller and Josh Katz, "What Researchers Discovered When They Sent 80,000 Fake Résumés to U.S. Jobs," *New York Times*, April 8, 2024, https://www.nytimes.com/2024/04/08/upshot/employment-discrimination-fake-resumes.html.

28. Justin Gomer and Shaun Ossei-Owusu, "Coaching While Black: Race, Leadership, and the National Football League," *Journal of Sport and Social Issues*, December 2022, 019372352211444, https://doi.org/10.1177/01937235221144435; Kenneth D. Gibbs, Jacob Basson, Imam M. Xierali, and David A. Broniatowski, "Decoupling of the Minority PhD Talent Pool and Assistant Professor Hiring in Medical School Basic Science Departments in the US," *eLife (Cambridge)* 5 (November 2016), https://doi.org/10.7554/elife.21393; Elizabeth Weise and Jessica Guynn, "Black and Hispanic Computer Scientists Have Degrees from Top Universities, but Don't Get Hired in Tech," *USA Today*, July 20, 2020, https://www.usatoday.com/story/tech/2014/10/12/silicon-valley-diversity-tech-hiring-computer-science-graduates-african-american-hispanic/14684211/; "Korn Ferry Study Reveals U.S. Black P&L Leaders Are Some of the Highest Performing Executives," Korn Ferry, October 8, 2019, https://www.kornferry.com/about-us/press/korn-ferry-study-reveals-united-states-black-pl-leaders-are-some-of-the-highest-performing-executives-in-the-us-c-suite#:~:text=Despite%20the%20wealth%20of%20talent,none%20of%20whom%20are%20women.

29. Miller and Katz.

30. Clémence Berson, Morgane Laouenan, and Emmanuel Valat, "Outsourcing Recruitment as a Solution to Prevent Discrimination: A Correspondence Study," 2020, https://econpapers.repec.org/article/eeelabeco/v_3a64_3ay_3a2020_3ai_3ac_3as0927537120300439.htm.

31. Miller and Katz, "What Researchers Discovered."

32. Miller and Katz.

33. Daniel Kahneman, *Thinking, Fast and Slow* (New York: Farrar, Straus & Giroux, 2011).

34. Daniel C. Quan, "The Demographic Context of Hiring Discrimination: Evidence from a Field Experiment in 50 Metropolitan Statistical Areas," *Work and Occupations* 50, 4 (2022): 463–98, https://doi.org/10.1177/07308884221134470.

35. Miller and Katz, "What Researchers Discovered."

36. Gomer and Ossei-Owusu, "Coaching While Black."

37. Miller and Katz, "What Researchers Discovered."

38. Miller and Katz.

39. "The Permanent Detour," https://stradaeducation.org/report /the-permanent-detour/; Matthew Loh, "Most US Graduates Who Start Their First Job Underemployed Can't Find College-Level Jobs 10 Years Later: Report," Business Insider, February 23, 2024, https://www.businessinsider.com/most-graduates -us-college-cant-find-job-underemployed-decade-2024-2. "Their findings were derived from a dataset of 60 million people's careers in the US, including those of 10.8 million people holding at least a bachelor's degree."

40. "The Permanent Detour"; Loh, "Most US Graduates."

41. "Korn Ferry Study."

42. "The Black P&L: Leader Insights and Lessons from Senior Black P&L Leaders in Corporate America," Korn Ferry, 2019, 47, chrome-extension://efaidnbmnnnibpcajpcglclefindmkaj/https ://www.kornferry.com/content/dam/kornferry/docs/pdfs /korn-ferry_theblack-pl-leader.pdf.

43. "The Black P&L."

44. Global Leadership Forecast Series, *Diversity & Inclusion Report*, 2020, chrome-extension://efaidnbmnnnibpcajpcglclefindmkaj/https:// media.ddiworld.com/research/GLF_DiversityandInclusionReport _2020.pdf.

45. Sandy J. Wayne, Jianguo Sun, Donald H. Kluemper, Gordon Weng-Kit Cheung, and Adaora Ubaka, "The Cost of Managing Impressions for Black Employees: An Expectancy Violation Theory Perspective," *Journal of Applied Psychology* 108, no. 2 (2023): 208–24, https://doi.org/10.1037/apl0001030.

46. Wayne et al.

47. Wayne et al.

48. Yashika Khandelwal, "How Lateral Hiring Can Enhance Your Teams Inclusivity," *Testlify* (blog), January 3, 2024, https://testlify.com /how-lateral-hiring-can-enhance-your-teams-inclusivity/.

49. Lauren Rollins, "The Myth of No Pipeline in Hiring Diverse Leadership," Western Massachusetts Policy Center, September 17, 2023, https://wmpolicy.org/the-myth-of-no-pipeline-in-hiring -diverse-leadership/.

50. Katherine W. Phillips, "Why Black Employees Hesitate to Open Up About Themselves," *Harvard Business Review*, August 27, 2021, https://hbr.org/2018/03/diversity-and-authenticity.

51. Phillips.

52. Phillips.

53. Kusum Crimmel, "What Is White Culture?" Dissecting Whiteness, January 13, 2020, https://www.dissectingwhiteness .com/blog/what-is-white-culture.

54. Dreama Moon, "Concept of 'Culture': Implications for Intercultural Communication Research," *Communication Quarterly* 44 (1996): 70–84.

55. "How Miscommunication Happens (and How to Avoid It)—Katherine Hampsten," TED-Ed, 2016, https://www.youtube .com/watch?v=gCfzeONu3Mo.

56. "How Miscommunication Happens."

57. "How Miscommunication Happens."

58. Ijeoma Oluo, *So You Want to Talk About Race* (New York: Seal Press, 2018).

59. "How Miscommunication Happens."

60. "Diversity Is Difficult," The Brink, Boston University, July 19, 2019, https://www.bu.edu/articles/2018/diversity-is-difficult/.

61. "How Miscommunication Happens."

62. Katie Rogers and Nicholas Fandos, "Trump Tells Congresswomen to 'Go Back' to the Countries They Came From," *New York Times*, July 16, 2019, https://www.nytimes.com/2019/07/14/us/politics /trump-twitter-squad-congress.html.

Epilogue

1. Julia Ingram and Alexander Hunter, "Some Republicans Attack Kamala Harris as 'DEI Hire.' Here's What That Means," CBS News, July 26, 2024, https://www.cbsnews.com/news /republicans-attack-kamala-harris-dei-hire/.

2. "GOP Lawmaker Makes Comment About Harris' Race. Hear What He Said," CNN, video, 2024, https://www.cnn .com/2024/07/22/politics/video/kamala-harris-burchett-dei -hire-charlamagne-tha-god-angela-rye-lead-digvid.

3. Philip Bump, "With Six Words, Michelle Obama Rewires America's Conversation on Race," *Washington Post*, August 23, 2024, https://www.washingtonpost.com/politics/2024/08/21/with -six-words-michelle-obama-rewires-americas-conversation-race/.

4. "Decline in Human Empathy Creates Global Risks in the 'Age of Anger,'" Zurich Insurance Company, n.d., https://www.zurich .com/en/knowledge/topics/global-risks/decline-human -empathy-creates-global-risks-age-of-anger.

5. "Decline in Human Empathy."

INDEX

ABOUT THE AUTHOR

SHARI DUNN was born and raised in a working-class, blue-collar, African American neighborhood in one of the most segregated cities in the nation, Milwaukee, Wisconsin. Growing up, she witnessed firsthand the devastating impact of racial discrimination on housing, health care, and employment for Black people. As part of the second wave of students bused to suburban schools, Shari understood that others had fought and died for her right to access education and opportunity. Her parents and family instilled in her the knowledge that the struggle for civil rights and affirmative action had created programs like the Educational Opportunity Program (EOP), which helped her and many other first-generation college students access higher education—not because they were unqualified, but because of historical inequities that provided an opportunity advantage to white people.

Among the most meaningful highlights of her career was the opportunity to interview and thank civil rights icons Harry Belafonte and Julian Bond. These conversations were profound moments when Shari felt it was her turn to pick up the baton and move the country forward.

In her groundbreaking book *Qualified*, Shari Dunn challenges the false narrative that diversity equates to a lack of qualifications. Through deep research, enlightening interviews, and anecdotes from her extensive career, Shari uncovers the impact of "Competency Checking," a practice that unjustly scrutinizes Black people and other people of color, forcing them to repeatedly prove their worth, intelligence, and even their right to be in the workplace. Shari argues that competency checking is a key reason why Black people and other people of color are underrepresented in many industries and why there continues to be a revolving door of Black talent, even after the hiring surges of 2020. *Qualified* illustrates the scope of this issue, exploring how we got here and how, through both identification and correction, we can go forward into a future where all people are truly seen and valued for their talents and contributions.